C-3994 CAREER EXAMINATION SERIES

This is your
PASSBOOK for...

Customs & Border Protection Officer

Test Preparation Study Guide
Questions & Answers

NATIONAL LEARNING CORPORATION®

COPYRIGHT NOTICE

This book is SOLELY intended for, is sold ONLY to, and its use is RESTRICTED to individual, bona fide applicants or candidates who qualify by virtue of having seriously filed applications for appropriate license, certificate, professional and/or promotional advancement, higher school matriculation, scholarship, or other legitimate requirements of education and/or governmental authorities.

This book is NOT intended for use, class instruction, tutoring, training, duplication, copying, reprinting, excerption, or adaptation, etc., by:

1) Other publishers
2) Proprietors and/or Instructors of "Coaching" and/or Preparatory Courses
3) Personnel and/or Training Divisions of commercial, industrial, and governmental organizations
4) Schools, colleges, or universities and/or their departments and staffs, including teachers and other personnel
5) Testing Agencies or Bureaus
6) Study groups which seek by the purchase of a single volume to copy and/or duplicate and/or adapt this material for use by the group as a whole without having purchased individual volumes for each of the members of the group
7) Et al.

Such persons would be in violation of appropriate Federal and State statutes.

PROVISION OF LICENSING AGREEMENTS – Recognized educational, commercial, industrial, and governmental institutions and organizations, and others legitimately engaged in educational pursuits, including training, testing, and measurement activities, may address request for a licensing agreement to the copyright owners, who will determine whether, and under what conditions, including fees and charges, the materials in this book may be used them. In other words, a licensing facility exists for the legitimate use of the material in this book on other than an individual basis. However, it is asseverated and affirmed here that the material in this book CANNOT be used without the receipt of the express permission of such a licensing agreement from the Publishers. Inquiries re licensing should be addressed to the company, attention rights and permissions department.

All rights reserved, including the right of reproduction in whole or in part, in any form or by any means, electronic or mechanical, including photocopying, recording, or by any information storage and retrieval system, without permission in writing from the Publisher.

Copyright © 2024 by
National Learning Corporation

212 Michael Drive, Syosset, NY 11791
(516) 921-8888 • www.passbooks.com
E-mail: info@passbooks.com

PUBLISHED IN THE UNITED STATES OF AMERICA

PASSBOOK® SERIES

THE *PASSBOOK® SERIES* has been created to prepare applicants and candidates for the ultimate academic battlefield – the examination room.

At some time in our lives, each and every one of us may be required to take an examination – for validation, matriculation, admission, qualification, registration, certification, or licensure.

Based on the assumption that every applicant or candidate has met the basic formal educational standards, has taken the required number of courses, and read the necessary texts, the *PASSBOOK® SERIES* furnishes the one special preparation which may assure passing with confidence, instead of failing with insecurity. Examination questions – together with answers – are furnished as the basic vehicle for study so that the mysteries of the examination and its compounding difficulties may be eliminated or diminished by a sure method.

This book is meant to help you pass your examination provided that you qualify and are serious in your objective.

The entire field is reviewed through the huge store of content information which is succinctly presented through a provocative and challenging approach – the question-and-answer method.

A climate of success is established by furnishing the correct answers at the end of each test.

You soon learn to recognize types of questions, forms of questions, and patterns of questioning. You may even begin to anticipate expected outcomes.

You perceive that many questions are repeated or adapted so that you can gain acute insights, which may enable you to score many sure points.

You learn how to confront new questions, or types of questions, and to attack them confidently and work out the correct answers.

You note objectives and emphases, and recognize pitfalls and dangers, so that you may make positive educational adjustments.

Moreover, you are kept fully informed in relation to new concepts, methods, practices, and directions in the field.

You discover that you are actually taking the examination all the time: you are preparing for the examination by "taking" an examination, not by reading extraneous and/or supererogatory textbooks.

In short, this PASSBOOK®, used directedly, should be an important factor in helping you to pass your test.

CUSTOMS AND BORDER PROTECTION (CBP) OFFICER

DUTIES
The Customs and Border Protection Officer must read and study laws, legal commentary, and regulations. They often must make critical decisions that require superior reasoning skills. Additionally, they may be called upon to prepare written incident reports and testify in court.

SCOPE OF THE EXAMINATION
The test will consist of three parts: Part A, which assesses logical reasoning in a verbal format, Part B, which assesses reasoning in a mathematical format (arithmetic reasoning), and Part C, which assesses writing skills involving the proper use of grammar, syntax, punctuation, spelling, organization of sentences in a paragraph, and organization of paragraphs in a passage.

HOW TO TAKE A TEST

I. YOU MUST PASS AN EXAMINATION

A. WHAT EVERY CANDIDATE SHOULD KNOW

Examination applicants often ask us for help in preparing for the written test. What can I study in advance? What kinds of questions will be asked? How will the test be given? How will the papers be graded?

As an applicant for a civil service examination, you may be wondering about some of these things. Our purpose here is to suggest effective methods of advance study and to describe civil service examinations.

Your chances for success on this examination can be increased if you know how to prepare. Those "pre-examination jitters" can be reduced if you know what to expect. You can even experience an adventure in good citizenship if you know why civil service exams are given.

B. WHY ARE CIVIL SERVICE EXAMINATIONS GIVEN?

Civil service examinations are important to you in two ways. As a citizen, you want public jobs filled by employees who know how to do their work. As a job seeker, you want a fair chance to compete for that job on an equal footing with other candidates. The best-known means of accomplishing this two-fold goal is the competitive examination.

Exams are widely publicized throughout the nation. They may be administered for jobs in federal, state, city, municipal, town or village governments or agencies.

Any citizen may apply, with some limitations, such as the age or residence of applicants. Your experience and education may be reviewed to see whether you meet the requirements for the particular examination. When these requirements exist, they are reasonable and applied consistently to all applicants. Thus, a competitive examination may cause you some uneasiness now, but it is your privilege and safeguard.

C. HOW ARE CIVIL SERVICE EXAMS DEVELOPED?

Examinations are carefully written by trained technicians who are specialists in the field known as "psychological measurement," in consultation with recognized authorities in the field of work that the test will cover. These experts recommend the subject matter areas or skills to be tested; only those knowledges or skills important to your success on the job are included. The most reliable books and source materials available are used as references. Together, the experts and technicians judge the difficulty level of the questions.

Test technicians know how to phrase questions so that the problem is clearly stated. Their ethics do not permit "trick" or "catch" questions. Questions may have been tried out on sample groups, or subjected to statistical analysis, to determine their usefulness.

Written tests are often used in combination with performance tests, ratings of training and experience, and oral interviews. All of these measures combine to form the best-known means of finding the right person for the right job.

II. HOW TO PASS THE WRITTEN TEST

A. NATURE OF THE EXAMINATION

To prepare intelligently for civil service examinations, you should know how they differ from school examinations you have taken. In school you were assigned certain definite pages to read or subjects to cover. The examination questions were quite detailed and usually emphasized memory. Civil service exams, on the other hand, try to discover your present ability to perform the duties of a position, plus your potentiality to learn these duties. In other words, a civil service exam attempts to predict how successful you will be. Questions cover such a broad area that they cannot be as minute and detailed as school exam questions.

In the public service similar kinds of work, or positions, are grouped together in one "class." This process is known as *position-classification*. All the positions in a class are paid according to the salary range for that class. One class title covers all of these positions, and they are all tested by the same examination.

B. FOUR BASIC STEPS

1) Study the announcement

How, then, can you know what subjects to study? Our best answer is: "Learn as much as possible about the class of positions for which you've applied." The exam will test the knowledge, skills and abilities needed to do the work.

Your most valuable source of information about the position you want is the official exam announcement. This announcement lists the training and experience qualifications. Check these standards and apply only if you come reasonably close to meeting them.

The brief description of the position in the examination announcement offers some clues to the subjects which will be tested. Think about the job itself. Review the duties in your mind. Can you perform them, or are there some in which you are rusty? Fill in the blank spots in your preparation.

Many jurisdictions preview the written test in the exam announcement by including a section called "Knowledge and Abilities Required," "Scope of the Examination," or some similar heading. Here you will find out specifically what fields will be tested.

2) Review your own background

Once you learn in general what the position is all about, and what you need to know to do the work, ask yourself which subjects you already know fairly well and which need improvement. You may wonder whether to concentrate on improving your strong areas or on building some background in your fields of weakness. When the announcement has specified "some knowledge" or "considerable knowledge," or has used adjectives like "beginning principles of…" or "advanced … methods," you can get a clue as to the number and difficulty of questions to be asked in any given field. More questions, and hence broader coverage, would be included for those subjects which are more important in the work. Now weigh your strengths and weaknesses against the job requirements and prepare accordingly.

3) Determine the level of the position

Another way to tell how intensively you should prepare is to understand the level of the job for which you are applying. Is it the entering level? In other words, is this the position in which beginners in a field of work are hired? Or is it an intermediate or advanced level? Sometimes this is indicated by such words as "Junior" or "Senior" in the class title. Other jurisdictions use Roman numerals to designate the level – Clerk I, Clerk II, for example. The word "Supervisor" sometimes appears in the title. If the level is not indicated by the title, check the description of duties. Will you be working under very close supervision, or will you have responsibility for independent decisions in this work?

4) Choose appropriate study materials

Now that you know the subjects to be examined and the relative amount of each subject to be covered, you can choose suitable study materials. For beginning level jobs, or even advanced ones, if you have a pronounced weakness in some aspect of your training, read a modern, standard textbook in that field. Be sure it is up to date and has general coverage. Such books are normally available at your library, and the librarian will be glad to help you locate one. For entry-level positions, questions of appropriate difficulty are chosen – neither highly advanced questions, nor those too simple. Such questions require careful thought but not advanced training.

If the position for which you are applying is technical or advanced, you will read more advanced, specialized material. If you are already familiar with the basic principles of your field, elementary textbooks would waste your time. Concentrate on advanced textbooks and technical periodicals. Think through the concepts and review difficult problems in your field.

These are all general sources. You can get more ideas on your own initiative, following these leads. For example, training manuals and publications of the government agency which employs workers in your field can be useful, particularly for technical and professional positions. A letter or visit to the government department involved may result in more specific study suggestions, and certainly will provide you with a more definite idea of the exact nature of the position you are seeking.

III. KINDS OF TESTS

Tests are used for purposes other than measuring knowledge and ability to perform specified duties. For some positions, it is equally important to test ability to make adjustments to new situations or to profit from training. In others, basic mental abilities not dependent on information are essential. Questions which test these things may not appear as pertinent to the duties of the position as those which test for knowledge and information. Yet they are often highly important parts of a fair examination. For very general questions, it is almost impossible to help you direct your study efforts. What we can do is to point out some of the more common of these general abilities needed in public service positions and describe some typical questions.

1) General information

Broad, general information has been found useful for predicting job success in some kinds of work. This is tested in a variety of ways, from vocabulary lists to questions about current events. Basic background in some field of work, such as sociology or economics, may be sampled in a group of questions. Often these are principles which have become familiar to most persons through exposure rather than through formal training. It is difficult to advise you how to study for these questions; being alert to the world around you is our best suggestion.

2) Verbal ability

An example of an ability needed in many positions is verbal or language ability. Verbal ability is, in brief, the ability to use and understand words. Vocabulary and grammar tests are typical measures of this ability. Reading comprehension or paragraph interpretation questions are common in many kinds of civil service tests. You are given a paragraph of written material and asked to find its central meaning.

3) Numerical ability

Number skills can be tested by the familiar arithmetic problem, by checking paired lists of numbers to see which are alike and which are different, or by interpreting charts and graphs. In the latter test, a graph may be printed in the test booklet which you are asked to use as the basis for answering questions.

4) Observation

A popular test for law-enforcement positions is the observation test. A picture is shown to you for several minutes, then taken away. Questions about the picture test your ability to observe both details and larger elements.

5) Following directions

In many positions in the public service, the employee must be able to carry out written instructions dependably and accurately. You may be given a chart with several columns, each column listing a variety of information. The questions require you to carry out directions involving the information given in the chart.

6) Skills and aptitudes

Performance tests effectively measure some manual skills and aptitudes. When the skill is one in which you are trained, such as typing or shorthand, you can practice. These tests are often very much like those given in business school or high school courses. For many of the other skills and aptitudes, however, no short-time preparation can be made. Skills and abilities natural to you or that you have developed throughout your lifetime are being tested.

Many of the general questions just described provide all the data needed to answer the questions and ask you to use your reasoning ability to find the answers. Your best preparation for these tests, as well as for tests of facts and ideas, is to be at your physical and mental best. You, no doubt, have your own methods of getting into an exam-taking mood and keeping "in shape." The next section lists some ideas on this subject.

IV. KINDS OF QUESTIONS

Only rarely is the "essay" question, which you answer in narrative form, used in civil service tests. Civil service tests are usually of the short-answer type. Full instructions for answering these questions will be given to you at the examination. But in case this is your first experience with short-answer questions and separate answer sheets, here is what you need to know:

1) Multiple-choice Questions

Most popular of the short-answer questions is the "multiple choice" or "best answer" question. It can be used, for example, to test for factual knowledge, ability to solve problems or judgment in meeting situations found at work.

A multiple-choice question is normally one of three types—

- It can begin with an incomplete statement followed by several possible endings. You are to find the one ending which *best* completes the statement, although some of the others may not be entirely wrong.
- It can also be a complete statement in the form of a question which is answered by choosing one of the statements listed.

- It can be in the form of a problem – again you select the best answer.

Here is an example of a multiple-choice question with a discussion which should give you some clues as to the method for choosing the right answer:

When an employee has a complaint about his assignment, the action which will *best* help him overcome his difficulty is to
    A. discuss his difficulty with his coworkers
    B. take the problem to the head of the organization
    C. take the problem to the person who gave him the assignment
    D. say nothing to anyone about his complaint

In answering this question, you should study each of the choices to find which is best. Consider choice "A" – Certainly an employee may discuss his complaint with fellow employees, but no change or improvement can result, and the complaint remains unresolved. Choice "B" is a poor choice since the head of the organization probably does not know what assignment you have been given, and taking your problem to him is known as "going over the head" of the supervisor. The supervisor, or person who made the assignment, is the person who can clarify it or correct any injustice. Choice "C" is, therefore, correct. To say nothing, as in choice "D," is unwise. Supervisors have and interest in knowing the problems employees are facing, and the employee is seeking a solution to his problem.

2) True/False Questions

The "true/false" or "right/wrong" form of question is sometimes used. Here a complete statement is given. Your job is to decide whether the statement is right or wrong.

SAMPLE: A roaming cell-phone call to a nearby city costs less than a non-roaming call to a distant city.

This statement is wrong, or false, since roaming calls are more expensive.

This is not a complete list of all possible question forms, although most of the others are variations of these common types. You will always get complete directions for answering questions. Be sure you understand *how* to mark your answers – ask questions until you do.

V. RECORDING YOUR ANSWERS

Computer terminals are used more and more today for many different kinds of exams.
For an examination with very few applicants, you may be told to record your answers in the test booklet itself. Separate answer sheets are much more common. If this separate answer sheet is to be scored by machine – and this is often the case – it is highly important that you mark your answers correctly in order to get credit.
An electronic scoring machine is often used in civil service offices because of the speed with which papers can be scored. Machine-scored answer sheets must be marked with a pencil, which will be given to you. This pencil has a high graphite content which responds to the electronic scoring machine. As a matter of fact, stray dots may register as answers, so do not let your pencil rest on the answer sheet while you are pondering the correct answer. Also, if your pencil lead breaks or is otherwise defective, ask for another.

Since the answer sheet will be dropped in a slot in the scoring machine, be careful not to bend the corners or get the paper crumpled.

The answer sheet normally has five vertical columns of numbers, with 30 numbers to a column. These numbers correspond to the question numbers in your test booklet. After each number, going across the page are four or five pairs of dotted lines. These short dotted lines have small letters or numbers above them. The first two pairs may also have a "T" or "F" above the letters. This indicates that the first two pairs only are to be used if the questions are of the true-false type. If the questions are multiple choice, disregard the "T" and "F" and pay attention only to the small letters or numbers.

Answer your questions in the manner of the sample that follows:

32. The largest city in the United States is
    A. Washington, D.C.
    B. New York City
    C. Chicago
    D. Detroit
    E. San Francisco

1) Choose the answer you think is best. (New York City is the largest, so "B" is correct.)
2) Find the row of dotted lines numbered the same as the question you are answering. (Find row number 32)
3) Find the pair of dotted lines corresponding to the answer. (Find the pair of lines under the mark "B.")
4) Make a solid black mark between the dotted lines.

VI. BEFORE THE TEST

Common sense will help you find procedures to follow to get ready for an examination. Too many of us, however, overlook these sensible measures. Indeed, nervousness and fatigue have been found to be the most serious reasons why applicants fail to do their best on civil service tests. Here is a list of reminders:

- Begin your preparation early – Don't wait until the last minute to go scurrying around for books and materials or to find out what the position is all about.
- Prepare continuously – An hour a night for a week is better than an all-night cram session. This has been definitely established. What is more, a night a week for a month will return better dividends than crowding your study into a shorter period of time.
- Locate the place of the exam – You have been sent a notice telling you when and where to report for the examination. If the location is in a different town or otherwise unfamiliar to you, it would be well to inquire the best route and learn something about the building.
- Relax the night before the test – Allow your mind to rest. Do not study at all that night. Plan some mild recreation or diversion; then go to bed early and get a good night's sleep.
- Get up early enough to make a leisurely trip to the place for the test – This way unforeseen events, traffic snarls, unfamiliar buildings, etc. will not upset you.
- Dress comfortably – A written test is not a fashion show. You will be known by number and not by name, so wear something comfortable.

- Leave excess paraphernalia at home – Shopping bags and odd bundles will get in your way. You need bring only the items mentioned in the official notice you received; usually everything you need is provided. Do not bring reference books to the exam. They will only confuse those last minutes and be taken away from you when in the test room.
- Arrive somewhat ahead of time – If because of transportation schedules you must get there very early, bring a newspaper or magazine to take your mind off yourself while waiting.
- Locate the examination room – When you have found the proper room, you will be directed to the seat or part of the room where you will sit. Sometimes you are given a sheet of instructions to read while you are waiting. Do not fill out any forms until you are told to do so; just read them and be prepared.
- Relax and prepare to listen to the instructions
- If you have any physical problem that may keep you from doing your best, be sure to tell the test administrator. If you are sick or in poor health, you really cannot do your best on the exam. You can come back and take the test some other time.

VII. AT THE TEST

The day of the test is here and you have the test booklet in your hand. The temptation to get going is very strong. Caution! There is more to success than knowing the right answers. You must know how to identify your papers and understand variations in the type of short-answer question used in this particular examination. Follow these suggestions for maximum results from your efforts:

1) Cooperate with the monitor
The test administrator has a duty to create a situation in which you can be as much at ease as possible. He will give instructions, tell you when to begin, check to see that you are marking your answer sheet correctly, and so on. He is not there to guard you, although he will see that your competitors do not take unfair advantage. He wants to help you do your best.

2) Listen to all instructions
Don't jump the gun! Wait until you understand all directions. In most civil service tests you get more time than you need to answer the questions. So don't be in a hurry. Read each word of instructions until you clearly understand the meaning. Study the examples, listen to all announcements and follow directions. Ask questions if you do not understand what to do.

3) Identify your papers
Civil service exams are usually identified by number only. You will be assigned a number; you must not put your name on your test papers. Be sure to copy your number correctly. Since more than one exam may be given, copy your exact examination title.

4) Plan your time
Unless you are told that a test is a "speed" or "rate of work" test, speed itself is usually not important. Time enough to answer all the questions will be provided, but this does not mean that you have all day. An overall time limit has been set. Divide the total time (in minutes) by the number of questions to determine the approximate time you have for each question.

5) Do not linger over difficult questions

If you come across a difficult question, mark it with a paper clip (useful to have along) and come back to it when you have been through the booklet. One caution if you do this – be sure to skip a number on your answer sheet as well. Check often to be sure that you have not lost your place and that you are marking in the row numbered the same as the question you are answering.

6) Read the questions

Be sure you know what the question asks! Many capable people are unsuccessful because they failed to *read* the questions correctly.

7) Answer all questions

Unless you have been instructed that a penalty will be deducted for incorrect answers, it is better to guess than to omit a question.

8) Speed tests

It is often better NOT to guess on speed tests. It has been found that on timed tests people are tempted to spend the last few seconds before time is called in marking answers at random – without even reading them – in the hope of picking up a few extra points. To discourage this practice, the instructions may warn you that your score will be "corrected" for guessing. That is, a penalty will be applied. The incorrect answers will be deducted from the correct ones, or some other penalty formula will be used.

9) Review your answers

If you finish before time is called, go back to the questions you guessed or omitted to give them further thought. Review other answers if you have time.

10) Return your test materials

If you are ready to leave before others have finished or time is called, take ALL your materials to the monitor and leave quietly. Never take any test material with you. The monitor can discover whose papers are not complete, and taking a test booklet may be grounds for disqualification.

VIII. EXAMINATION TECHNIQUES

1) Read the general instructions carefully. These are usually printed on the first page of the exam booklet. As a rule, these instructions refer to the timing of the examination; the fact that you should not start work until the signal and must stop work at a signal, etc. If there are any *special* instructions, such as a choice of questions to be answered, make sure that you note this instruction carefully.

2) When you are ready to start work on the examination, that is as soon as the signal has been given, read the instructions to each question booklet, underline any key words or phrases, such as *least, best, outline, describe* and the like. In this way you will tend to answer as requested rather than discover on reviewing your paper that you *listed without describing*, that you selected the *worst* choice rather than the *best* choice, etc.

3) If the examination is of the objective or multiple-choice type – that is, each question will also give a series of possible answers: A, B, C or D, and you are called upon to select the best answer and write the letter next to that answer on your answer paper – it is advisable to start answering each question in turn. There may be anywhere from 50 to 100 such questions in the three or four hours allotted and you can see how much time would be taken if you read through all the questions before beginning to answer any. Furthermore, if you come across a question or group of questions which you know would be difficult to answer, it would undoubtedly affect your handling of all the other questions.

4) If the examination is of the essay type and contains but a few questions, it is a moot point as to whether you should read all the questions before starting to answer any one. Of course, if you are given a choice – say five out of seven and the like – then it is essential to read all the questions so you can eliminate the two that are most difficult. If, however, you are asked to answer all the questions, there may be danger in trying to answer the easiest one first because you may find that you will spend too much time on it. The best technique is to answer the first question, then proceed to the second, etc.

5) Time your answers. Before the exam begins, write down the time it started, then add the time allowed for the examination and write down the time it must be completed, then divide the time available somewhat as follows:
    - If 3-1/2 hours are allowed, that would be 210 minutes. If you have 80 objective-type questions, that would be an average of 2-1/2 minutes per question. Allow yourself no more than 2 minutes per question, or a total of 160 minutes, which will permit about 50 minutes to review.
    - If for the time allotment of 210 minutes there are 7 essay questions to answer, that would average about 30 minutes a question. Give yourself only 25 minutes per question so that you have about 35 minutes to review.

6) The most important instruction is to *read each question* and make sure you know what is wanted. The second most important instruction is to *time yourself properly* so that you answer every question. The third most important instruction is to *answer every question*. Guess if you have to but include something for each question. Remember that you will receive no credit for a blank and will probably receive some credit if you write something in answer to an essay question. If you guess a letter – say "B" for a multiple-choice question – you may have guessed right. If you leave a blank as an answer to a multiple-choice question, the examiners may respect your feelings but it will not add a point to your score. Some exams may penalize you for wrong answers, so in such cases *only*, you may not want to guess unless you have some basis for your answer.

7) Suggestions
    a. Objective-type questions
        1. Examine the question booklet for proper sequence of pages and questions
        2. Read all instructions carefully
        3. Skip any question which seems too difficult; return to it after all other questions have been answered
        4. Apportion your time properly; do not spend too much time on any single question or group of questions

5. Note and underline key words – *all, most, fewest, least, best, worst, same, opposite,* etc.
6. Pay particular attention to negatives
7. Note unusual option, e.g., unduly long, short, complex, different or similar in content to the body of the question
8. Observe the use of "hedging" words – *probably, may, most likely,* etc.
9. Make sure that your answer is put next to the same number as the question
10. Do not second-guess unless you have good reason to believe the second answer is definitely more correct
11. Cross out original answer if you decide another answer is more accurate; do not erase until you are ready to hand your paper in
12. Answer all questions; guess unless instructed otherwise
13. Leave time for review

b. Essay questions
1. Read each question carefully
2. Determine exactly what is wanted. Underline key words or phrases.
3. Decide on outline or paragraph answer
4. Include many different points and elements unless asked to develop any one or two points or elements
5. Show impartiality by giving pros and cons unless directed to select one side only
6. Make and write down any assumptions you find necessary to answer the questions
7. Watch your English, grammar, punctuation and choice of words
8. Time your answers; don't crowd material

8) Answering the essay question

Most essay questions can be answered by framing the specific response around several key words or ideas. Here are a few such key words or ideas:

M's: manpower, materials, methods, money, management
P's: purpose, program, policy, plan, procedure, practice, problems, pitfalls, personnel, public relations

a. Six basic steps in handling problems:
1. Preliminary plan and background development
2. Collect information, data and facts
3. Analyze and interpret information, data and facts
4. Analyze and develop solutions as well as make recommendations
5. Prepare report and sell recommendations
6. Install recommendations and follow up effectiveness

b. Pitfalls to avoid
1. *Taking things for granted* – A statement of the situation does not necessarily imply that each of the elements is necessarily true; for example, a complaint may be invalid and biased so that all that can be taken for granted is that a complaint has been registered

2. *Considering only one side of a situation* – Wherever possible, indicate several alternatives and then point out the reasons you selected the best one
3. *Failing to indicate follow up* – Whenever your answer indicates action on your part, make certain that you will take proper follow-up action to see how successful your recommendations, procedures or actions turn out to be
4. *Taking too long in answering any single question* – Remember to time your answers properly

IX. AFTER THE TEST

Scoring procedures differ in detail among civil service jurisdictions although the general principles are the same. Whether the papers are hand-scored or graded by machine we have described, they are nearly always graded by number. That is, the person who marks the paper knows only the number – never the name – of the applicant. Not until all the papers have been graded will they be matched with names. If other tests, such as training and experience or oral interview ratings have been given, scores will be combined. Different parts of the examination usually have different weights. For example, the written test might count 60 percent of the final grade, and a rating of training and experience 40 percent. In many jurisdictions, veterans will have a certain number of points added to their grades.

After the final grade has been determined, the names are placed in grade order and an eligible list is established. There are various methods for resolving ties between those who get the same final grade – probably the most common is to place first the name of the person whose application was received first. Job offers are made from the eligible list in the order the names appear on it. You will be notified of your grade and your rank as soon as all these computations have been made. This will be done as rapidly as possible.

People who are found to meet the requirements in the announcement are called "eligibles." Their names are put on a list of eligible candidates. An eligible's chances of getting a job depend on how high he stands on this list and how fast agencies are filling jobs from the list.

When a job is to be filled from a list of eligibles, the agency asks for the names of people on the list of eligibles for that job. When the civil service commission receives this request, it sends to the agency the names of the three people highest on this list. Or, if the job to be filled has specialized requirements, the office sends the agency the names of the top three persons who meet these requirements from the general list.

The appointing officer makes a choice from among the three people whose names were sent to him. If the selected person accepts the appointment, the names of the others are put back on the list to be considered for future openings.

That is the rule in hiring from all kinds of eligible lists, whether they are for typist, carpenter, chemist, or something else. For every vacancy, the appointing officer has his choice of any one of the top three eligibles on the list. This explains why the person whose name is on top of the list sometimes does not get an appointment when some of the persons lower on the list do. If the appointing officer chooses the second or third eligible, the No. 1 eligible does not get a job at once, but stays on the list until he is appointed or the list is terminated.

X. HOW TO PASS THE INTERVIEW TEST

The examination for which you applied requires an oral interview test. You have already taken the written test and you are now being called for the interview test – the final part of the formal examination.

You may think that it is not possible to prepare for an interview test and that there are no procedures to follow during an interview. Our purpose is to point out some things you can do in advance that will help you and some good rules to follow and pitfalls to avoid while you are being interviewed.

What is an interview supposed to test?

The written examination is designed to test the technical knowledge and competence of the candidate; the oral is designed to evaluate intangible qualities, not readily measured otherwise, and to establish a list showing the relative fitness of each candidate – as measured against his competitors – for the position sought. Scoring is not on the basis of "right" and "wrong," but on a sliding scale of values ranging from "not passable" to "outstanding." As a matter of fact, it is possible to achieve a relatively low score without a single "incorrect" answer because of evident weakness in the qualities being measured.

Occasionally, an examination may consist entirely of an oral test – either an individual or a group oral. In such cases, information is sought concerning the technical knowledges and abilities of the candidate, since there has been no written examination for this purpose. More commonly, however, an oral test is used to supplement a written examination.

Who conducts interviews?

The composition of oral boards varies among different jurisdictions. In nearly all, a representative of the personnel department serves as chairman. One of the members of the board may be a representative of the department in which the candidate would work. In some cases, "outside experts" are used, and, frequently, a businessman or some other representative of the general public is asked to serve. Labor and management or other special groups may be represented. The aim is to secure the services of experts in the appropriate field.

However the board is composed, it is a good idea (and not at all improper or unethical) to ascertain in advance of the interview who the members are and what groups they represent. When you are introduced to them, you will have some idea of their backgrounds and interests, and at least you will not stutter and stammer over their names.

What should be done before the interview?

While knowledge about the board members is useful and takes some of the surprise element out of the interview, there is other preparation which is more substantive. It *is* possible to prepare for an oral interview – in several ways:

1) Keep a copy of your application and review it carefully before the interview

This may be the only document before the oral board, and the starting point of the interview. Know what education and experience you have listed there, and the sequence and dates of all of it. Sometimes the board will ask you to review the highlights of your experience for them; you should not have to hem and haw doing it.

2) Study the class specification and the examination announcement

Usually, the oral board has one or both of these to guide them. The qualities, characteristics or knowledges required by the position sought are stated in these documents. They offer valuable clues as to the nature of the oral interview. For example, if the job involves supervisory responsibilities, the announcement will usually indicate that knowledge of modern supervisory methods and the qualifications of the candidate as a supervisor will be tested. If so, you can expect such questions, frequently in the form of a hypothetical situation which you are expected to solve. NEVER go into an oral without knowledge of the duties and responsibilities of the job you seek.

3) Think through each qualification required

Try to visualize the kind of questions you would ask if you were a board member. How well could you answer them? Try especially to appraise your own knowledge and background in each area, *measured against the job sought*, and identify any areas in which you are weak. Be critical and realistic – do not flatter yourself.

4) Do some general reading in areas in which you feel you may be weak

For example, if the job involves supervision and your past experience has NOT, some general reading in supervisory methods and practices, particularly in the field of human relations, might be useful. Do NOT study agency procedures or detailed manuals. The oral board will be testing your understanding and capacity, not your memory.

5) Get a good night's sleep and watch your general health and mental attitude

You will want a clear head at the interview. Take care of a cold or any other minor ailment, and of course, no hangovers.

What should be done on the day of the interview?

Now comes the day of the interview itself. Give yourself plenty of time to get there. Plan to arrive somewhat ahead of the scheduled time, particularly if your appointment is in the fore part of the day. If a previous candidate fails to appear, the board might be ready for you a bit early. By early afternoon an oral board is almost invariably behind schedule if there are many candidates, and you may have to wait. Take along a book or magazine to read, or your application to review, but leave any extraneous material in the waiting room when you go in for your interview. In any event, relax and compose yourself.

The matter of dress is important. The board is forming impressions about you – from your experience, your manners, your attitude, and your appearance. Give your personal appearance careful attention. Dress your best, but not your flashiest. Choose conservative, appropriate clothing, and be sure it is immaculate. This is a business interview, and your appearance should indicate that you regard it as such. Besides, being well groomed and properly dressed will help boost your confidence.

Sooner or later, someone will call your name and escort you into the interview room. *This is it.* From here on you are on your own. It is too late for any more preparation. But remember, you asked for this opportunity to prove your fitness, and you are here because your request was granted.

What happens when you go in?

The usual sequence of events will be as follows: The clerk (who is often the board stenographer) will introduce you to the chairman of the oral board, who will introduce you to the other members of the board. Acknowledge the introductions before you sit down. Do not be surprised if you find a microphone facing you or a stenotypist sitting by. Oral interviews are usually recorded in the event of an appeal or other review.

Usually the chairman of the board will open the interview by reviewing the highlights of your education and work experience from your application – primarily for the benefit of the other members of the board, as well as to get the material into the record. Do not interrupt or comment unless there is an error or significant misinterpretation; if that is the case, do not hesitate. But do not quibble about insignificant matters. Also, he will usually ask you some question about your education, experience or your present job – partly to get you to start talking and to establish the interviewing "rapport." He may start the actual questioning, or turn it over to one of the other members. Frequently, each member undertakes the questioning on a particular area, one in which he is perhaps most competent, so you can expect each member to participate in the examination. Because time is limited, you may also expect some rather abrupt switches in the direction the questioning takes, so do not be upset by it. Normally, a board member will not pursue a single line of questioning unless he discovers a particular strength or weakness.

After each member has participated, the chairman will usually ask whether any member has any further questions, then will ask you if you have anything you wish to add. Unless you are expecting this question, it may floor you. Worse, it may start you off on an extended, extemporaneous speech. The board is not usually seeking more information. The question is principally to offer you a last opportunity to present further qualifications or to indicate that you have nothing to add. So, if you feel that a significant qualification or characteristic has been overlooked, it is proper to point it out in a sentence or so. Do not compliment the board on the thoroughness of their examination – they have been sketchy, and you know it. If you wish, merely say, "No thank you, I have nothing further to add." This is a point where you can "talk yourself out" of a good impression or fail to present an important bit of information. Remember, *you close the interview yourself.*

The chairman will then say, "That is all, Mr. _____, thank you." Do not be startled; the interview is over, and quicker than you think. Thank him, gather your belongings and take your leave. Save your sigh of relief for the other side of the door.

How to put your best foot forward

Throughout this entire process, you may feel that the board individually and collectively is trying to pierce your defenses, seek out your hidden weaknesses and embarrass and confuse you. Actually, this is not true. They are obliged to make an appraisal of your qualifications for the job you are seeking, and they want to see you in your best light. Remember, they must interview all candidates and a non-cooperative candidate may become a failure in spite of their best efforts to bring out his qualifications. Here are 15 suggestions that will help you:

1) **Be natural – Keep your attitude confident, not cocky**

If you are not confident that you can do the job, do not expect the board to be. Do not apologize for your weaknesses, try to bring out your strong points. The board is interested in a positive, not negative, presentation. Cockiness will antagonize any board member and make him wonder if you are covering up a weakness by a false show of strength.

2) **Get comfortable, but don't lounge or sprawl**

Sit erectly but not stiffly. A careless posture may lead the board to conclude that you are careless in other things, or at least that you are not impressed by the importance of the occasion. Either conclusion is natural, even if incorrect. Do not fuss with your clothing, a pencil or an ashtray. Your hands may occasionally be useful to emphasize a point; do not let them become a point of distraction.

3) **Do not wisecrack or make small talk**

This is a serious situation, and your attitude should show that you consider it as such. Further, the time of the board is limited – they do not want to waste it, and neither should you.

4) Do not exaggerate your experience or abilities

In the first place, from information in the application or other interviews and sources, the board may know more about you than you think. Secondly, you probably will not get away with it. An experienced board is rather adept at spotting such a situation, so do not take the chance.

5) If you know a board member, do not make a point of it, yet do not hide it

Certainly you are not fooling him, and probably not the other members of the board. Do not try to take advantage of your acquaintanceship – it will probably do you little good.

6) Do not dominate the interview

Let the board do that. They will give you the clues – do not assume that you have to do all the talking. Realize that the board has a number of questions to ask you, and do not try to take up all the interview time by showing off your extensive knowledge of the answer to the first one.

7) Be attentive

You only have 20 minutes or so, and you should keep your attention at its sharpest throughout. When a member is addressing a problem or question to you, give him your undivided attention. Address your reply principally to him, but do not exclude the other board members.

8) Do not interrupt

A board member may be stating a problem for you to analyze. He will ask you a question when the time comes. Let him state the problem, and wait for the question.

9) Make sure you understand the question

Do not try to answer until you are sure what the question is. If it is not clear, restate it in your own words or ask the board member to clarify it for you. However, do not haggle about minor elements.

10) Reply promptly but not hastily

A common entry on oral board rating sheets is "candidate responded readily," or "candidate hesitated in replies." Respond as promptly and quickly as you can, but do not jump to a hasty, ill-considered answer.

11) Do not be peremptory in your answers

A brief answer is proper – but do not fire your answer back. That is a losing game from your point of view. The board member can probably ask questions much faster than you can answer them.

12) Do not try to create the answer you think the board member wants

He is interested in what kind of mind you have and how it works – not in playing games. Furthermore, he can usually spot this practice and will actually grade you down on it.

13) Do not switch sides in your reply merely to agree with a board member

Frequently, a member will take a contrary position merely to draw you out and to see if you are willing and able to defend your point of view. Do not start a debate, yet do not surrender a good position. If a position is worth taking, it is worth defending.

14) Do not be afraid to admit an error in judgment if you are shown to be wrong

The board knows that you are forced to reply without any opportunity for careful consideration. Your answer may be demonstrably wrong. If so, admit it and get on with the interview.

15) Do not dwell at length on your present job

The opening question may relate to your present assignment. Answer the question but do not go into an extended discussion. You are being examined for a *new* job, not your present one. As a matter of fact, try to phrase ALL your answers in terms of the job for which you are being examined.

Basis of Rating

Probably you will forget most of these "do's" and "don'ts" when you walk into the oral interview room. Even remembering them all will not ensure you a passing grade. Perhaps you did not have the qualifications in the first place. But remembering them will help you to put your best foot forward, without treading on the toes of the board members.

Rumor and popular opinion to the contrary notwithstanding, an oral board wants you to make the best appearance possible. They know you are under pressure – but they also want to see how you respond to it as a guide to what your reaction would be under the pressures of the job you seek. They will be influenced by the degree of poise you display, the personal traits you show and the manner in which you respond.

ABOUT THIS BOOK

This book contains tests divided into Examination Sections. Go through each test, answering every question in the margin. We have also attached a sample answer sheet at the back of the book that can be removed and used. At the end of each test look at the answer key and check your answers. On the ones you got wrong, look at the right answer choice and learn. Do not fill in the answers first. Do not memorize the questions and answers, but understand the answer and principles involved. On your test, the questions will likely be different from the samples. Questions are changed and new ones added. If you understand these past questions you should have success with any changes that arise. Tests may consist of several types of questions. We have additional books on each subject should more study be advisable or necessary for you. Finally, the more you study, the better prepared you will be. This book is intended to be the last thing you study before you walk into the examination room. Prior study of relevant texts is also recommended. NLC publishes some of these in our Fundamental Series. Knowledge and good sense are important factors in passing your exam. Good luck also helps. So now study this Passbook, absorb the material contained within and take that knowledge into the examination. Then do your best to pass that exam.

EXAMINATION SECTION

EXAMINATION SECTION

TEST 1

DIRECTIONS: Each question or incomplete statement is followed by several suggested answers or completions. Select the one that BEST answers the question or completes the statement. *PRINT THE LETTER OF THE ANSWER YOU CHOOSE IN THE SPACE AT THE RIGHT.*

PART A: LOGICAL REASONING TEST

Questions 1-9.
To answer questions 1 through 9, you should select the only answer that can be validly concluded from the paragraph that is given. You must use ONLY the information provided in the paragraph, without using any outside information whatsoever. In some questions, you will be asked to select the only answer that can be validly inferred from the paragraph, and in other questions, you will be asked to select the only answer that CANNOT be validly inferred from the paragraph. Mark the letter of your choice in the space at the right.

1. In order to make a valid arrest, a police officer must have probable cause, a "reasonable ground for belief in guilt," as Supreme Court Justice Rutledge stated in a 1949 opinion. This is a belief based on probabilities: more than suspicion but far less than certainty. This standard of probable cause prevents a police officer from arresting someone and finding the crime later. A police officer may make an arrest if and only if he or she has formed a reasonable belief, based on the facts, that someone has committed a crime. Courts have widely held that flight from a police officer is sufficient to justify probable cause. In a recent case a subject fled from Officer D.F.

   From the information given above it can be validly concluded that

   A) Officer D.F. may arrest the subject who fled from him
   B) Officer D.F. may not arrest the subject who fled from him
   C) no valid arrests are made with probable cause
   D) some valid arrests are made without probable cause
   E) some arrests made with probable cause are not valid arrests

   1._____

2. A trucking company can act as a common carrier -- for hire to the general public at published rates. As a common carrier, it is liable for any cargo damage, unless the company can show that it is not negligent, then it is not liable for cargo damage. In contrast, a contract carrier (a trucking company hired by a shipper under a specific contract) is responsible only for cargo damage as spelled out in the contract. A Weeks Inc. tractor-trailer, acting under common carrier authority, was in a 5-vehicle accident that damaged its cargo. An Ankum Inc. tractor-trailer, acting under contract carrier authority, was involved in the same accident, and its cargo was also damaged.

   2._____

From the information given above it can be validly concluded that, in reference to the accident,

- A) if Weeks Inc. is liable, then it can show that it was not negligent
- B) if Weeks Inc. cannot show that it was not negligent, then it is not liable
- C) if Weeks Inc. can show that it was not negligent, then it is not liable
- D) if Ankum Inc. is liable, then it cannot show that it is negligent
- E) if Ankum Inc. can show that it is not negligent, then it is not liable

3. Under the Internal Revenue Code, the theft or damage of some kinds of uninsured property may be treated as a casualty loss and a tax deduction may be taken for that loss. The amount of the loss equals the reduction in the fair market value of the item. If the IRS determines that an appraisal of its lost value is difficult or impossible to obtain, the cost of the repairs is accepted as establishing the value of that reduction. G.B. claimed a casualty loss on her tax return, but the cost of the repairs was not accepted by the IRS as establishing the amount of that loss.

3._____

From the information given above it can be validly concluded that, the IRS determined that an appraisal of the item's lost value

- A) is both difficult and impossible to obtain
- B) is impossible to obtain
- C) is quite difficult, or even impossible to obtain
- D) is difficult to obtain
- E) is neither difficult nor impossible to obtain

4. Despite the fact that HIV is not easily transmitted, its deadly potential requires that law enforcement officers protect themselves from becoming infected by it. At the Callen Precinct, officers use only disposable items for collecting evidence whenever blood is present. While investigating a particular crime scene where blood was present, Detective R.C. of the Callen Precinct used only disposable items for collecting evidence.

4._____

From the information given above it can be validly concluded that, when collecting evidence at a crime scene,

- A) Detective R.C. does not always use disposable items when blood is present
- B) whenever blood is not present, Detective R.C. does not use only disposable items
- C) Detective R.C. uses only disposable items whenever blood is not present
- D) no officers at the Callen Precinct fail to use only disposable items whenever blood is present
- E) some officers at the Callen Precinct do not use disposable items exclusively whenever blood is present

5. Often, crimes are characterized as either *malum in se* -- inherently evil – or *malum prohibitum* -- criminal because they are declared as offenses by a legislature. Murder is an example of *malum in se*. Failing to file a tax return illustrates *malum prohibitum*. Some jurisdictions no longer distinguish between *malum in se* and *malum prohibitum*, although many still do.

5._____

From the information given above it can be validly concluded that

- A) many jurisdictions no longer distinguish between crimes *malum in se* and *malum prohibitum*
- B) some jurisdictions still distinguish between crimes *malum in se* and *malum prohibitum*
- C) some crimes characterized as *malum in se* are not inherently evil
- D) some crimes characterized as *malum prohibitum* are not declared by a legislature to be an offense
- E) sometimes failing to file a tax return is characterized as *malum in se*

6. All Treasury securities, including T-bills, notes, and bonds, are now issued in book-entry form. Instead of being issued as paper certificates to investors, these securities are now electronically logged as accounting entries with the U.S. Treasury, a Federal Reserve Bank, or some other custodian.

6._____

From the information given above it can be validly concluded that

- A) some Treasury securities are now issued as paper certificates
- B) any securities that are not issued in book-entry form are not Treasury securities
- C) no Treasury securities are now issued in book-entry form
- D) it is not true that some securities now issued in book-entry form are Treasury securities
- E) it is not true that all securities issued as paper certificates are non-Treasury securities

7. Some 350,000 immigrants were admitted to the United States in 1977. By 1993, 42 percent of them had been naturalized as U.S. citizens. Among these immigrants, the ones engaged in health diagnosing occupations had the highest percentage of naturalization -- 64%. Of course, 1977 immigrants in many professional occupations were naturalized at rates above 50%.

7._____

From the information given above it can be validly concluded that, among 1977 immigrants to the United States,

- A) many employee subgroups who were naturalized at rates above 50% were in professional occupations
- B) it is not true that some employee subgroups who were naturalized at rates above 50% were in professional occupations
- C) no immigrants in professional occupations were naturalized at rates above 50%

D) many in professional occupations were not naturalized at rates above 50%
   E) almost all who were in professional occupations were naturalized at rates below 50%

8. The Supreme Court's power to invalidate legislation that violates the Constitution is a strong restriction on the powers of Congress. If an act of Congress is deemed unconstitutional by the Supreme Court, then the Act is voided. Unlike a presidential veto, which can be overridden by two-thirds vote of the House and Senate, a constitutional ruling by the Supreme Court must be accepted by the Congress.

8._____

From the information given above it can be validly concluded that

   A) If an act of Congress is voided, then it has been deemed unconstitutional by the Supreme Court
   B) If an act of Congress has not been voided, then it has not been deemed unconstitutional by the Supreme Court
   C) If an act of Congress has not been deemed unconstitutional by the Supreme Court, then it is voided
   D) If an act of Congress is deemed unconstitutional by the Supreme Court, then it is not voided
   E) If an act of Congress has not been voided, then it has been deemed unconstitutional by the Supreme Court

9. A rapidly changing technical environment in government is promoting greater reliance on electronic mail (email) systems. As this usage grows, there are increasing chances of conflict between the users' expectations of privacy and public access rights. In some investigations, access to all email, including those messages stored in archival files and messages outside the scope of the investigation, has been sought and granted. In spite of this, some people send messages through email that would never be said face-to-face or written formally.

9._____

From the information given above it CANNOT be validly concluded that

   A) some email messages that have been requested as part of investigations have contained messages that would never be said face-to-face
   B) some messages that people would never say face-to-face are sent in email messages
   C) some email messages have been requested as part of investigations
   D) email messages have not been exempted from investigations
   E) some email messages contain information that would be omitted from formal writing

PART B: ARITHMETIC REASONING

DIRECTIONS: The questions in this part of the test require you to solve math word problems involving operations such as addition, subtraction, multiplication, division, calculating percentages and averages, solving rate problems, and calculating simple probabilities. These operations reflect the type of mathematical operations that are performed routinely in CBP Officer work. Mark the letter of the answer you choose in the space at right.

10. Staff at a law enforcement training academy purchases badges at $32 each for all the graduates of the academy. The last training class graduated 25 new officers. What is the total amount of money the academy staff will spend for the badges for these new officers, if the badge vendor provided the Academy a 20% discount on each badge?

    A) $800
    B) $790
    C) $640
    D) $ 16
    E) None of these

    10._____

11. The gross weight of merchandise in a container examined by an officer was 108 pounds. According to policy, the officer was required to convert this weight into kilograms. If the formula for conversion is 1.8 pounds for each kilogram, what was the gross weight of the container load in kilograms (rounded to the nearest tenth)?

    A) 194.0
    B) 166.6
    C) 60.0
    D) 45.0
    E) None of these

    11._____

12. On a typical day, 4/5 of all the objects inspected at a large international airport are not passenger luggage. Therefore, for a piece of passenger luggage located anywhere in the airport, the probability that it is not subject to inspection is

    A) zero
    B) 20%
    C) 75%
    D) 80%
    E) None of these

    12._____

13. A CBP Officer and her dog found a total of 1,500 packages wrapped in plain brown paper hidden in a large mail container. Upon inspection, the officer found that some of the packages had legal CBP stickers on them and some had illegal stickers from another country. The proportion or ratio of packages with legal stickers to packages with illegal stickers was 2:3. How many packages contained illegal stickers?

    A) 1,000
    B)   900
    C)   600
    D)   500
    E) None of these

13._____

14. While working the evening shift, Officer K took 8 hours to complete a task at his work station and Officer M took 10 hours to complete the same task at his work station. How long would it take Officer K and Officer M to complete the same task working together, each working at his own work station?

    A) 9
    B) 8 1/9
    C) 4 4/9
    D) 6 3/4
    E) None of these

14._____

15. There are three dogs in a canine team in charge of inspecting cargo at an international airport. Last week, one of these dogs identified 20 packages of narcotics among 120 packages of incoming freight in a flight arriving from a certain country. Assuming that the dog selected the first package to be inspected totally at random, the probability that this package contained a shipment of narcotics was

    A) 1/3
    B) 1/4
    C) 1/5
    D) 1/6
    E) None of these

15._____

16. One day, Officer Ferong spent 4 hours processing passengers from a flight from Brazil at a rate of 16 passengers every 40 minutes. The next day, she spent 4 hours processing passengers at a rate of 18 every 40 minutes. What was the average number of passengers she processed during the 4-hour periods on day one and day two?

    A) 283
    B) 204
    C) 141.5
    D) 102
    E) None of these

16._____

PART C: WRITING SKILLS

DIRECTIONS: For questions 17, 18, 19, and 20 choose the one answer that represents a correction that should be made to the sentence. If no correction is necessary, choose (D).

17. Once a request to carry firearms into a foreign country are approved, an officer must notify the Office of Foreign Operations for coordination of the request.

    A) insert a comma after Operations
    B) change are to is
    C) change coordination to coordinating
    D) no correction is necessary

    17._____

18. Officer Smith knows that it is important for his CBP Officers to understand each of the fundamental principals that apply to all methods of dog training.

    A. change knows to know
    B. insert a comma after Officers
    C. change principals to principles
    D. no correction is necessary

    18._____

19. The geographical area composing much of the border between the U.S. and Mexico is considered to have a desert climate.

    A. change between to from
    B. insert a comma after area
    C. change is to are
    D. no correction is necessary

    19._____

20. When writing a report on a drug smuggling incident, it is important to add all dates, times, names, and quotes associated from the case for future reference.

    A. change incident to incedent
    B. remove the comma after names
    C. change from to with
    D. no correction is necessary

    20._____

DIRECTIONS: For sample questions 21 and 22, choose the one sentence which is correct in grammar, syntax, punctuation, and spelling and which exemplifies usage suitable to a formal letter or report.

21. A) The impact of this training requirement will be measured by the number of new CBP Officers who successfully complete the probationary period.
    B) The impact that this training requirement has will be measured by the number of new CBP Officers who successfully complete the probationary period.
    C) The impact of this training requirement will be measured by the number of new CBP Officers which successfully complete the probationary period.
    D) The impact that this training requirement has will be measured by the number of new CBP Officers which successfully complete the probationary period.
    E) The impact of this training requirement will be measured by the number of new CBP Officers whom successfully complete the probationary period.

21._____

22. A) In order to deceive the Special Agents and become a hindrance to the investigation, the informant gave a fraudulant description of the drug smugglers.
    B) In order to deceive the Special Agents and become a hindrence to the investigation, the informant gave a fraudelant description of the drug smugglers.
    C) In order to deceive the Special Agents and become a hindrance to the investigation, the informant gave a fraudulent description of the drug smugglers.
    D) In order to deceive the Special Agents and become a hindrance to the investigation, the informant gave a fraudelent description of the drug smugglers.

22._____

DIRECTIONS: For question 23, select the correct paragraph order to create a passage that is well-organized, clear, and coherent. If no correction is necessary, choose (D).

23. 1) First used on a wide scale in 1970, narcotic detector dogs save countless staff hours in locating narcotics in vehicles, mail, unaccompanied baggage, and on cargo ships. A dog and its handler can check 500 packages in 30 minutes; it would take a mail examiner several days to inspect as many. At border ports, a dog can inspect a vehicle in about two minutes; the same search by a CBP Officer would take at least 20 minutes. Therefore, the use of narcotic detector dogs has greatly enhanced the fight against illegal drug smuggling into the United States.
    2) While not exactly high-tech, a unique tool in CBP's drug fight is its force of drug detector dogs, their trainers, and the CBP Officers who work with these canine detectors.
    3) This fight continues today, extending into the high-tech world of the 21st Century. Through diligence, close inspection, sophisticated technology, and the sacrifice of lives, CBP has given an excellent account of itself in fighting the flow of illegal drugs into this country.

23._____

4) Since the repeal of Prohibition in 1933, liquor smuggling has naturally decreased. In recent years, however, the illegal entry of narcotics and dangerous drugs has increased to threatening proportions. During the 1960s, '70s, and '80s, CBP Officers have faced the almost overwhelming task of fighting the influx of opium, heroin, cocaine, hashish, marijuana, and amphetamines into the United States.

    A) 4,3,2,1
    B) 3,4,1,2
    C) 2,3,4,1
    D) no change to the sentence order is necessary

KEY (CORRECT ANSWERS)

Explanations for the Logical Reasoning Questions

1. **Correct Answer: A** Officer D. F. may arrest the subject.

The paragraph says, essentially, that "An officer may make an arrest if and only if the officer has probable cause." In the case of Officer D. F., the subject's fleeing is probable cause. Therefore, Officer D. F. may arrest the subject (Response A) and, therefore, it cannot be said that Officer D. F. may <u>not</u> arrest the subject (Response B).

The first sentence in the paragraph means that all valid arrests are made with probable cause. Response C is the opposite of this meaning, and is, therefore, false. Since all valid arrests are made with probable cause, it cannot be the case that some valid arrests are made without probable cause, Response D. The paragraph never tells us if either all, none, or some of the arrests made with probable cause are invalid, so Response E is unsupported.

2. **Correct Answer: C** If Weeks Inc. can show that it was not negligent, then it is not liable.

The second sentence states the liability rule for common carriers: all common carriers are liable for cargo damages unless they can show that they are not negligent; if they can show that they are not negligent, then they are not liable for cargo damage. Weeks Inc. is a common carrier, and accordingly, this rule applies to them. From this rule it follows that if Weeks Inc. can show it was not negligent, then it is not liable, Response C. Response A contradicts this rule by claiming that when Weeks Inc. is liable it can show that it was not negligent. Response B contradicts this rule by claiming that Weeks Inc. is not liable even when it cannot show that it is not negligent. Responses D and E concern Ankum Inc., a contract carrier. However, the terms of the Ankum Inc. contract were not disclosed in the paragraph, so neither response is supported.

3. **Correct Answer: E** The IRS determined that an appraisal of the item's lost value is neither difficult nor impossible to obtain.

This question's primary logical structure is an if-then structure. <u>If</u> an appraisal is either difficult or impossible to obtain, <u>then</u> the cost of repairs is accepted as establishing lost value. The IRS did NOT accept the use of the cost of repairs. Therefore, the appraisal is NOT "either difficult or impossible to obtain." If it had been "difficult or impossible to obtain" the appraisal, the IRS would have accepted the cost of repairs to establish the lost value. Response C says that the appraisal is "difficult or impossible to obtain," which contradicts the correct conclusion. Since the appraisal is not "either difficult or impossible to obtain," we can say that the appraisal is both easy and possible to obtain. Contrary to this, Response A says that the appraisal is both difficult and impossible to obtain. Since the appraisal is easy and possible to obtain, it cannot be impossible to obtain (Response B), nor can it be difficult to obtain (Response D).

4. **Correct Answer: D**   No officers at the Callen Precinct fail to use only disposable items whenever blood is present.

The second sentence of the paragraph states that whenever blood is present, all officers at the Callen precinct use only disposable items for collecting evidence. This is equivalent in meaning to answer D, that no officers fail to use only disposable items when collecting evidence in the presence of blood. Response E contradicts the second sentence in the paragraph by stating that some officers do not use disposable items exclusively when blood is present. Responses A, B, and C refer to the evidence gathering procedures of Detective R.C., who is identified in the third sentence of the paragraph as working for the Callen Precinct. Response A contradicts the sense of the second sentence by stating that Detective R.C. does not always use disposable items when blood is present. Responses B and C refer to R.C.'s evidence gathering when blood is not present. However, the paragraph does not give us information about evidence gathering in that case.

5. **Correct Answer: B**   Some jurisdictions still distinguish between crimes *malum in se* and *malum prohibitum*.

This question is concerned with classification of crimes into categories - that is, with the classification of crimes as either *malum in se,* which is one category, or *malum prohibitum*, which is another category. The last sentence tells us that many jurisdictions still make the distinction between these two categories of crimes. Response B is a valid conclusion based on that sentence because, if **many** jurisdictions make the distinction, then **some** jurisdictions make the distinction. However, the reverse of this is not necessarily true. The fact the **some** jurisdictions no longer make the distinction, does not necessarily mean that **many** jurisdictions no longer make the distinction because, obviously, **some** does not necessarily mean **many**. The paragraph does not tell us how many jurisdictions no longer make the distinction, except to say that **some** no longer do it. That is why Response A is not correct.

Responses C, D, and E are based on erroneous definitions of the two categories of crimes. The paragraph tells us that **all** crimes characterized as *malum in se* are inherently evil. Response C is false because it cannot be the case that SOME crimes characterized as *malum in se* are NOT inherently evil. The paragraph also tells us that **all** crimes characterized as *malum prohibitum* are declared offenses by law (legislature). Response D is false because it cannot be the case that *some* crimes characterized as *malum prohibitum* are NOT declared by law (legislature) to be an offense. We are told that filing a tax return late is *malum prohibitum,* rather than *malum in se*. Response E is incorrect because it cannot be the case that failing to file a tax return is *malum in se*.

6. **Correct Answer: B**   Any securities that are not issued in book-entry form are not Treasury securities.

This question refers to a category of securities (a security is an evidence of indebtedness) and a subcategory of Treasury securities that may include 1 bills, notes, or bonds. It states that all Treasury securities are now issued in book-entry form, which means that they are not issued as paper certificates to investors, but, instead, are now electronically logged as accounting entries with some custodian.

The correct response, B, can be concluded from the first sentence of the paragraph. Since <u>all</u> Treasury securities are issued in book-entry form, there cannot be any Treasury securities that are <u>not</u> issued in that form. All of the incorrect responses are inconsistent with the first sentence of the paragraph. Response A states that "some Treasury securities are now issued as paper certificates." That contradicts the information in the paragraph that said all Treasury securities are now issued in book-entry form. Response C states that "no Treasury securities are now issued in book-entry form," which also is contrary to the first sentence of the paragraph. Response D denies any overlap in the book-entry and Treasury subcategories, which is contradicted by the paragraph. And, since the paragraph states that the new book-entry form replaces the issuance of paper certificates, Response E is false, since any paper certificate <u>must</u> be a non-Treasury security.

7. **Correct Answer: A**   Many of those naturalized at rates above 50% were in professional occupations.

There are many possible conclusions that might be drawn about these statistics, but by reviewing all the possible answers, it is clear that the choice must be made among different statements about people in professional occupations. About this group, the paragraph says that "1977 immigrants in many professional occupations were naturalized at rates above 50%."

This example is illustrative of categories and subcategories. We do not know exactly how many is "many." We have to treat this sentence the same way we would treat one that said "some." Given this treatment, Response A is correct; it restates the final sentence in terms of the overlap between occupations with naturalization rates above 50% and professional occupations. Response B <u>must</u> be false because it denies that there is any overlap between occupations that have naturalization rates above 50% and professional occupations, even though this overlap is clear from the last sentence of the paragraph. And Response C does the same thing by stating that no members of the professional occupations achieved these rates.

Response D goes beyond the paragraph to draw conclusions about how many professional occupations had naturalization rates at or below 50%. We have no information about these occupations. Finally, Response E expands the proportion of occupational groups who can be assumed to be naturalized at rates at or below 50% to "almost all" -- a conclusion that again we cannot conclude because we were not given that information. In addition, Response E is contrary to the information given that many professional groups were above (rather than below) 50%.

8. **Correct Answer: B**   If an act of Congress has not been voided, then it has not been deemed unconstitutional by the Supreme Court.

The essential information from which Response B can be concluded is contained in the second sentence, which states that if an Act of Congress has been deemed unconstitutional, then it is voided. It follows logically that, if an Act of Congress is not voided, then it has **not** been deemed unconstitutional by the Supreme Court.

Response A is not supported by the paragraph because the paragraph does not indicate whether an Act of Congress is voided **only** when it has been deemed unconstitutional or if it could be voided for other reasons.

Response C, like Response A, cannot be concluded from the paragraph because the paragraph does not indicate whether or not an Act of Congress would be voided if the Supreme Court did not declare it to be unconstitutional.

Responses D and E are incorrect because they both contradict the paragraph.

Note that in this question, the correct answer follows basically from one sentence in the paragraph -- the second sentence. The rest of the paragraph presents additional information about the relationship between the Supreme Court and the Congress, which is relevant to the discussion, but not necessary to draw a conclusion. In this test, you will find some questions which will require you to use all or most of the statements presented in the paragraph in order to conclude the correct answer.

9. **Correct Answer: A**   Some email messages that have been requested as part of investigations have contained messages that would never be said face-to-face.

This is an example of a question with a negative lead-in statement. It asks for the conclusion that is NOT supported by the paragraph. That means that four of the statements are valid conclusions from the paragraph while one is not. It is also a question that concerns categories and subcategories. Response B (some messages that people would never say face-to-face are sent in email messages) correctly restates a fact given in the last sentence of the paragraph. Response E (some email messages contain information that would be omitted from formal writing) correctly restates the other fact in that sentence.

The next-to-last sentence is the source of both Response C (email messages have not been exempted from investigations) and Response D (email messages have not been exempted from investigations). Both of these choices restate information in that sentence, based on the fact that access to email messages was sought and granted. This leaves only the first option, Response A. This is the only choice that does not represent a valid conclusion, because even though we know from the paragraph that there is a subcategory of email messages that are requested in investigations and also that there is a subcategory of messages that contain information that people would not say face-to-face, there is nothing that says that these subcategories overlap. We simply do not know.

Solutions to the Arithmetic Reasoning Questions

10. **Correct Answer: C** $32 x 25 = $800; $800 x .20 = $160; $800 - $160 = $640. The second way to calculate the problem is, $800 x .80 = $640.
11. **Correct Answer: C**   108 ÷ 1.8 = 60 kgs
12. **Correct Answer: E**   None of these. The probability cannot be determined because we have no information on how much luggage located anywhere in the airport was inspected.

13. **Correct Answer: B** Legal stickers = 2/5; illegal stickers = 3/5; 3/5 x 1,500 900.
14. **Correct Answer: C** Let Officer K's hours be represented by 1/8 and Officer M's hours be represented by 1/10. This says that Officer K completes 1/8 of the job per hour and Officer M completes 1/10 of the job per hour. Together, they work 1/8 + 1/10 = 18/80 of the job per hour, which when reduced to its lowest terms, is 9/40.

    Therefore, if T is the amount of time it takes the two of them to finish the job, then 9/40 of the job per hour x T (hours) has to equal 1 job. So, 9/40 x T = 1 and T = 40/9 = 4 4/9 hours (four and four-ninths hours).
15. **Correct Answer: D** The probability is 20/120 = 1/6.
16. **Correct Answer: D** 16/40 = .40 (this says Officer Ferong processed passengers at a rate of .40 per minute); .40 x 60 = 24 passengers per hour; and 24 x 4 = 96 passengers every four hours. For the next day, the calculations are 18/40 = .45 x 60 = 27 x 4 108. The average of 108 and 96 is 108 + 96 2 = 102.

Answers to the Writing Skills Questions

17. **Correct Answer: B**   A verb must agree with its subject in number. The subject, *request*, is singular and, therefore, the verb should be changed from "are" to "is."

18. **Correct Answer: C**   The correct use of the word *principles* refers to *rules*, *laws*, or *standards that are applied* to the method of dog training. By contrast, the word *principal* means *first* or *foremost in importance*.

19. **Correct Answer: D**   No change to the sentence is necessary.

20. **Correct Answer: C**   The correct term is "associated with" and not "associated from." Objects are "associated with" one another which means they are related to each other in some way.

21. **Correct Answer: A**   The correct answer is (A). The sentence should read as follows: *The impact of this training will be measured by the number of new CBP Officers who successfully complete the probationary period.* This is a well constructed sentence in both grammar and syntax.

22. **Correct Answer: C**   The correct spelling of the words "hindrance" and "fraudulent" are used in this sentence while various incorrect spellings of these words are used in A, B, and D.

23. **Correct Answer: A**   The most logical order of the passages is 4, 3, 2, 1. It is not logical to begin the passages with paragraphs 2 or 3, as indicated in Responses B and C, because they appear to complete information that has been presented earlier and, therefore, depend on information in the other two

paragraphs in order to be understood. This also eliminates Response D. This leaves Response A, which begins with paragraph 4. The paragraphs presented in this order form a well-organized, coherent passage.

EXAMINATION SECTION
TEST 1

DIRECTIONS: Each question or incomplete statement is followed by several suggested answers or completions. Select the one the BEST answers the question or completes the statement. *PRINT THE LETTER OF THE CORRECT ANSWER IN THE SPACE AT THE RIGHT.*

1. Aliens who are immediate relatives of a U.S. citizen are eligible to receive a green card, and the number of relatives who may receive green cards is not limited by a quota. Those who are considered immediate relatives include spouses of U.S. citizens; widows and widowers who apply within two years of the U.S. citizen spouse's death; unmarried people under the age of 21 who have at least one U.S. citizen parent; and parents of U.S. citizens, if the U.S. citizen child is over the age of 21.
Alma Gonzalez, age 56, is an alien who was married to a U.S. citizen and lived for most of their marriage in Oaxaca, and they had a child together when Alma was 32 years old. Alma's husband died three years ago.
From the information above, it CANNOT be validly concluded that

    A. if Alma is not eligible for a green card, she has not remarried since her husband's death
    B. it's possible that Alma may be eligible for a green card if her child is still alive
    C. Alma is still eligible for a green card
    D. Alma is not eligible for a green card if she has not remarried since her husband's death

1.____

2. Border Patrol agents are often required to carry firearms, and for many agents, patrolling is the activity that accounts for most of the time spent at work. All the agents in the X sector carry firearms on patrol. Sometimes Moreno, an agent, doesn't carry a firearm when he is at work. Another agent, Robinson, carries a firearm the whole time she is at work.
From the information above, it can be validly concluded that

    A. Robinson patrols every time she is at work
    B. Most of the agents carry firearms
    C. Moreno does not always go on patrol while at work
    D. Agents who are not on patrol do not carry firearms

2.____

3. Some immigrants who applied for permits to work in the tool-and-die industry in the month of August were denied, while most of the immigrants in other industries were approved. Reporters from the local newspapers say a labor shortage in industries other than tool-and-die accounted for the lower approval rate.
Which of the following, if true, would most strengthen the conclusion of the reporters' argument?

    A. More immigrants applied for tool-and-die permits than in any other single industry.
    B. Several immigrants who applied for work in the tool-and-die industry also applied for work in at least one other industry.
    C. Demand for labor in the tool-and-die industry has not declined significantly.
    D. One of the industries that resulted in more approvals did not have a labor shortage.

3.____

17

4. Of three officers—Rodriguez, Parks, and Anton—each received a grade of A, C, and F on the firearms safety exam. Anton did not receive an F on her exam. Which of the following pieces of additional information makes it possible to determine who received each grade?

   A. Rodriguez received a C.
   B. Anton received an A.
   C. Parks received an F.
   D. Anton did not receive a C.

5. Twelve immigrants at a port of entry are arbitrarily divided into three groups for inspection: Groups A, B, and C. On the issue of green card eligibility, Group A includes two first preference immigrants and two third preference immigrants. Group B includes two third preference immigrants and two second preference; while Group C includes 2 second preference immigrants and two fourth preference.
   To be guaranteed of meeting one immigrant from each of the four preference categories, a person must meet

   A. three people each from Group A and Group C.
   B. one person from Group A, two people from Group B, and three from Group
   C. two people from each of the three groups.
   D. four people from Group A, three people from group B, and two from Group

6. A law enforcement office decides to contract the maintenance of its information network out to an independent contractor. The current marketplace is such that some information technology contractors offer products and services for both data and voice communications. If the office signed a contract with a medium-sized IT contractor and was not offered products and services for voice communications, either it was dealing with a company that serves only municipal governments, or it was dealing with a company that serves county governments.
   Which of the following statements most clearly leads to the above conclusion?

   A. Often, salespeople for IT companies that serve municipal and county governments forget to offer voice communications solutions.
   B. IT companies that serve only municipal governments are the only ones other than those serving county governments that do not offer voice communications solutions.
   C. Most IT companies rarely offer voice solutions.
   D. If the law enforcement office wants to hire an IT firm for the maintenance of its network, it should try companies other than those that serve municipal or county governments.

7. Each agent in the Border Patrol's Sector Y office speaks at least one foreign language, but no member speaks more than four foreign language. Five members speak Spanish; three speak French; four speak Tagalog; four speak Hindi; and five speak a foreign language other than Spanish.
   From the information above, it can be validly concluded that in Sector Y,

   A. there are no more than nine agents.
   B. agents who speak Spanish also speak French.
   C. agents who speak a language other than Spanish do not speak Spanish at all.
   D. there are no fewer than seven agents.

8. A spartan is worth 2 nobles. You can trade 2 cressidas for a dido. You can trade 3 spartans for 2 cressidas.   8.____
   From the information given above, it can be validly concluded that of the items listed above,

   A. the spartan is the most valuable
   B. the noble is the least valuable
   C. the cressida is the least valuable
   D. the dido is the most valuable

9. Border Patrol agents were led to believe that many of the border crossings that occurred   9.____
   within the last week at Nogales were illegal crossings. Upon investigating, the agents learned that all of the immigrants that crossed at Nogales in the past week were legal immigrants. Also, none of the illegal crossings were made by agricultural workers.
   From the information above, it can be validly concluded that, concerning immigrants who crossed the Nogales border within the past week,

   A. all of the agricultural workers crossed legally
   B. none of the agricultural workers crossed at Nogales
   C. some of the crossings made at Nogales were made illegally
   D. all of the immigrants who were agricultural workers crossed at Nogales

10. Telstar International faces a difficult audit from the Internal Revenue Service, and discovers that its records are in disarray. Mr. Ruhl, the star accountant for Telstar, will work for the company in New York only if his petition for a green card is approved. If the company ultimately passes the audit without penalty, then Mr. Ruhl's petition had not been approved.   10.____
    Before the audit, Mr. Ruhl's petition for a green card was approved.
    From the information above, it can be validly concluded that

    A. Mr. Ruhl worked for Telstar, but Telstar failed the audit anyway.
    B. Mr. Ruhl worked for Telstar, which passed the audit without penalty.
    C. Telstar passed the audit even though Mr. Ruhl did not do any accounting work for them
    D. Mr. Ruhl was never able to do any accounting work for Telstar

11. The penalties against employers who hire undocumented immigrants are now so severe   11.____
    that it would cost an employer far more to pay the fine than it would have cost to simply pay the wage of a legal worker. Therefore, since employers wants to keep costs down, those that hire immigrants will simply stick to those who have the proper documentation.
    Which of the following, if true, most seriously weakens the argument above?

    A. Employers are as concerned with long-term profit as they are with short-term strategies.
    B. Employers generally only do the "right" thing only if it makes good business sense.
    C. Employers tend to treat fines levied against them as an ordinary business expense.
    D. Employers generally underestimate the likelihood that they'll get caught for hiring illegal workers.

12. There are currently no census figures available for determining what proportion of American businesses are conducted from the home and do not report revenues to the IRS. On the other hand, at least some private industrial surveys, such as those conducted by the publishing or child-care industries, include IRS-revenues from home-based businesses that are run by husband-and-wife teams.
    From the information above, it can be validly concluded that

    A. there are at least some home businesses run by husband-and-wife teams that do not report their revenues to the IRS.
    B. there are at least some businesses run from the home that report revenues to the IRS.
    C. no businesses that are run at home by husband-and-wife teams fail to report revenues to the IRS.
    D. there are at least some home businesses that do not report to the IRS, but for which census figures are available.

13. Although many of the most popular destinations for legal immigrants these days are urban centers that have a large and varied job market and opportunities for advancement, many of the increasingly popular destinations-including rural areas of states such as Oregon, Washington, or many Midwestern states-offer a quality of life that can't be matched by the big cities. A clean environment, good schools, and a sense of community are all important factors in determining where an immigrant will decide to live.
    From the information above it can be validly concluded that

    A. good schools, a clean environment, and a sense of community are all important factors in drawing people to live in rural Oregon
    B. most Midwestern states, along with the rural areas of Oregon and Washington, don't typically draw as many immigrants as the big American cities
    C. if a person decides to live in a place such as rural Washington State, the decision will rely more on issues other than economic factors
    D. most immigrants to the United States are interested in quality-of-life factors other than simply finding a good, stable job

14. Banning drug use in films and on network television programs will not reduce the number of people who use drugs—they know about what drugs are being used, and how to get them, and don't need to see drug use in the media to get that kind of information.
    Which of the following, if true, would most seriously weaken the above argument?

    A. Older people tend to be less influenced by mass media content than younger people.
    B. Those who oppose drug use have always spoken out or advertised against it in the mass media.
    C. Seeing or hearing a celebrity using a particular drug tends to increase a person's curiosity about the drug.
    D. Removing drug use from mass media content will increase the direct pressure of illegal drug dealers and distributors on people, especially in the inner cities, to use drugs.

Questions 15 and 16 refer to the information below.

Five businesses each occupy one story of a five-story office building. The chiropractor's office is above the dentist's. The private detective's office is between the chiropractor's and the aromatherapist's. The gem trader's office is somewhere between the aromatherapist's and the dentist's. The private detective occupies the fourth story.

15. From the information above, it can be validly concluded that the

    A. chiropractor occupies the top story
    B. gem trader occupies the second story
    C. aromatherapist occupies the third story
    D. dentist occupies the third story

16. From the information above, the occupant of the _____ story CANNOT be validly determined.

    A. first
    B. second
    C. third
    D. fourth

17. Agent Polonsky did 200 sit-ups the night before his physical examination. In a six-level rating system with the highest possible rating of "excellent," his doctor gave him a rating of "good"—one level below "excellent." Six months later, the night before his next physical examination, Agent Polonsky did 300 sit-ups. Which of the following mistakes did he make in his reasoning?

    A. He overgeneralized from one specific occurrence.
    B. He incorrectly calculated the ratio of sit-ups to level achieved on the exam.
    C. He assumed that more is better.
    D. He assumed that an event is caused by another event simply because on preceded the other.

18. Studies show that without vaccinations for the HIB bacteria, the incidence of bacterial meningitis among children would increase by as much as 95%. Before the approval of the first HIB vaccine in 1990 for infants, HIB was the leading cause of bacterial meningitis, but today Streptococcus pneumoniae is one of the leading causes of bacterial meningitis. It is estimated that each year in the U.S. there are about 16,000 cases of pneumococcal bacteremia and 1400 cases of pneumococcal meningitis among children under age five. Children under the age of two are at highest risk for infection. In up to half the cases of meningitis, brain damage and hearing loss occurs and about 10 percent die. From the information above it CANNOT be validly concluded that

    A. HIB used to cause more cases of bacterial meningitis than Streptococcus pneumoniae
    B. in any given year, at least 700 cases of meningitis among children under five, brain damage and hearing loss occur
    C. some time before 1990, the incidence of bacterial meningitis was 95% higher among children than it is today
    D. according to studies, if the rate of bacterial meningitis begins to rise among children, it will be because of declining rates of HIB vaccination

19. Two trucking companies, XYZ and Nando Incorporated, compete for business across the U.S.-Mexican border. One of the trucking companies hauls loads under 5 tons. One of the companies does not have a contract with Gem Motor Company, and focuses its business on the Arizona border. The company that focuses on the Arizona border hauls loads under 5 tons. One company hauls agricultural produce. Nando has contracts with Gem Motor Company and Tarbell Freight.
From the information above, it can be validly concluded that

   A. Nando focuses its business on the Arizona border.
   B. XYZ hauls loads under 5 tons.
   C. The company that focuses on the Arizona border hauls agricultural produce.
   D. XYZ hauls agricultural produce.

20. Most immigrants into Sector C are agricultural workers. All immigrants in Sector C are native Spanish speakers. Therefore, some agricultural workers are Spanish speakers.
Which of the following arguments is formed most like the argument above?

   A. All law enforcement officer candidates in La Cruz receive language instruction. Arnold is a law enforcement officer candidate. Therefore, Arnold must receive language instruction.
   B. Of the people who are on the swim team, most also run cross country. All swim team members play soccer. Therefore, some cross country runners play soccer.
   C. Studies show that most people who work out regularly are in good health. Therefore, anyone who wants to be in good health should work out regularly.
   D. Some immigrants from Country Z speak two languages. Most immigrants from Country Z are college educated. Therefore, some immigrants from Country Z who speak two languages are also college educated.

21. Edgar G., the owner of Lifeways Insurance, signed a contract with each of his salespeople promising an automatic $1000 bonus to anyone who sells more than 12 flood insurance policies in a calendar month. Talbot Nevin, an insurance salesperson, sold 18 flood insurance policies in March, but did not receive a bonus.
From the information above, it can be validly concluded that

   A. Talbot Nevin does not work for Edgar G.
   B. Talbot Nevin neglected to sign his contract.
   C. If Edgar G. has not violated any contract, he is not Talbot Nevin's employer.
   D. If Talbot Nevin is Edgar G.'s employee, Edgar G. has not violated their contract.

Questions 22 and 23 refer to the following information.

On the examination to determine agents' promotion to GS-7 status, Lee outscored Foster. Clark outscored Prieto, but did not score as high as Torres. Prieto outscored Foster.

22. From the information above, it can be validly concluded that

   A. Lee received the highest score on the examination.
   B. Foster received the lowest score.
   C. Clark outscored Lee.
   D. Foster outscored Clark.

23. Which of the following pieces of information would allow all five competitors to be ranked in the order of their scores? 23.____

    A. Lee outscored Prieto.
    B. Torres outscored Lee.
    C. Lee outscored Clark.
    D. Prieto outscored Lee.

24. People within the Staunton town limit are required to display slow-moving vehicle signs while driving a horse carriage on any state or federal roads. Mrs. Nightingale drove all the way to Staunton's town plaza without displaying a slow-moving vehicle sign.
    From the information given above, it can be validly concluded that 24.____

    A. if Mrs. Nightingale did not receive a citation, she drove only on county roads.
    B. if Mrs. Nightingale was driving a horse carriage on a state or federal road within the town limit, she broke the law.
    C. the Staunton town plaza is not within the town limit.
    D. if Mrs. Nightingale did not break the law, she was driving on either a state or federal road within the Staunton town limit.

25. A rapidly changing security environment in the United States is leading to more serious penalties for making statements about "bombs" or "hijackings" at U.S. airports. Passengers are observed more closely than ever-by surveillance audio/video and by screening personnel-to discover the content of their conversations with other passengers. In spite of this, some passengers still make jokes or flippant remarks about bombs and hijacking that they would never make to airport security personnel.
    From the information above, it CANNOT be validly concluded that 25.____

    A. during some conversations between passengers, people say things they would not stay to airport security personnel
    B. some passengers that have been detained by security personnel have made private jokes or flippant remarks that they would never have said to security personnel
    C. a passenger's statements alone are enough to incur a possible penalty at U.S. airports
    D. some things that people would never say to airport security personnel are uttered in conversations with other passengers.

KEY (CORRECT ANSWERS)

1. D
2. C
3. C
4. A
5. A

6. B
7. D
8. D
9. A
10. A

11. D
12. B
13. A
14. C
15. B

16. C
17. D
18. D
19. B
20. B

21. C
22. B
23. D
24. B
25. B

TEST 2

DIRECTIONS: Each question or incomplete statement is followed by several suggested answers or completions. Select the one the BEST answers the question or completes the statement. *PRINT THE LETTER OF THE CORRECT ANSWER IN THE SPACE AT THE RIGHT.*

1. Border Patrol agents are granted the authority by law to have access to privates lands— but not dwellings—for the purpose of patrolling. This authority applies to

    A. an area extending 25 miles into U.S. territory from any external boundary
    B. an area extending 25 miles on either side of an external boundary
    C. any land under U.S. sovereignty
    D. any land that directly abuts an external boundary

    1.____

2. A Border Crossing Identification Card

    I. is an identity card issued to an alien who is lawfully admitted for permanent residence
    II. may be issued to any resident of Mexico or Canada
    III. includes a machine-readable biometric identifier, such as a fingerprint
    IV. may be issued for the purpose of day labor

    A. I only
    B. I and II
    C. I, II and III
    D. I, II, III and IV

    2.____

3. An alien commuter engaged in seasonal work will be presumed to have taken up residence in the United States if he or she is present in the country for more than _____ in any continuous twelve-month period.

    A. three months consecutively
    B. six months consecutively
    C. six months in the aggregate
    D. nine months in the aggregate

    3.____

4. Legislation passed in 1925 gave Border Patrol officers the authority to

    A. seize goods brought into the United States in violation of import/ export laws
    B. interrogate any alien or person believed to be an alien about his/her right to be or remain in the United States
    C. arrest a deportable alien found in the United States
    D. board and search vehicles/conveyances in which they believe aliens are being brought into the United States

    4.____

5. When a person suffers a neck or back injury, the ideal way to care for him/her is to

    A. apply a splint to the neck and back
    B. stabilize the neck and back and wait for EMS personnel
    C. stabilize the neck and back and transport the victim with a stretcher
    D. leave the person alone until EMS personnel arrive

    5.____

6. The "harboring of aliens" provisions of U.S. immigrant law holds that usually, a first instance of _____ is NOT a crime.
   I. hiring an undocumented worker
   II. providing church sanctuary to undocumented refugees
   III. warn undocumented aliens of the presence of an INS officer
   IV. paying for an apartment for an undocumented alien

   A. I only
   B. I and II
   C. II, III and IV
   D. I, II, III and IV

6.____

7. "Green card" is simply another term for INS Form

   A. I-94; arrival/departure record
   B. I-551; permanent resident visa
   C. G-14; information form
   D. I-9; employment eligibility verification

7.____

8. The Border Patrol was originally created in response to the large-scale smuggling of aliens to states

   A. along the U.S./Mexico land border
   B. along the Great Lakes border region
   C. on the Eastern Seaboard
   D. on the Gulf of Mexico

8.____

9. In the United States, most of the authority in the field of immigration lies with

   A. the Supreme Court
   B. Congress
   C. state governments
   D. the Executive Branch

9.____

10. An agent comes across several people in a very hot part of the desert. The people have been exposed for a long time and their skin is very hot and dry. The agent should suspect heat

    A. stroke
    B. cramps
    C. exhaustion
    D. syncope

10.____

11. The total length of international land and water boundary protected by the Border Patrol is about _____ miles.

    A. 1,200
    B. 3,000
    C. 8,000
    D. 12,500

11.____

12. The best way to re-warm a frostbitten body part is to 12.____

    A. gently rub the body part
    B. apply warm water
    C. place the body part next to a warm body
    D. use a hot water bottle

13. The first treatment for severe sunburn should be to apply 13.____

    A. antiseptic cream
    B. burn ointment
    C. a warm, moist dressing
    D. a cold pack

14. The basic operation of the Border Patrol is 14.____

    A. traffic check
    B. line watch
    C. air patrol
    D. transportation check

15. Each of the following is a procedure in the treatment of heat exhaustion, EXCEPT 15.____

    A. giving the victim salt tablets
    B. using wet towels to cool the victim
    C. elevating the victim's legs
    D. moving the victim to a cool place

16. Immigration-related services performed by the Border Patrol include 16.____
    I. adjustment of status requests
    II. processing requests for employment authorization documents
    III. port-of-entry admissions
    IV. processing naturalization requests

    A. I only
    B. I and II
    C. III only
    D. I, II, III and IV

17. The purpose of drag trails and sand traps is to 17.____

    A. detect illegal narcotics
    B. enhance the detection capabilities of electronic sensor alarms
    C. ensure that footprints left by trespassers are fresh and can be tracked
    D. disable vehicles that are transporting illegal aliens across the U.S. border

18. In one-rescuer CPR, the best way to tell if your breaths are effective is to 18.____

    A. observe the stomach rise
    B. listen for exhalations
    C. observe the chest rise
    D. observe the victim's skin color

19. The largest percentage of border violators are

    A. uninformed or poorly advised
    B. smugglers of aliens or contraband
    C. carrying fraudulent documents
    D. armed and dangerous

20. Prior to the Illegal Reform and Immigrant Responsibility Act (IIRIRA) of 1996, a person who entered secretly along a border or who made a false claim of U.S. citizenship in order to get into the United States was said to be

    A. inadmissible
    B. undocumented
    C. entered without inspection
    D. excludable

21. An agent encounters a person who has suffered a severe leg wound from attempting to climb a border fence. The wound is bleeding profusely. The first method that should be tried for controlling the bleeding is

    A. applying a tourniquet
    B. exposing the wound to air
    C. direct pressure
    D. using the femoral pressure point

22. Sectors in the Border Patrol organization are supervised directly by a

    A. Deputy Director
    B. Regional Commissioner
    C. Sector Captain
    D. Chief Patrol Inspector

23. Signs of heat stroke include
    I. heavy perspiration
    II. normal body temperature
    III. hot, dry skin
    IV. unequal pupils of the eye

    A. I only
    B. I and II
    C. III only
    D. III and IV

24. What was the term for the U.S.-Mexico agreement for providing Mexican agricultural workers to farms during World War II and afterward?

    A. Operation Gatekeeper
    B. Operation Jobs
    C. Operation Wetback
    D. Bracero Program

25. Before administering CPR, the victim should be placed with the
    A. body level or head higher than the heart
    B. head and feet elevated
    C. body level or head lower than the heart
    D. feet lower than the head

25.____

KEY (CORRECT ANSWERS)

1. A	11. C
2. C	12. B
3. C	13. C
4. C	14. B
5. B	15. A
6. A	16. D
7. B	17. C
8. D	18. C
9. B	19. A
10. A	20. C

21. C
22. D
23. C
24. D
25. C

INDIVIDUAL ACHIEVEMENT RECORD
EXAMINATION SECTION
TEST 1

DIRECTIONS: Each question or incomplete statement is followed by several suggested answers or completions. Select the one that BEST answers the question or completes the statement. *PRINT THE LETTER OF THE CORRECT ANSWER IN THE SPACE AT THE RIGHT.*

1. While a senior in high school, I was absent

   A. never
   B. seldom
   C. frequently
   D. more than 10 days
   E. only when I felt bored

   1._____

2. While in high school, I failed classes

   A. never
   B. once
   C. twice
   D. more than twice
   E. at least four times

   2._____

3. During class discussions in my high school classes, I usually

   A. listened without participating
   B. participated as much as possible
   C. listened until I had something to add to the discussion
   D. disagreed with others simply for the sake of argument
   E. laughed at stupid ideas

   3._____

4. My high school grade point average (on a 4.0 scale) was

   A. 2.0 or lower   B. 2.1 to 2.5   C. 2.6 to 3.0
   D. 3.1 to 3.5   E. 3.6 to 4.0

   4._____

5. As a high school student, I completed my assignments

   A. as close to the due date as I could manage
   B. whenever the teacher gave me an extension
   C. frequently
   D. on time
   E. when they were interesting

   5._____

6. While in high school, I participated in

   A. athletic and nonathletic extracurricular activities
   B. athletic extracurricular activities
   C. nonathletic extracurricular activities
   D. no extracurricular activities
   E. mandatory after-school programs

   6._____

7. In high school, I made the honor roll

   A. several times
   B. once
   C. more than once
   D. twice
   E. I can't remember if I made the honor roll

   7._____

8. Upon graduation from high school, I received

    A. academic and nonacademic honors
    B. academic honors
    C. nonacademic honors
    D. no honors
    E. I can't remember if I received honors

9. While attending high school, I worked at a paid job or as a volunteer

    A. never
    B. every so often
    C. 5 to 10 hours a month
    D. more than 10 hours a month
    E. more than 15 hours a month

10. During my senior year of high school, I skipped school

    A. whenever I could   B. once a week
    C. several times a week   D. not at all
    E. when I got bored

11. I was suspended from high school

    A. not at all
    B. once or twice
    C. once or twice, for fighting
    D. several times
    E. more times than I can remember

12. During high school, my fellow students and teachers considered me

    A. above average
    B. below average
    C. average
    D. underachieving
    E. underachieving and prone to fighting

13. The ability to _____ is most important to a Border Patrol Agent.

    A. draw his/her gun quickly
    B. see over great distances and difficult terrain
    C. verbally and physically intimidate illegal aliens
    D. communicate effectively in circumstances which can be dangerous
    E. hear over great distances

14. I began planning for college

    A. when my parents told me to
    B. when I entered high school
    C. during my junior year
    D. during my senior year
    E. when I signed up for my SAT (or other standardized) exam

15. An effective leader is someone who   15.____

    A. inspires confidence in his/her followers
    B. inspires fear in his/her followers
    C. tells subordinates exactly what they should do
    D. creates an environment in which subordinates feel insecure about their job security and performance
    E. makes as few decisions as possible

16. I prepared myself for college by   16.____

    A. learning how to get extensions on major assignments
    B. working as many hours as possible at my after-school job
    C. spending as much time with my friends as possible
    D. getting good grades and participating in extracurricular activities
    E. watching television shows about college kids

17. I paid for college by   17.____

    A. supplementing my parents contributions with my own earnings
    B. relying on scholarships, loans, and my own earnings
    C. relying on my parents and student loans
    D. relying on my parents to pay my tuition, room and board
    E. relying on sources not listed here

18. While a college student, I spent my summers and holiday breaks   18.____

    A. in summer or remedial classes
    B. traveling
    C. working
    D. relaxing
    E. spending time with my friends

19. My final college grade point average (on a 4.0 scale) was   19.____

    A. 3.8 to 4.0   B. 3.5 to 3.8   C. 3.0 to 3.5
    D. 2.5 to 3.0   E. 2.0 to 2.5

20. As a college student, I cut classes   20.____

    A. frequently   B. when I didn't like them
    C. sometimes   D. rarely
    E. when I needed the sleep

21. In college, I received academic honors   21.____

    A. not at all
    B. once
    C. twice
    D. several times
    E. I can't remember if I received academic honors

22. While in college, I declared a major 22.____

    A. during my first year
    B. during my sophomore year
    C. during my junior year
    D. during my senior year
    E. several times

23. While on patrol as a Border Patrol Agent, you spot someone attempting to cross the border illegally. Your first reaction is to 23.____

    A. draw your weapon
    B. observe the person until he or she completes the crossing
    C. identify yourself as an agent of the Border Patrol
    D. fire your weapon over the person's head in order to scare him or her
    E. call immediately for backup

24. As a college student, I failed _____ classes. 24.____

    A. no   B. two
    C. three   D. four
    E. more than four

25. Friends describe me as 25.____

    A. introverted   B. hot-tempered
    C. unpredictable   D. quiet
    E. easygoing

KEY (CORRECT ANSWERS)

PLEASE NOTE: The answers listed are the best answers. However, you are to answer the exam honestly. Your personal answer may differ from the *best* answers.

1.	A	11.	A
2.	A	12.	A
3.	C	13.	D
4.	E	14.	B
5.	D	15.	A
6.	A	16.	D
7.	A	17.	B
8.	A	18.	C
9.	E	19.	A
10.	D	20.	D

21. D
22. A
23. C
24. A
25. E

TEST 2

DIRECTIONS: Each question or incomplete statement is followed by several suggested answers or completions. Select the one that BEST answers the question or completes the statement. *PRINT THE LETTER OF THE CORRECT ANSWER IN THE SPACE AT THE RIGHT.*

1. As a Border Patrol Agent, you apprehend three men whom you believe crossed the border illegally. However, none of the men speaks English, and you don't speak their language. Your reaction should be to

   A. draw your weapon so that they understand the seriousness of the situation
   B. take them into custody, where they will have access to a translator
   C. attempt to communicate through hand gestures and shouting
   D. call for a translator to come and meet you at your location
   E. pretend you understand their language and apprehend them

1.____

2. During my college classes, I preferred to

   A. remain silent during class discussions
   B. do other homework during class discussions
   C. participate frequently in class discussions
   D. argue with others as much as possible
   E. laugh at the stupid opinions of others

2.____

3. As a Border Patrol Agent, you are chasing a small group of people who have just crossed the border illegally. During your pursuit, one member of the group is left behind. You see that she is injured and in need of medical attention.
Your reaction is to

   A. fire your weapon at the group members to get them to stop
   B. cease pursuit of the group members and take the woman into custody
   C. continue pursuit of the group members, leaving the woman behind since acting ill is a common trick
   D. radio for backup to stay with the woman while medical help arrives while you continue pursuit of the group members
   E. radio for backup to continue pursuit of the group members while you stay with the woman and wait for medical help to arrive

3.____

4. As a college student, I was placed on academic probation

   A. not at all   B. once
   C. twice   D. three times
   E. more than three times

4.____

5. At work, being a team player means to

   A. compromise your ideals and beliefs
   B. compensate for the incompetence of others
   C. count on others to compensate for my inexperience
   D. cooperate with others to get a project finished
   E. rely on others to get the job done

5.____

6. As a Border Patrol Agent, you confront someone you believe has just crossed the border illegally. After identifying yourself, you notice the suspect holding something that looks like a knife. Your FIRST reaction should be to

    A. draw your weapon and fire
    B. call immediately for backup
    C. keep your weapon drawn until you get the suspect into a position that is controllable
    D. ask the suspect if he is armed
    E. talk to the suspect without drawing your weapon

7. My friends from college remember me primarily as a(n)

    A. person who loved to party
    B. ambitious student
    C. athlete
    D. joker
    E. fighter

8. My college experience is memorable primarily because of

    A. the friends I made
    B. the sorority/fraternity I was able to join
    C. the social activities I participated in
    D. my academic achievements
    E. the money I spent

9. A friend who is applying for a job asks you to help him pass the mandatory drug test by substituting a sample of your urine for his. You should

    A. help him by supplying the sample
    B. help him by supplying the sample and insisting he seek drug counseling
    C. supply the sample, but tell him that this is the only time you'll help in this way
    D. call the police
    E. refuse

10. As a college student, I handed in my assignments

    A. when they were due
    B. whenever I could get an extension
    C. when they were interesting
    D. when my friends reminded me to
    E. when I was able to

11. At work you are accused of a minor infraction which you didn't commit. Your first reaction is to

    A. call a lawyer
    B. speak to your supervisor about the mistake
    C. call the police
    D. yell at the person who did commit the infraction
    E. accept the consequences regardless of your guilt or innocence

12. While on patrol, you are surprised by a large group of illegal aliens who have just crossed the border. You are greatly outnumbered.
    As a Border Patrol Agent, your first reaction is to

    A. draw your weapon and identify yourself
    B. get back into your vehicle and wait for help to arrive
    C. call for backup
    D. pretend you are part of a large group of agents in the area
    E. identify yourself and get the group members into a controllable position

13. As a college student, I began to prepare for final exams

    A. the night before taking them
    B. when the professor handed out the review sheets
    C. several weeks before taking them
    D. when my friends began to prepare for their exams
    E. the morning of the exam

14. As a Border Patrol Agent in the field, you confront a small group of people you believe to be illegal aliens. Your most important consideration during this exchange should be

    A. apprehension of illegal aliens
    B. safety of American citizens in nearby towns
    C. safety of the illegal aliens
    D. number of illegal aliens you must apprehend in order to receive a commendation
    E. the amount of respect the illegal aliens show to you and your position

15. At work, I am known as

    A. popular   B. quiet   C. intense
    D. easygoing   E. dedicated

16. The most important quality in a coworker is

    A. friendliness   B. cleanliness
    C. a good sense of humor   D. dependability
    E. good listening skills

17. In the past year, I have stayed home from work

    A. frequently
    B. only when I felt depressed
    C. rarely
    D. only when I felt overwhelmed
    E. only to run important errands

18. As a Border Patrol Agent, the best way to collect information from a suspect during an interview is to

    A. physically intimidate the suspect
    B. verbally intimidate the suspect
    C. threaten the suspect's family and/or friends with criminal prosecution
    D. encourage a conversation with the suspect
    E. sit in silence until the suspect begins speaking

19. For me, the best thing about college was the

    A. chance to strengthen my friendships and develop new ones
    B. chance to test my abilities and develop new ones
    C. number of extracurricular activities and clubs
    D. chance to socialize
    E. chance to try several different majors

20. As an employee, my weakest skill is

    A. controlling my temper
    B. my organizational ability
    C. my ability to effectively understand directions
    D. my ability to effectively manage others
    E. my ability to communicate my thoughts in writing

21. As a Border Patrol Agent, my greatest strength would be

    A. my sense of loyalty
    B. my organizational ability
    C. punctuality
    D. dedication
    E. my ability to intimidate others

22. As a Border Patrol Agent, you find a group of illegal aliens gathered around a truck which is on fire. Your first reaction is to

    A. call the fire department
    B. arrest them all for destruction of property
    C. draw your weapon and begin questioning them
    D. return to your vehicle and wait for the fire department
    E. instruct the group to remain while you return to your vehicle and request backup

23. If asked by my company to learn a new job-related skill, my reaction would be to

    A. ask for a raise
    B. ask for overtime pay
    C. question the necessity of the skill
    D. cooperate with some reluctance
    E. cooperate with enthusiasm

24. When I disagree with others, I tend to

    A. listen quietly despite my disagreement
    B. laugh openly at the person I disagree with
    C. ask the person to explain their views before I respond
    D. leave the conversation before my anger gets the best of me
    E. point out exactly why the person is wrong

25. When I find myself in a situation which is confusing or unclear, my reaction is to
    A. pretend I am not confused
    B. remain calm and, if necessary, ask someone else for clarification
    C. grow frustrated and angry
    D. walk away from the situation
    E. immediately insist that someone explain things to me

KEY (CORRECT ANSWERS)

PLEASE NOTE: The answers listed are the best answers. However, you are to answer the exam honestly. Your personal answer may differ from the *best* answers.

1. B
2. C
3. E
4. A
5. D

6. C
7. B
8. D
9. E
10. A

11. B
12. E
13. C
14. A
15. E

16. D
17. C
18. D
19. B
20. E

21. D
22. A
23. E
24. C
25. B

TEST 3

DIRECTIONS: Each question or incomplete statement is followed by several suggested answers or completions. Select the one that BEST answers the question or completes the statement. *PRINT THE LETTER OF THE CORRECT ANSWER IN THE SPACE AT THE RIGHT.*

1. While on patrol as a Border Patrol Agent, you find a dead body lying in the open. Hiding a few feet away, behind some rocks, you find an illegal alien who is holding items which seem to have been taken from the dead body, including a pair of shoes and some jewelry.
You should

    A. apprehend the illegal alien and bring him to the station for further questioning
    B. arrest the illegal alien for murder and robbery
    C. arrest the illegal alien for murder
    D. subdue the illegal alien with force and check the area for his accomplices
    E. subdue the illegal alien with force and call for backup to check the area for his accomplices

1.____

2. If you were placed in a supervisory position, which of the following abilities would you consider to be most important to your job performance?

    A. Stubbornness
    B. The ability to hear all sides of a story before making a decision
    C. Kindness
    D. The ability to make and stick to a decision
    E. Patience

2.____

3. What is your highest level of education?

    A. Less than a high school diploma
    B. A high school diploma or equivalency
    C. A graduate of community college
    D. A graduate of a four-year accredited college
    E. A degree from graduate school

3.____

4. When asked to supervise other workers, your approach should be to

    A. ask for management wages since you're doing management work
    B. give the workers direction and supervise every aspect of the process
    C. give the workers direction and then allow them to do the job
    D. hand the workers their job specifications
    E. do the work yourself, since you're uncomfortable supervising others

4.____

5. Which of the following best describes you?

    A. Need little or no supervision
    B. Resent too much supervision
    C. Require as much supervision as my peers
    D. Require slightly more supervision than my peers
    E. Require close supervision

5.____

6. You accept a job which requires an ability to perform several tasks at once. What is the best way to handle such a position?

   A. With strong organizational skills and a close attention to detail
   B. By delegating the work to someone with strong organizational skills
   C. Staying focused on one task at a time, no matter what happens
   D. Working on one task at a time until each task is successfully completed
   E. Asking my supervisor to help me

7. As a Border Patrol Agent, you take a suspected illegal alien into custody. After returning to the field, you notice that your gun is missing. You should

   A. retrace your steps to see if you dropped it somewhere
   B. report the loss immediately
   C. ask your partner to borrow his or her gun
   D. pretend that nothing's happened
   E. rely on your hands for defense and protection

8. Which of the following best describes your behavior when you disagree with someone? You

   A. state your own point of view as quickly and loudly as you can
   B. listen quietly and keep your opinions to yourself
   C. listen to the other person's perspective and then carefully point out all the flaws in their logic
   D. list all of the ignorant people who agree with the opposing point of view
   E. listen to the other person's perspective and then explain your own perspective

9. As a new Border Patrol Agent, you make several mistakes during your first week of work. You react by

   A. learning from your mistakes and moving on
   B. resigning
   C. blaming it on your supervisor
   D. refusing to talk about it
   E. blaming yourself

10. My ability to communicate effectively with others is

    A. below average
    B. average
    C. above average
    D. far above average
    E. far below average

11. In which of the following areas are you most highly skilled?

    A. Written communication
    B. Oral communication
    C. Ability to think quickly in difficult situations
    D. Ability to work with a broad diversity of people and personalities
    E. Organizational skills

12. As a Border Patrol Agent, you are assigned to work with a partner whom you dislike. You should

    A. immediately report the problem to your supervisor
    B. ask your partner not to speak to you during working hours
    C. tell your colleagues about your differences
    D. tell your partner why you dislike him/her
    E. work with your partner regardless of your personal feelings

13. During high school, what was your most common after-school activity?

    A. Remaining after school to participate in various clubs and organizations (such as band, sports, etc.)
    B. Remaining after school to make up for missed classes
    C. Remaining after school as punishment (detention, etc.)
    D. Going straight to an after-school job
    E. Spending the afternoon at home or with friends

14. During high school, in which of the following subjects did you receive the highest grades?

    A. English, History, Social Studies
    B. Math, Science
    C. Vocational classes
    D. My grades were consistent in all subjects
    E. Classes I liked

15. When faced with an overwhelming number of duties at work, your reaction is to

    A. do all of the work yourself, no matter what the cost
    B. delegate some responsibilities to capable colleagues
    C. immediately ask your supervisor for help
    D. put off as much work as possible until you can get to it
    E. take some time off to relax and clear your mind

16. As a Border Patrol Agent, your supervisor informs you that a prisoner whom you arrested has accused you of beating him. You know you are innocent. You react by

    A. quitting your job
    B. hiring a lawyer
    C. challenging your supervisor to prove the charges against you
    D. calmly telling your supervisor what really happened and presenting evidence to support your position
    E. insisting that you be allowed to speak alone to the prisoner

17. Which of the following best describes your desk at your current or most recent job?

    A. Messy and disorganized
    B. Neat and organized
    C. Messy but organized
    D. Neat but disorganized
    E. Messy

18. The _____ BEST describes your reasons for wanting to become a Border Patrol Agent.

    A. ability to carry and use a weapon
    B. excitement and challenges of the career
    C. excellent salary and benefits package
    D. chance to tell other people what to do
    E. chance to help people find a better life

19. As a Border Patrol Agent in the field, you are approached by a man who is frantic but unable to speak English. After several minutes of trying to communicate, you realize that the man is asking you to come with him in order to help someone who has been hurt. You should

    A. ignore him, since it might be a trap
    B. call for backup
    C. immediately offer to help the man
    D. return to your vehicle and wait for the man to leave
    E. radio your position and situation to another Agent, and then go with the man to offer help

19.____

20. When asked to take on extra responsibility at work, in order to help out a coworker who is overwhelmed, your response is to

    A. ask for overtime pay
    B. complain to your supervisor that you are being taken advantage of
    C. help the coworker to the best of your ability
    D. ask the coworker to come back some other time
    E. give the coworker some advice on how to get his/her job done

20.____

21. At my last job, I was promoted

    A. not at all
    B. once
    C. twice
    D. three times
    E. more than three times

21.____

22. As a Border Patrol Agent, you discover the body of a person whom you suspect to be an illegal alien. You also suspect that there are several other illegal aliens hiding in the nearby vicinity.
    Your first reaction should be to

    A. begin a search of the nearby area for the other illegal aliens
    B. return to your vehicle and call for backup
    C. return to your vehicle with the body of the person you found
    D. check whether the person you found is dead or alive
    E. draw your weapon and identify yourself

22.____

23. You are faced with an overwhelming deadline at work. Your reaction is to

    A. procrastinate until the last minute
    B. procrastinate until someone notices you need some help
    C. notify your supervisor that you can't complete the work on your own
    D. work in silence without asking any questions
    E. arrange your schedule so that you can get the work done before the deadline

23.____

24. When you feel yourself under deadline pressures at work, your response is to

    A. make sure you keep to a schedule which allows you to complete the work on time
    B. wait until just before the deadline to complete the work
    C. ask someone else to do the work
    D. grow so obsessive about the work that your coworkers feel compelled to help you
    E. ask your supervisor immediately for help

24.____

25. Which of the following best describes your appearance at your current or most recent position?   25._____

    A. Well-groomed, neat, and clean
    B. Unkempt, but dressed neatly
    C. Messy and dirty clothing
    D. Unshaven and untidy
    E. Clean-shaven, but sloppily dressed

KEY (CORRECT ANSWERS)

PLEASE NOTE: The answers listed are the best answers. However, you are to answer the exam honestly. Your personal answers may differ from the *best* answers.

1. A	11. C
2. D	12. E
3. E	13. A
4. C	14. D
5. A	15. B
6. A	16. D
7. B	17. B
8. E	18. B
9. A	19. E
10. C	20. C

21. C
22. D
23. E
24. A
25. A

TEST 4

DIRECTIONS: Each question or incomplete statement is followed by several suggested answers or completions. Select the one that BEST answers the question or completes the statement. *PRINT THE LETTER OF THE CORRECT ANSWER IN THE SPACE AT THE RIGHT.*

1. Which of the following best describes the way you react to making a difficult decision? 1.____

    A. Consult with the people you're closest to before making the decision
    B. Make the decision entirely on your own
    C. Consult only with those people whom your decision will affect
    D. Consult with everyone you know, in an effort to make a decision that will please everyone
    E. Forget about the decision until you have to make it

2. If placed in a supervisory role, which of the following characteristics would you rely on most heavily when dealing with the employees you supervise? 2.____

    A. Kindness   B. Cheeriness   C. Honesty
    D. Hostility   E. Aloofness

3. As a Border Patrol Agent, you are pursuing an illegal alien when he turns and pulls something out of his jacket that looks like a gun. You should 3.____

    A. run away and call for backup
    B. assure the man that you mean him no harm
    C. draw your gun and order the man to stop and drop his weapon
    D. draw your gun and fire a warning shot
    E. draw your gun and fire immediately

4. In addition to English, in which of the following languages are you also fluent? 4.____

    A. Spanish   B. French   C. Italian
    D. German   E. Other

5. When confronted with gossip at work, your typical reaction is to 5.____

    A. participate
    B. listen without participating
    C. notify your supervisor
    D. excuse yourself from the discussion
    E. confront your coworkers about their problem

6. In the past two years, how many jobs have you held? 6.____

    A. None   B. One
    C. Two   D. Three
    E. More than three

7. In your current or most recent job, your favorite part of the job is the part which involves 7.____

    A. telling other people what they're doing wrong
    B. supervising others
    C. working without supervision to finish a project
    D. written communication
    E. oral communication

8. Your supervisor asks you about a colleague who is applying for a position which you also want. You react by

   A. commenting honestly on the person's work performance
   B. enhancing the person's negative traits
   C. informing your supervisor about your colleague's personal problems
   D. telling your supervisor that you would be better in the position
   E. refusing to comment

9. As a Border Patrol Agent, you confiscate some contraband which was being imported by an illegal alien who is now in your custody. Your partner asks you not to turn the contraband in to your supervisors.
   Your response is to

   A. inform your supervisor of your partner's request immediately
   B. tell your partner you feel uncomfortable with his request
   C. pretend you didn't hear your partner's request
   D. tell your supervisor and all your colleagues about your partner's request
   E. give the contraband to your partner and let him handle it

10. Which of the following best describes your responsibilities in your last job?

    A. Entirely supervisory
    B. Much supervisory responsibility
    C. Equal amounts of supervisory and nonsupervisory responsibility
    D. Some supervisory responsibilities
    E. No supervisory responsibilities

11. How much written communication did your previous or most recent job require of you?

    A. A great deal of written communication
    B. Some written communication
    C. I don't remember
    D. A small amount of written communication
    E. No written communication

12. In the past two years, how many times have you been fired from a job?

    A. None
    B. Once
    C. Twice
    D. Three times
    E. More than three times

13. How much time have you spent working for volunteer organizations in the past year?

    A. 10 to 20 hours per week
    B. 5 to 10 hours per week
    C. 3 to 5 hours per week
    D. 1 to 3 hours per week
    E. I have spent no time volunteering in the past year

14. Your efforts at volunteer work usually revolve around which of the following types of organizations?	14.____

    A. Religious
    B. Community-based organizations working to improve the community
    C. Charity organizations working on behalf of the poor
    D. Charity organizations working on behalf of the infirm or handicapped
    E. Other

15. Which of the following best describes your professional history?	15.____
    Promoted at

    A. a much faster rate than coworkers
    B. a slightly faster rate than coworkers
    C. the same rate as coworkers
    D. a slightly slower rate than coworkers
    E. a much slower rate than coworkers

16. Which of the following qualities do you most appreciate in a coworker?	16.____

    A. Friendliness   B. Dependability
    C. Good looks   D. Silence
    E. Forgiveness

17. When you disagree with a supervisor's instructions or opinion about how to complete a	17.____
    project, your reaction is to

    A. inform your supervisor that you refuse to complete the project according to his or her instructions
    B. inform your colleagues of your supervisor's incompetence
    C. accept your supervisor's instructions in silence
    D. voice your concerns and then complete the project according to your own instincts
    E. voice your concerns and then complete the project according to your supervisor's instructions

18. Which of the following best describes your reaction to close supervision and specific	18.____
    direction from your supervisors?
    You

    A. listen carefully to the directions, and then figure out a way to do the job more efficiently
    B. complete the job according to the given specifications
    C. show some initiative by doing the job your way
    D. ask someone else to do the job for you
    E. listen carefully to the directions, and then figure out a better way to do the job which will save more money

19. How should a Border Patrol Agent handle a situation in which he or she is offered a bribe	19.____
    to enter the United States illegally?

    A. Pretend the bribe was never offered
    B. Accept the money as evidence and release the aliens
    C. Draw your weapon and call for backup

D. Refuse the bribe and then arrest the illegal aliens
E. Accept the bribe and then arrest the illegal aliens

20. At work, you are faced with a difficult decision. You react by

    A. seeking advice from your colleagues
    B. following your own path regardless of the consequences
    C. asking your supervisor what you should do
    D. keeping the difficulties to yourself
    E. working for a solution which will please everyone

20.____

21. If asked to work with a person whom you dislike, your response would be

    A. to ask your supervisor to allow you to work with someone else
    B. to ask your coworker to transfer to another department or project
    C. talk to your coworker about the proper way to behave at work
    D. pretend the coworker is your best friend for the sake of your job
    E. to set aside your personal differences in order to complete the job

21.____

22. As a supervisor, which of the following incentives would you use to motivate your employees?

    A. Fear of losing their jobs
    B. Fear of their supervisors
    C. Allowing employees to provide their input on a number of policies
    D. Encouraging employees to file secret reports regarding colleagues' transgressions
    E. All of the above

22.____

23. A fellow Border Patrol Agent, with whom you enjoy a close friendship, has a substance-abuse problem which has gone undetected. You suspect the problem may be affecting his job.
    You would

    A. ask the Border Patrol Agent if the problem is affecting his job performance
    B. warn the Border Patrol Agent that he must seek counseling or you will report him
    C. wait a few weeks to see whether the Agent's problem really is affecting his job
    D. discuss it with your supervisor
    E. wait for the supervisor to discover the problem

23.____

24. In the past two months, you have missed work

    A. zero times   B. once
    C. twice   D. three times
    E. more than three times

24.____

25. As a Border Patrol Agent, you are pursuing a group of illegal aliens when you discover several small children who have been abandoned near a crossing point. You should

    A. tell the children to stay put while you continue your pursuit
    B. lock the children in your vehicle and continue your pursuit
    C. stay with the children and radio for help in the pursuit of the illegal aliens
    D. use the children to set a trap for the illegal aliens
    E. ignore the children and continue your pursuit

25.____

KEY (CORRECT ANSWERS)

PLEASE NOTE: The answers listed are the best answers. However, you are to answer the exam honestly. Your personal answer may differ from the *best* answers.

1. A
2. C
3. C
4. A
5. D

6. B
7. C
8. A
9. A
10. D

11. B
12. A
13. C
14. B
15. A

16. B
17. E
18. B
19. D
20. A

21. E
22. C
23. D
24. A
25. C

READING COMPREHENSION
UNDERSTANDING AND INTERPRETING WRITTEN MATERIAL

EXAMINATION SECTION
TEST 1

DIRECTIONS: Each question or incomplete statement is followed by several suggested answers or completions. Select the one that BEST answers the question or completes the statement. *PRINT THE LETTER OF THE CORRECT ANSWER IN THE SPACE AT THE RIGHT.*

Questions 1-5.

DIRECTIONS: Questions 1 through 5 are to be answered on the basis of the following passage.

The laws with which criminal courts are concerned contain threats of punishment for infraction of specified rules. Consequently, the courts are organized primarily for implementation of the punitive societal reaction of crime. While the informal organization of most courts allows the judge to use discretion as to which guilty persons actually are to be punished, the threat of punishment for all guilty persons always is present. Also, in recent years a number of formal provisions for the use of non-punitive and treatment methods by the criminal courts have been made, but the threat of punishment remains, even for the recipients of the treatment and non-punitive measures. For example, it has become possible for courts to grant probation, which can be non-punitive, to some offenders, but the probationer is constantly under the threat of punishment, for, if he does not maintain the conditions of his probation, he may be imprisoned. As the treatment reaction to crime becomes more popular, the criminal courts may have as their sole function the determination of the guilt or innocence of the accused persons, leaving the problem of correcting criminals entirely to outsiders. Under such conditions, the organization of the court system, the duties and activities of court personnel, and the nature of the trial all would be decidedly different.

1. Which one of the following is the BEST description of the subject matter of the above passage?
The

    A. value of non-punitive measures for criminals
    B. effect of punishment on guilty individuals
    C. punitive functions of the criminal courts
    D. success of probation as a deterrent of crime

1.____

2. It may be INFERRED from the above passage that the present traditional organization of the criminal court system is a result of

    A. the nature of the laws with which these courts are concerned
    B. a shift from non-punitive to punitive measures for correctional purposes
    C. an informal arrangement between court personnel and the government
    D. a formal decision made by court personnel to increase efficiency

2.____

3. All persons guilty of breaking certain specified rules, according to the above passage, are subject to the threat of

   A. treatment
   B. punishment
   C. probation
   D. retrial

4. According to the above passage, the decision whether or not to punish a guilty person is a function USUALLY performed by

   A. the jury
   B. the criminal code
   C. the judge
   D. corrections personnel

5. According to the above passage, which one of the following is a possible effect of an increase in the *treatment reactions to crime?*

   A. A decrease in the number of court personnel
   B. An increase in the number of criminal trials
   C. Less reliance on probation as a non-punitive treatment measure
   D. A decrease in the functions of the court following determination of guilt

Questions 6-8.

DIRECTIONS: Questions 6 through 8 are to be answered on the basis of the following passage.

A glaring exception to the usual practice of the judicial trial as a means of conflict resolution is the utilization of administrative hearings. The growing tendency to create administrative bodies with rule-making and quasi-judicial powers has shattered many standard concepts. A comprehensive examination of the legal process cannot neglect these newer patterns.

In the administrative process, the legislative, executive, and judicial functions are mixed together, and many functions, such as investigating, advocating, negotiating, testifying, rule making, and adjudicating, are carried out by the same agency. The reason for the breakdown of the separation-of-powers formula is not hard to find. It was felt by Congress, and state and municipal legislatures, that certain regulatory tasks could not be performed efficiently, rapidly, expertly, and with due concern for the public interest by the traditional branches of government. Accordingly, regulatory agencies were delegated powers to consider disputes from the earliest stage of investigation to the final stages of adjudication entirely within each agency itself, subject only to limited review in the regular courts.

6. The above passage states that the usual means for conflict resolution is through the use of

   A. judicial trial
   B. administrative hearing
   C. legislation
   D. regulatory agencies

7. The above passage IMPLIES that the use of administrative hearing in resolving conflict is a(n) _____ approach.

   A. traditional
   B. new
   C. dangerous
   D. experimental

8. The above passage states that the reason for the breakdown of the separation-of-powers formula in the administrative process is that

A. Congress believed that certain regulatory tasks could be better performed by separate agencies
B. legislative and executive functions are incompatible in the same agency
C. investigative and regulatory functions are not normally reviewed by the courts
D. state and municipal legislatures are more concerned with efficiency than with legality

Questions 9-10.

DIRECTIONS: Questions 9 and 10 are to be answered SOLELY on the basis of the information given in the following paragraph.

An assumption commonly made in regard to the reliability of testimony is that when a number of persons report upon the same matter, those details upon which there is an agreement may, in general, be considered as substantiated. Experiments have shown, however, that there is a tendency for the same errors to appear in the testimony of different individuals, and that, quite apart from any collusion, agreement of testimony is no proof of dependability.

9. According to the above paragraph, it is commonly assumed that details of an event are substantiated when 9.____

    A. a number of persons report upon them
    B. a reliable person testifies to them
    C. no errors are apparent in the testimony of different individuals
    D. several witnesses are in agreement about them

10. According to the above paragraph, agreement in the testimony of different witnesses to the same event is 10.____

    A. evaluated more reliably when considered apart from collusion
    B. not the result of chance
    C. not a guarantee of the accuracy of the facts
    D. the result of a mass reaction of the witnesses

Questions 11-12.

DIRECTIONS: Questions 11 and 12 are to be answered SOLELY on the basis of the information given in the following paragraph.

The accuracy of the information about past occurrence obtainable in an interview is so low that one must take the stand that the best use to be made of the interview in this connection is a means of finding clues and avenues of access to more reliable sources of information. On the other hand, feelings and attitudes have been found to be clearly and correctly revealed in a properly conducted personal interview.

11. According to the above paragraph, information obtained in a personal interview 11.____

    A. can be corroborated by other clues and more reliable sources of information revealed at the interview
    B. can be used to develop leads to other sources of information about past events
    C. is not reliable
    D. is reliable if it relates to recent occurrences

12. According to the above paragraph, the personal interview is suitable for obtaining

    A. emotional reactions to a given situation
    B. fresh information on factors which may be forgotten
    C. revived recollection of previous events for later use as testimony
    D. specific information on material already reduced to writing

Questions 13-15.

DIRECTIONS: Questions 13 through 15 are to be answered on the basis of the following paragraph.

Admissibility of handwriting standards (samples of handwriting for the purpose of comparison) as a basis for expert testimony is frequently necessary when the authenticity of disputed documents may be at issue. Under the older rules of common law, only that writing relating to the issues in the case could be used as a basis for handwriting testimony by an expert. Today, most jurisdictions admit irrelevant writings as standards for comparison. However, their genuineness, in all instances, must be established to the satisfaction of the court. There are a number of types of documents, however, not ordinarily relevant to the issues which are seldom acceptable to the court as handwriting standards, such as bail bonds, signatures on affidavits, depositions, etc. These are usually already before the court as part of the record in a case. Exhibits written in the presence of a witness or prepared voluntarily for a law enforcement officer are readily admissible in most jurisdictions. Testimony of a witness who is considered familiar with the writing is admissible in some jurisdictions. In criminal cases, it is possible that the signature on the fingerprint card obtained in connection with the arrest of the defendant for the crime currently charged may be admitted as a handwriting standard. In order to give the defendant the fairest possible treatment, most jurisdictions do not admit the signatures on fingerprint cards pertaining to prior arrests. However, they are admitted sometimes. In such instances, the court usually requires that the signature be photographed or removed from the card and no reference be made to the origin of the signature.

13. Of the following, the types of handwriting standards MOST likely to be admitted in evidence by most jurisdictions are those

    A. appearing on depositions and bail bonds
    B. which were written in the presence of a witness or voluntarily given to a law enforcement officer
    C. identified by witnesses who claim to be familiar with the handwriting
    D. which are in conformity with the rules of common law only

14. The PRINCIPAL factor which generally determines the acceptance of handwriting standards by the courts is

    A. the relevance of the submitted documents to the issues of the case
    B. the number of witnesses who have knowledge of the submitted documents
    C. testimony that the writing has been examined by a handwriting expert
    D. acknowledgment by the court of the authenticity of the submitted documents

15. The MOST logical reason for requiring the removal of the signature of a defendant from fingerprint cards pertaining to prior arrests, before admitting the signature in court as a handwriting standard, is that

A. it simplifies the process of identification of the signature as a standard for comparison
B. the need for identifying the fingerprints is eliminated
C. mention of prior arrests may be prejudicial to the defendant
D. a handwriting expert does not need information pertaining to prior arrests in order to make his identification

Questions 16-20.

DIRECTIONS: Questions 16 through 20 are to be answered SOLELY on the basis of the information contained in the following paragraph.

A statement which is offered in an attempt to prove the truth of the matters therein stated, but which is not made by the author as a witness before the court at the particular trial in which it is so offered, is hearsay. This is so whether the statement consists of words (oral or written), of symbols used as a substitute for words, or of signs or other conduct offered as the equivalent of a statement. Subject to some well-established exceptions, hearsay is not generally acceptable as evidence, and it does not become competent evidence just because it is received by the court without objection. One basis for this rule is simply that a fact cannot be proved by showing that somebody stated it was a fact. Another basis for the rule is the fundamental principle that in a criminal prosecution the testimony of the witness shall be taken before the court, so that at the time he gives the testimony offered in evidence he will be sworn and subject to cross-examination, the scrutiny of the court, and confrontation by the accused.

16. Which of the following is hearsay? 16.____
    A(n)

    A. written statement by a person not present at the court hearing where the statement is submitted as proof of an occurrence
    B. oral statement in court by a witness of what he saw
    C. written statement of what he saw by a witness present in court
    D. re-enactment by a witness in court of what he saw

17. In a criminal case, a statement by a person not present in court is 17.____

    A. *acceptable* evidence if not objected to by the prosecutor
    B. *acceptable* evidence if not objected to by the defense lawyer
    C. *not acceptable* evidence except in certain well-settled circumstances
    D. *not acceptable* evidence under any circumstances

18. The rule on hearsay is founded on the belief that 18.____

    A. proving someone said an act occurred is not proof that the act did occur
    B. a person who has knowledge about a case should be willing to appear in court
    C. persons not present in court are likely to be unreliable witnesses
    D. permitting persons to testify without appearing in court will lead to a disrespect for law

19. One reason for the general rule that a witness in a criminal case must give his testimony in court is that

    A. a witness may be influenced by threats to make untrue statements
    B. the opposite side is then permitted to question him
    C. the court provides protection for a witness against unfair questioning
    D. the adversary system is designed to prevent a miscarriage of justice

20. Of the following, the MOST appropriate title for the above passage would be

    A. WHAT IS HEARSAY?
    B. RIGHTS OF DEFENDANTS
    C. TRIAL PROCEDURES
    D. TESTIMONY OF WITNESSES

21. A person's statements are independent of who he is or what he is. Statements made by a person are not proved true or false by questioning his character or his position. A statement should stand or fall on its merits, regardless of who makes the statement. Truth is determined by evidence only. A person's character or personality should not be the determining factor in logic. Discussions should not become incidents of name calling. According to the above, whether or not a statement is true depends on the

    A. recipient's conception of validity
    B. maker's reliability
    C. extent of support by facts
    D. degree of merit the discussion has

Question 22-25.

DIRECTIONS: Questions 22 through 25 are to be answered on the basis of the following passage.

The question, whether an act, repugnant to the Constitution, can become the law of the land, is a question deeply interesting to the United States; but, happily, not of an intricacy proportioned to its interest. It seems only necessary to recognize certain principles, supposed to have been long and well-established, to decide it. That the people have an original right to establish, for their future government, such principles as, in their opinion, shall most conduce to their own happiness, is the basis on which the whole American fabric has been erected. The exercise of this original right is a very great exertion; nor can it, nor ought it, to be frequently repeated. The principles, therefore, so established are deemed fundamental; and as the authority from which they proceed is supreme, and can seldom act, they are designed to be permanent.

22. The BEST title for the above passage would be

    A. PRINCIPLES OF THE CONSTITUTION
    B. THE ROOT OF CONSTITUTIONAL CHANGE
    C. ONLY PEOPLE CAN CHANGE THE CONSTITUTION
    D. METHODS OF CONSTITUTIONAL CHANGE

23. According to the above passage, original right is

    A. fundamental to the principle that the people may choose their own form of government
    B. established by the Constitution

C. the result of a very great exertion and should not often be repeated
D. supreme, can seldom act, and is designed to be permanent

24. Whether an act not in keeping with Constitutional principles can become law is, according to the above passage, 24.____

    A. an intricate problem requiring great thought and concentration
    B. determined by the proportionate interests of legislators
    C. determined by certain long established principles, fundamental to Constitutional Law
    D. an intricate problem, but less intricate than it would seem from the interest shown in it

25. According to the above passage, the phrase *and can seldom act* refers to the 25.____

    A. principle enacted early into law by Americans when they chose their future form of government
    B. original rights of the people as vested in the Constitution
    C. original framers of the Constitution
    D. established, fundamental principles of government

KEY (CORRECT ANSWERS)

1.	C	11.	B
2.	A	12.	A
3.	B	13.	B
4.	C	14.	D
5.	D	15.	C
6.	A	16.	A
7.	B	17.	C
8.	A	18.	A
9.	D	19.	B
10.	C	20.	A

21. C
22. B
23. A
24. D
25. A

TEST 2

DIRECTIONS: Each question or incomplete statement is followed by several suggested answers or completions. Select the one that BEST answers the question or completes the statement. *PRINT THE LETTER OF THE CORRECT ANSWER IN THE SPACE AT THE RIGHT.*

Questions 1-3.

DIRECTIONS: Questions 1 through 3 are to be answered SOLELY on the basis of the following paragraph.

The police laboratory performs a valuable service in crime investigation by assisting in the reconstruction of criminal action and by aiding in the identification of persons and things. When studied by a technician, physical things found at crime scenes often reveal facts useful in identifying the criminal and in determining what has occurred. The nature of substances to be examined and the character of the examination to be made vary so widely that the services of a large variety of skilled scientific persons are needed in crime investigations. To employ such a complete staff and to provide them with equipment and standards needed for all possible analysis and comparisons is beyond the means and the needs of any but the largest police departments. The search of crime scenes for physical evidence also calls for the services of specialists supplied with essential equipment and assigned to each tour of duty so as to provide service at any hour.

1. If a police department employs a large staff of technicians of various types in its laboratory, it will affect crime investigations to the extent that

    A. most crimes will be speedily solved
    B. identification of criminals will be aided
    C. search of crime scenes for physical evidence will become of less importance
    D. investigation by police officers will not usually be required

2. According to the above paragraph, the MOST complete study of objects found at the scenes of crimes is

    A. always done in all large police departments
    B. based on assigning one technician to each tour of duty
    C. probably done only in large police departments
    D. probably done in police departments of communities with low crime rates

3. According to the above paragraph, a large variety of skilled technicians is useful in criminal investigations because

    A. crimes cannot be solved without their assistance as part of the police team
    B. large police departments need large staffs
    C. many different kinds of tests on various substances can be made
    D. the police cannot predict what methods may be tried by wily criminals

Questions 4-6.

DIRECTIONS: Questions 4 through 6 are to be answered SOLELY on the basis of the following passage.

Probably the most important single mechanism for bringing the resources of science and technology to bear on the problems of crime would be the establishment of a major prestigious science and technology research program within a research institute. The program would create interdisciplinary teams of mathematicians, computer scientists, electronics engineers, physicists, biologists, and other natural scientists, psychologists, sociologists, economists, and lawyers. The institute and the program must be significant enough to attract the best scientists available, and, to this end, the director of this institute must himself have a background in science and technology and have the respect of scientists. Because it would be difficult to attract such a staff into the Federal government, the institute should be established by a university, a group of universities, or an independent nonprofit organization, and should be within a major metropolitan area. The institute would have to establish close ties with neighboring criminal justice agencies that would receive the benefit of serving as experimental laboratories for such an institute. In fact, the proposal for the institute might be jointly submitted with the criminal justice agencies. The research program would require, in order to bring together the necessary *critical mass* of competent staff, an annual budget which might reach 5 million dollars, funded with at least three years of lead time to assure continuity. Such a major scientific and technological research institute should be supported by the Federal government.

4. Of the following, the MOST appropriate title for the foregoing passage is

   A. RESEARCH - AN INTERDISCIPLINARY APPROACH TO FIGHTING CRIME
   B. A CURRICULUM FOR FIGHTING CRIME
   C. THE ROLE OF THE UNIVERSITY IN THE FIGHT AGAINST CRIME
   D. GOVERNMENTAL SUPPORT OF CRIMINAL RESEARCH PROGRAMS

5. According to the above passage, in order to attract the best scientists available, the research institute should

   A. provide psychologists and sociologists to counsel individual members of interdisciplinary teams
   B. encourage close ties with neighboring criminal justice agencies
   C. be led by a person who is respected in the scientific community
   D. be directly operated and funded by the Federal government

6. The term *critical mass,* as used in the above passage, refers MAINLY to

   A. a staff which would remain for three years of continuous service to the institute
   B. staff members necessary to carry out the research program of the institute successfully
   C. the staff necessary to establish relations with criminal justice agencies which will serve as experimental laboratories for the institute
   D. a staff which would be able to assist the institute in raising adequate funds

Questions 7-9.

DIRECTIONS: Questions 7 through 9 are to be answered SOLELY on the basis of the following paragraph.

The use of modern scientific methods in the examination of physical evidence often provides information to the investigator which he could not otherwise obtain. This applies particularly to small objects and materials present in minute quantities or trace evidence because the quantities here are such that they may be overlooked without methodical searching, and often special means of detection are needed. Whenever two objects come in contact with one another, there is a transfer of material, however slight. Usually, the softer object will transfer to the harder, but the transfer may be mutual. The quantity of material transferred differs with the type of material involved and the more violent the contact the greater the degree of transference. Through scientific methods of determining physical properties and chemical composition, we can add to the facts observable by the investigator's unaided senses, and thereby increase the chances of identification.

7. According to the above paragraph, the amount of material transferred whenever two objects come in contact with one another

    A. varies directly with the softness of the objects involved
    B. varies directly with the violence of the contact of the objects
    C. is greater when two soft, rather than hard, objects come into violent contact with each other
    D. is greater when coarse-grained, rather than smooth-grained, materials are involved

8. According to the above paragraph, the PRINCIPAL reason for employing scientific methods in obtaining trace evidence is that

    A. other methods do not involve a methodical search of the crime scene
    B. scientific methods of examination frequently reveal physical evidence which did not previously exist
    C. the amount of trace evidence may be so sparse that other methods are useless
    D. trace evidence cannot be properly identified unless special means of detection are employed

9. According to the above paragraph, the one of the following statements which BEST describes the manner in which scientific methods of analyzing physical evidence assists the investigator is that such methods

    A. add additional valuable information to the investigator's own knowledge of complex and rarely occurring materials found as evidence
    B. compensate for the lack of important evidential material through the use of physical and chemical analyses
    C. make possible an analysis of evidence which goes beyond the ordinary capacity of the investigator's senses
    D. identify precisely those physical characteristics of the individual which the untrained senses of the investigator are unable to discern

Questions 10-13.

DIRECTIONS: Questions 10 through 13 are to be answered SOLELY on the basis of the information contained in the following paragraph.

Under the provisions of the Bank Protection Act of 1968, enacted July 8, 1968, each Federal banking supervisory agency, as of January 7, 1969, had to issue rules establishing minimum standards with which financial institutions under their control must comply with respect to the installation, maintenance, and operation of security devices and procedures, reasonable in cost, to discourage robberies, burglaries, and larcenies, and to assist in the identification and apprehension of persons who commit such acts. The rules set the time limits within which the affected banks and savings and loan associations must comply with the standards, and the rules require the submission of periodic reports on the steps taken. A violator of a rule under this Act is subject to a civil penalty not to exceed $100 for each day of the violation. The enforcement of these regulations rests with the responsible banking supervisory agencies.

10. The Bank Protection Act of 1968 was designed to

    A. provide Federal police protection for banks covered by the Act
    B. have organizations covered by the Act take precautions against criminals
    C. set up a system for reporting all bank robberies to the FBI
    D. insure institutions covered by the Act from financial loss due to robberies, burglaries, and larcenies

11. Under the provisions of the Bank Protection Act of 1968, each Federal banking supervisory agency was required to set up rules for financial institutions covered by the Act governing the

    A. hiring of personnel
    B. punishment of burglars
    C. taking of protective measures
    D. penalties for violations

12. Financial institutions covered by the Bank Protection Act of 1968 were required to

    A. file reports at regular intervals on what they had done to prevent theft
    B. identify and apprehend persons who commit robberies, burglaries, and larcenies
    C. draw up a code of ethics for their employees
    D. have fingerprints of their employees filed with the FBI

13. Under the provisions of the Bank Protection Act of 1968, a bank which is subject to the rules established under the Act and which violates a rule is liable to a penalty of NOT _____ than $100 for each _____.

    A. more; violation   B. less; day of violation
    C. less; violation   D. more; day of violation

Questions 14-17.

DIRECTIONS: Questions 14 through 17 are to be answered SOLELY on the basis of the following passage.

Specific measures for prevention of pilferage will be based on careful analysis of the conditions at each agency. The most practical and effective method to control casual pilferage is the establishment of psychological deterrents.

One of the most common means of discouraging casual pilferage is to search individuals leaving the agency at unannounced times and places. These spot searches may occasionally detect attempts at theft, but greater value is realized by bringing to the attention of individuals the fact that they may be apprehended if they do attempt the illegal removal of property.

An aggressive security education program is an effective means of convincing employees that they have much more to lose than they do to gain by engaging in acts of theft. It is important for all employees to realize that pilferage is morally wrong no matter how insignificant the value of the item which is taken. In establishing any deterrent to casual pilferage, security officers must not lose sight of the fact that most employees are honest and disapprove of thievery. Mutual respect between security personnel and other employees of the agency must be maintained if the facility is to be protected from other more dangerous forms of human hazards. Any security measure which infringes on the human rights or dignity of others will jeopardize, rather than enhance, the overall protection of the agency.

14. The $100,000 yearly inventory of an agency revealed that $50 worth of goods had been stolen; the only individuals with access to the stolen materials were the employees. Of the following measures, which would the author of the above passage MOST likely recommend to a security officer?

    A. Conduct an intensive investigation of all employees to find the culprit.
    B. Make a record of the theft, but take no investigative or disciplinary action against any employee.
    C. Place a tight security check on all future movements of personnel.
    D. Remove the remainder of the material to an area with much greater security.

15. What does the passage imply is the percentage of employees whom a security officer should expect to be honest?

    A. No employee can be expected to be honest all of the time
    B. Just 50%
    C. Less than 50%
    D. More than 50%

16. According to the above passage, the security officer would use which of the following methods to minimize theft in buildings with many exits when his staff is very small?

    A. Conduct an inventory of all material and place a guard near that which is most likely to be pilfered
    B. Inform employees of the consequences of legal prosecution for pilfering
    C. Close off the unimportant exits and have all his men concentrate on a few exits
    D. Place a guard at each exit and conduct a casual search of individuals leaving the premises

17. Of the following, the title BEST suited for this passage is

    A. CONTROL MEASURES FOR CASUAL PILFERING
    B. DETECTING THE POTENTIAL PILFERER
    C. FINANCIAL LOSSES RESULTING FROM PILFERING
    D. THE USE OF MORAL PERSUASION IN PHYSICAL SECURITY

Questions 18-24.

DIRECTIONS: Questions 18 through 24 are to be answered SOLELY on the basis of the following passage.

Burglar alarms are designed to detect intrusion automatically. Robbery alarms enable a victim of a robbery or an attack to signal for help. Such devices can be located in elevators, hallways, homes and apartments, businesses and factories, and subways, as well as on the street in high-crime areas. Alarms could deter some potential criminals from attacking targets so protected. If alarms were prevalent and not visible, then they might serve to suppress crime generally. In addition, of course, the alarms can summon the police when they are needed.

All alarms must perform three functions: sensing or initiation of the signal, transmission of the signal and annunciation of the alarm. A burglar alarm needs a sensor to detect human presence or activity in an unoccupied enclosed area like a building or a room. A robbery victim would initiate the alarm by closing a foot or wall switch, or by triggering a portable transmitter which would send the alarm signal to a remote receiver. The signal can sound locally as a loud noise to frighten away a criminal, or it can be sent silently by wire to a central agency. A centralized annunciator requires either private lines from each alarmed point, or the transmission of some information on the location of the signal.

18. A conclusion which follows LOGICALLY from the above passage is that

    A. burglar alarms employ sensor devices; robbery alarms make use of initiation devices
    B. robbery alarms signal intrusion without the help of the victim; burglar alarms require the victim to trigger a switch
    C. robbery alarms sound locally; burglar alarms are transmitted to a central agency
    D. the mechanisms for a burglar alarm and a robbery alarm are alike

19. According to the above passage, alarms can be located

    A. in a wide variety of settings
    B. only in enclosed areas
    C. at low cost in high-crime areas
    D. only in places where potential criminals will be deterred

20. According to the above passage, which of the following is ESSENTIAL if a signal is to be received in a central office?

    A. A foot or wall switch
    B. A noise-producing mechanism
    C. A portable reception device
    D. Information regarding the location of the source

21. According to the above passage, an alarm system can function WITHOUT a

    A. centralized annunciating device
    B. device to stop the alarm
    C. sensing or initiating device
    D. transmission device

22. According to the above passage, the purpose of robbery alarms is to

    A. find out automatically whether a robbery has taken place
    B. lower the crime rate in high-crime areas
    C. make a loud noise to frighten away the criminal
    D. provide a victim with the means to signal for help

23. According to the above passage, alarms might aid in lessening crime if they were 23.____

    A. answered promptly by police
    B. completely automatic
    C. easily accessible to victims
    D. hidden and widespread

24. Of the following, the BEST title for the above passage is 24.____

    A. DETECTION OF CRIME BY ALARMS
    B. LOWERING THE CRIME RATE
    C. SUPPRESSION OF CRIME
    D. THE PREVENTION OF ROBBERY

25. Although the rural crime reporting area is much less developed than that for cities and 25.____
    towns, current data are collected in sufficient volume to justify the generalization that
    rural crime rates are lower than those or urban communities.
    According to this statement,

    A. better reporting of crime occurs in rural areas than in cities
    B. there appears to be a lower proportion of crime in rural areas than in cities
    C. cities have more crime than towns
    D. crime depends on the amount of reporting

KEY (CORRECT ANSWERS)

1.	B	11.	C
2.	C	12.	A
3.	C	13.	D
4.	A	14.	B
5.	C	15.	D
6.	B	16.	B
7.	B	17.	A
8.	C	18.	A
9.	C	19.	A
10.	B	20.	D

21.	A
22.	D
23.	D
24.	A
25.	B

READING COMPREHENSION
UNDERSTANDING AND INTERPRETING WRITTEN MATERIAL
EXAMINATION SECTION
TEST 1

DIRECTIONS: Each question or incomplete statement is followed by several suggested answers or completions. Select the one that BEST answers the question or completes the statement. *PRINT THE LETTER OF THE CORRECT ANSWER IN THE SPACE AT THE RIGHT.*

Questions 1-4.

DIRECTIONS: Questions 1 through 4 are to be answered SOLELY on the basis of the following passage.

Those engaged in the exercise of First Amendment rights by pickets, marches, parades, and open-air assemblies are not exempted from obeying valid local traffic ordinances. In a recent pronouncement, Mr. Justice Baxter, speaking for the Supreme Court, wrote:

The rights of free speech and assembly, while fundamental to our democratic society, still do not mean that everyone with opinions or beliefs to express may address a group at any public place and at any time. The constitutional guarantee of liberty implies the existence of an organized society maintaining public order, without which liberty itself would be lost in the excesses of anarchy. The control of travel on the streets is a clear example of governmental responsibility to insure this necessary order. A restriction in that relation, designed to promote the public convenience in the interest of all, and not susceptible to abuses of discriminatory application, cannot be disregarded by the attempted exercise of some civil rights which, in other circumstances, would be entitled to protection. One would not be justified in ignoring the familiar red light because this was thought to be a means of social protest. Governmental authorities have the duty and responsibility to keep their streets open and available for movement. A group of demonstrators could not insist upon the right to cordon off a street, or entrance to a public or private building, and allow no one to pass who did not agree to listen to their exhortations.

1. Which of the following statements BEST reflects Mr. Justice Baxter's view of the relationship between liberty and public order?

    A. Public order cannot exist without liberty.
    B. Liberty cannot exist without public order.
    C. The existence of liberty undermines the existence of public order.
    D. The maintenance of public order insures the existence of liberty.

2. According to the above passage, local traffic ordinances result from

    A. governmental limitations on individual liberty
    B. governmental responsibility to insure public order
    C. majority rule as determined by democratic procedures
    D. restrictions on expression of dissent

3. The above passage suggests that government would be acting improperly if a local traffic ordinance

   A. was enforced in a discriminatory manner
   B. resulted in public inconvenience
   C. violated the right of free speech and assembly
   D. was not essential to public order

4. Of the following, the MOST appropriate title for the above passage is

   A. THE RIGHTS OF FREE SPEECH AND ASSEMBLY
   B. ENFORCEMENT OF LOCAL TRAFFIC ORDINANCES
   C. FIRST AMENDMENT RIGHTS AND LOCAL TRAFFIC ORDINANCES
   D. LIBERTY AND ANARCHY

Questions 5-8

DIRECTIONS: Questions 5 through 8 are to be answered SOLELY on the basis of the following passage

On November 8, 1976, the Supreme Court refused to block the payment of Medicaid funds for elective abortions. The Court's action means that a new Federal statute that bars the use of Federal funds for abortions unless abortion is necessary to save the life of the mother will not go into effect for many months, if at all.

A Federal District Court in Brooklyn ruled the following month that the statute was unconstitutional and ordered that Federal reimbursement for the costs of abortions continue on the same basis as reimbursements for the costs of pregnancy and childbirth-related services.

Technically, what the Court did today was to deny a request by Senator Howard Ramsdell and others for a stay blocking enforcement of the District Court order pending appeal. The Court's action was a victory for New York City. The City's Health and Hospitals Corporation initiated one of the two lawsuits challenging the new statute that led to the District Court's decision. The Corporation also opposed the request for a Supreme Court stay of that decision, telling the Court in a memorandum that a stay would subject the Corporation to a *grave and irreparable injury*.

5. According to the above passage, it would be CORRECT to state that the Health and Hospitals Corporation

   A. joined Senator Ramsdell in his request for a stay
   B. opposed the statute which limited reimbursement for the cost of abortions
   C. claimed that it would experience a loss if the District Court order was enforced
   D. appealed the District Court decision

6. The above passage indicates that the Supreme Court acted in DIRECT response to

   A. a lawsuit initiated by the Health and Hospitals Corporation
   B. a ruling by a Federal District Court
   C. a request for a stay
   D. the passage of a new Federal statute

3 (#1)

7. According to the above passage, it would be CORRECT to state that the Supreme Court 7.____

   A. blocked enforcement of the District Court order
   B. refused a request for a stay to block enforcement of the Federal statute
   C. ruled that the new Federal statute was unconstitutional
   D. permitted payment of Federal funds for abortion to continue

8. Following are three statements concerning abortion that might be correct: 8.____
   I. Abortion costs are no longer to be Federally reimbursed on the same basis as those for pregnancy and childbirth
   II. Federal funds have not been available for abortions except to save the life of the mother
   III. Medicaid has paid for elective abortions in the past

   According to the passage above, which of the following CORRECTLY classifies the above statements into those that are true and those that are not true?

   A. I is true, but II and III are not.
   B. I and III are true, but II is not.
   C. I and II are true, but III is not.
   D. III is true, but I and II are not.

Questions 9-12.

DIRECTIONS: Questions 9 through 12 are to be answered SOLELY on the basis of the following passage.

A person may use physical force upon another person when and to the extent he reasonably believes such to be necessary to defend himself or a third person from what he reasonably believes to be the use or imminent use of unlawful physical force by such other person, unless (a) the latter's conduct was provoked by the actor himself with intent to cause physical injury to another person; or (b) the actor was the initial aggressor; or (c) the physical force involved is the product of a combat by agreement not specifically authorized by law.

A person may not use deadly physical force upon another person under the circumstances specified above unless (a) he reasonably believes that such other person is using or is about to use deadly physical force. Even in such case, however, the actor may not use deadly physical force if he knows he can, with complete safety, as to himself and others avoid the necessity of doing so by retreating; except that he is under no duty to retreat if he is in his dwelling and is not the initial aggressor; or (b) he reasonably believes that such other person is committing or attempting to commit a kidnapping, forcible rape, or forcible sodomy.

9. Jones and Smith, who have not met before, get into an argument in a tavern. Smith takes a punch at Jones, but misses. Jones then hits Smith on the chin with his fist. Smith falls to the floor and suffers minor injuries. 9.____
   According to the above passage, it would be CORRECT to state that _____ justified in using physical force.

   A. only Smith was   B. only Jones was
   C. both Smith and Jones were   D. neither Smith nor Jones was

10. While walking down the street, Brady observes Miller striking Mrs. Adams on the head with his fist in an attempt to steal her purse.
    According to the above passage, it would be CORRECT to state that Brady would

    A. not be justified in using deadly physical force against Miller since Brady can safely retreat
    B. be justified in using physical force against Miller but not deadly physical force
    C. not be justified in using physical force against Miller since Brady himself is not being attacked
    D. be justified in using deadly physical force

11. Winters is attacked from behind by Sharp, who attempts to beat up Winters with a blackjack. Winters disarms Sharp and succeeds in subduing him with a series of blows to the head. Sharp stops fighting and explains that he thought Winters was the person who had robbed his apartment a few minutes before, but now realizes his mistake.
    According to the above passage, it would be CORRECT to state that

    A. Winters was justified in using physical force on Sharp only to the extent necessary to defend himself
    B. Winters was not justified in using physical force on Sharp since Sharp's attack was provoked by what he believed to be Winters' behavior
    C. Sharp was justified in using physical force on Winters since he reasonably believed that Winters had unlawfully robbed him
    D. Winters was justified in using physical force on Sharp only because Sharp was acting mistakenly in attacking him

12. Roberts hears a noise in the cellar of his home, and, upon investigation, discovers an intruder, Welch. Welch moves towards Roberts in a threatening manner, thrusts his hand into a bulging pocket, and withdraws what appears to be a gun. Roberts thereupon strikes Welch over the head with a golf club. He then sees that the *gun* is a toy. Welch later dies of head injuries. According to the above passage, it would be CORRECT to state that Roberts was

    A. justified in using deadly physical force because he reasonably believed Welch was about to use deadly physical force
    B. not justified in using deadly physical force
    C. justified in using deadly physical force only because he did not provoke Welch's conduct
    D. justified in using deadly physical force only because he was not the initial aggressor

Questions 13-16.

DIRECTIONS: Questions 13 through 16 are to be answered SOLELY on the basis of the following passage.

From the beginning, the Supreme Court has supervised the fairness of trials conducted by the Federal government. But the Constitution, as originally drafted, gave the court no such general authority in state cases. The court's power to deal with state cases comes from the Fourteenth Amendment, which became part of the Constitution in 1868. The crucial provision forbids any state to *deprive any person of life, liberty, or property without due process of law.*

The guarantee of *due process* would seem, at the least, to require fair procedure in criminal trials. But curiously the Supreme Court did not speak on the question for many decades. During that time, however, the due process clause was interpreted to bar *unreasonable* state economic regulations, such as minimum wage laws.

In 1915, there came the case of Leo M. Frank, a Georgian convicted of murder in a trial that he contended was dominated by mob hysteria. Historians now agree that there was such hysteria, with overtones of anti-semitism.

The Supreme Court held that it could not look past the findings of the Georgia courts that there had been no mob atmosphere at the trial. Justices Oliver Wendell Holmes and Charles Evans Hughes dissented, arguing that the constitutional guarantee would be *a barren one* if the Federal courts could not make their own inferences from the facts.

In 1923, the case of Moore v. Dempsey involved five Arkansas Blacks convicted of murder and sentenced to death in a community so aroused against them that at one point they were saved from lynching only by Federal troops. Witnesses against them were said to have been beaten into testifying.

The court, though not actually setting aside the convictions, directed a lower Federal court to hold a habeas corpus hearing to find out whether the trial had been fair, or whether the whole proceeding had been *a mask—that counsel, jury, and judge were swept to the fatal end by an irresistible wave of public passion.*

13. According to the above passage, the Supreme Court's INITIAL interpretation of the Fourteenth Amendment

    A. protected state supremacy in economic matters
    B. increased the scope of Federal jurisdiction
    C. required fair procedures in criminal trials
    D. prohibited the enactment of minimum wage laws

14. According to the above passage, the Supreme Court in the Frank case

    A. denied that there had been mob hysteria at the trial
    B. decided that the guilty verdict was supported by the evidence
    C. declined to question the state court's determination of the facts
    D. found that Leo Frank had not received *due process*

15. According to the above passage, the dissenting judges in the Frank case maintained that

    A. due process was an empty promise in the circumstances of that case
    B. the Federal courts could not guarantee certain provisions of the Constitution
    C. the Federal courts should not make their own inferences from the facts in state cases
    D. the Supreme Court had rendered the Constitution *barren*

16. Of the following, the MOST appropriate title for the above passage is 16.____
    A. THE CONDUCT OF FEDERAL TRIALS
    B. THE DEVELOPMENT OF STATES' RIGHTS: 1868-1923
    C. MOORE V. DEMPSEY: A CASE STUDY IN CRIMINAL JUSTICE
    D. DUE PROCESS-THE EVOLUTION OF A CONSTITUTIONAL CORNERSTONE

Questions 17-20.

DIRECTIONS: Questions 17 through 20 are to be answered SOLELY on the basis of the following passage.

The difficulty experienced in determining which party has the burden of proving payment or non-payment is due largely to a lack of consistency between the rules of pleading and the rules of proof. In some cases, a plaintiff is obligated by a rule of pleading to allege non-payment on his complaint, yet is not obligated to prove non-payment on the trial. An action upon a contract for the payment of money will serve as an illustration. In such a case, the plaintiff must allege non-payment in his complaint, but the burden of proving payment on the trial is upon the defendant. An important and frequently cited case on this problem is Conkling v. Weatherwax. In that case, the action was brought to establish and enforce a legacy as a lien upon real property. The defendant alleged in her answer that the legacy had been paid. There was no witness competent to testify for the plaintiff to show that the legacy had not been paid. Therefore, the question of the burden of proof became of primary importance since, if the plaintiff had the burden of proving non-payment, she must fail in her action; whereas if the burden of proof was on the defendant to prove payment, the plaintiff might win. The Court of Appeals held that the burden of proof was on the plaintiff. In the course of his opinion, Judge Vann attempted to harmonize the conflicting cases on this subject, and for that purpose formulated three rules. These rules have been construed and applied to numerous subsequent cases. As so construed and applied, these may be summarized as follows:

Rule 1. In an action upon a contract for the payment of money only, where the complaint does not allege a balance due over and above all payments made, the plaintiff must allege nonpayment in his complaint, but the burden of proving payment is upon the defendant. In such a case, payment is an affirmative defense which the defendant must plead in his answer. If the defendant fails to plead payment, but pleads a general denial instead, he will not be permitted to introduce evidence of payment.

Rule 2. Where the complaint sets forth a balance in excess of all payments, owing to the structure of the pleading, burden is upon the plaintiff to prove his allegation. In this case, the defendant is not required to plead payment as a defense in his answer but may introduce evidence of payment under a general denial.

Rule 3. When the action is not upon contract for the payment of money, but is upon an obligation created by operation of law, or is for the enforcement of a lien where non-payment of the amount secured is part of the cause of action, it is necessary both to allege and prove the fact of nonpayment.

17. In the above passage, the case of Conkling v. Weatherwax was cited PRIMARILY to illustrate   17.____

    A. a case where the burden of proof was on the defendant to prove payment
    B. how the question of the burden of proof can affect the outcome of a case
    C. the effect of a legacy as a lien upon real property
    D. how conflicting cases concerning the burden of proof were harmonized

18. According to the above passage, the pleading of payment is a defense in Rule(s)   18.____

    A. 1, but not Rules 2 and 3
    B. 2, but not Rules 1 and 3
    C. 1 and 3, but not Rule 2
    D. 2 and 3, but not Rule 1

19. The facts in Conkling v. Weatherwax CLOSELY resemble the conditions described in   19.____

    A. Rule #1
    B. Rule #2
    C. Rule #3
    D. none of the rules

20. The MAJOR topic of the above passage may BEST be described as   20.____

    A. determining the ownership of property
    B. providing a legal definition
    C. placing the burden of proof
    D. formulating rules for deciding cases

Questions 21-25.

DIRECTIONS: Questions 21 through 25 are to be answered SOLELY on the basis of the following passage.

The law is quite clear that evidence obtained in violation of Section 605 of the Federal Communications Act is not admissible in Federal court. However, the law as to the admissibility of evidence in state court is far from clear. Had the Supreme Court of the United States made the wiretap exclusionary rule applicable to the states, such confusion would not exist.

In the case of Alton v. Texas, the Supreme Court was called upon to determine whether wiretapping by state and local officers came within the proscription of the Federal statute and, if so, whether Section 605 required the same remedies for its vindication in state courts. In answer to the first question, Mr. Justice Minton, speaking for the court, flatly stated that Section 605 made it a federal crime for anyone to intercept telephone messages and divulge what he learned. The court went on to say that a state officer who testified in state court concerning the existence, contents, substance, purport, effect, or meaning of an intercepted conversation violated the Federal law and committed a criminal act. In regard to the second question, how-ever, the Supreme Court felt constrained by due regard for federal-state relations to answer in the negative. Mr. Justice Minton stated that the court would not presume, in the absence of a clear manifestation of congressional intent, that Congress intended to supersede state rules of evidence.

Because the Supreme Court refused to apply the exclusionary rule to wiretap evidence that was being used in state courts, the states respectively made this decision for themselves. According to hearings held before a congressional committee in 1975, six states authorize wiretapping by statute, 33 states impose total bans on wiretapping, and 11 states have no definite statute on the subject. For examples of extremes, a statute in Pennsylvania will be compared with a statute in New York.

The Pennsylvania statute provides that no communications by telephone or telegraph can be intercepted without permission of both parties. It also specifically prohibits such interception by public officials and provides that evidence obtained cannot be used in court.

The lawmakers in New York, recognizing the need for legal wire-tapping, authorized wiretapping by statute. A New York law authorizes the issuance of an ex parte order upon oath or affirmation for limited wiretapping. The aim of the New York law is to allow court-ordered wiretapping and to encourage the testimony of state officers concerning such wiretapping in court. The New York law was found to be constitutional by the New York State Supreme Court in 1975. Other states, including Oregon, Maryland, Nevada, and Massachusetts, enacted similar laws which authorize court-ordered wiretapping.

To add to this legal disarray, the vast majority of the states, including New Jersey and New York, permit wiretapping evidence to be received in court even though obtained in violation of the state laws and of Section 605 of the Federal act. However, some states, such as Rhode Island, have enacted statutory exclusionary rules which provide that illegally procured wiretap evidence is incompetent in civil as well as criminal actions.

21. According to the above passage, a state officer who testifies in New York State court concerning the contents of a conversation he overheard through a court-ordered wire-tap is in violation of _____ law.

    A. state law but not federal
    B. federal law but not state
    C. federal law and state
    D. neither federal nor state

22. According to the above passage, which of the following statements concerning states statutes on wiretapping is CORRECT?

    A. The number of states that impose total bans on wiretapping is three times as great as the number of states with no definite statute on wiretapping.
    B. The number of states having no definite statute on wiretapping is more than twice the number of states authorizing wiretapping.
    C. The number of states which authorize wiretapping by statute and the number of states having no definite statute on wiretapping exceed the number of states imposing total bans on wiretapping.
    D. More states authorize wiretapping by statute than impose total bans on wiretapping.

23. Following are three statements concerning wiretapping that might be valid:
    I. In Pennsylvania, only public officials may legally intercept telephone communications.
    II. In Rhode Island, evidence obtained through an illegal wiretap is incompetent in criminal, but not civil, actions.
    III. Neither Massachusetts nor Pennsylvania authorizes wiretapping by public officials.

    According to the above passage, which of the following CORRECTLY classifies these statements into those that are valid and those that are not?

    A. I is valid, but II and III are not.
    B. II is valid, but I and III are not.
    C. II and III are valid, but I is not.
    D. None of the statements is valid.

24. According to the above passage, evidence obtained in violation of Section 605 of the Federal Communications Act is inadmissible in

    A. federal court but not in any state courts
    B. federal court and all state courts
    C. all state courts but not in federal court
    D. federal court and some state courts

25. In regard to state rules of evidence, Mr. Justice Minton expressed the Court's opinion that Congress

    A. intended to supersede state rules of evidence, as manifested by Section 605 of the Federal Communications Act
    B. assumed that federal statutes would govern state rules of evidence in all wiretap cases
    C. left unclear whether it intended to supersede state rules of evidence
    D. precluded itself from superseding state rules of evidence through its regard for federal-state relations

KEY (CORRECT ANSWERS)

1. B
2. B
3. A
4. C
5. B

6. C
7. D
8. D
9. B
10. B

11. A
12. A
13. D
14. C
15. A

16. D
17. B
18. A
19. C
20. C

21. B
22. A
23. D
24. D
25. C

TEST 2

DIRECTIONS: Each question or incomplete statement is followed by several suggested answers or completions. Select the one that BEST answers the question or completes the Statement. *PRINT THE LETTER OF THE CORRECT ANSWER IN THE SPACE AT THE RIGHT.*

Questions 1-3.

DIRECTIONS: Questions 1 through 3 are to be answered SOLELY on the basis of the following passage.

    The State Assembly has passed a bill that would require all state agencies, public authorities, and local governments to refuse bids in excess of $2,000 from any foreign firm or corporation. The only exceptions to this outright prohibition against public buying of foreign goods or services would be for products not available in this country, goods of a quality unobtainable from an American supplier, and products using foreign materials that are *substantially* manufactured in the United States.

    This bill is a flagrant violation of the United States' officially espoused trade principles. It would add to the costs of state and local governments. It could provoke retaliatory action from many foreign governments against the state and other American producers, and foreign governments would be fully entitled to take such retaliatory action under the General Agreement on Tariffs and Trade, which the United States has signed.

    The State Senate, which now has the Assembly bill before it, should reject this protectionist legislation out of enlightened regard for the interests of the taxpayers and producers of the State—as well as for those of the nation and its trading partners generally. In this time of unemployment and international monetary disorder, the State—with its reputation for intelligent and progressive law-making—should avoid contributing to what could become a tidal wave of protectionism here and overseas.

1. Under the requirements of the bill passed by the State Assembly, a bid from a foreign manufacturer in excess of $2,000 can be accepted by a state agency or local government only if it meets which one of the following requirements?
The

    A. bid is approved individually by the State Legislature
    B. bidder is willing to accept payment in United States currency
    C. bid is for an item of a quality unobtainable from an American supplier
    D. bid is for an item which would be more expensive if it were purchased from an American supplier

1.____

2. The author of the above passage feels that the bill passed by the State Assembly should be

    A. passed by the State Senate and put into effect
    B. passed by the State Senate but vetoed by the Governor
    C. reintroduced into the State Assembly and rejected
    D. rejected by the State Senate

2.____

3. The author of the above passage calls the practice of prohibiting purchase of products manufactured by foreign countries

   A. prohibition
   B. protectionism
   C. retaliatory action
   D. isolationism

Questions 4-7.

DIRECTIONS: Questions 4 through 7 are to be answered SOLELY on the basis of the following passage.

    Data processing is by no means a new invention. In one form or another, it has been carried on throughout the entire history of civilization. In its most general sense, data processing means organizing data so that it can be used for a specific purpose-a procedure commonly known simply as *record-keeping* or *paperwork*. With the development of modern office equipment, and particularly with the recent introduction of computers, the techniques of data processing have become highly elaborate and sophisticated, but the basic purpose remains the same: Turning raw data into useful information.

    The key concept here is usefulness. The data, or input, that is to be processed can be compared to the raw material that is to go into a manufacturing process. The information, or output, that results from data processing—like the finished product of a manufacturer—should be clearly usable. A collection of data has little value unless it is converted into information that serves a specific function.

4. The expression *paperwork*, as it is used in this passage,

   A. shows that the author regards such operations as a waste of time
   B. has the same general meaning as *data processing*
   C. refers to methods of record-keeping that are no longer in use
   D. indicates that the public does not understand the purpose of data processing

5. The above passage indicates that the use of computers has

   A. greatly simplified the clerical work in an office
   B. led to more complicated systems for the handling of data
   C. had no effect whatsoever on data processing
   D. made other modern office machines obsolete

6. Which of the following BEST expresses the basic principle of data processing as it is described in the above passage?

   A. Input-processing-output
   B. Historical record-keeping-modern techniques -specific functions
   C. Office equipment-computer-accurate data
   D. Raw material-manufacturer-retailer

7. According to the above passage, data processing may be described as

   A. a new management technique
   B. computer technology
   C. information output
   D. record-keeping

Questions 8-10.

DIRECTIONS: Questions 8 through 10 are to be answered SOLELY on the basis of the following passage.

A loan receipt is an instrument devised to permit the insurance company to bring an action against the wrongdoer in the name of the insured despite the fact that the insured no longer has any financial interest in the outcome. It provides, in effect, that the amount of the loss is advanced to the insured as a loan which is repayable only up to the extent of any recovery made from the wrongdoer. The insured further agrees to enter and prosecute suit against the wrongdoer in his own name. Such a receipt substitutes a loan for a payment for the purpose of permitting the insurance company to press its action against the wrongdoer in the name of the insured.

8. According to the above passage, the purpose behind the use of a loan receipt is to   8.____

    A. guarantee that the insurance company gets repayment from the person insured
    B. insure repayment of all expenditures to the named insured
    C. make it possible for the insurance company to sue in the name of the policyowner
    D. prevent the wrongdoer from escaping the natural consequences of his act

9. According to the above passage, the amount of the loan which must be paid back to the   9.____
   insurance company equals but does NOT exceed the amount

    A. of the loss
    B. on the face of the policy
    C. paid to the insured
    D. recovered from the wrongdoer

10. According to the above passage, by giving a loan receipt, the person insured agrees to   10.____

    A. a suit against the wrongdoer in his own name
    B. forego any financial gain from the outcome of the suit
    C. institute an action on behalf of the insurance company
    D. repay the insurance company for the loan received

Questions 11-12.

DIRECTIONS: Questions 11 and 12 are to be answered SOLELY on the basis of the following passage.

Open air markets originally came into existence spontaneously when groups of pushcart peddlers congregated in spots where business was good. Good business induced them to return to these spots daily and, thus, unofficial open air markets arose. These peddlers paid no fees, and the city received no revenue from them. Confusion and disorder reigned in these unsupervised markets; the earliest arrivals secured the best locations, unless or until forcibly ejected by stronger or tougher peddlers. Although the open air markets supplied a definite need in the community, there were many detrimental factors involved in their operation. They were unsightly, created unsanitary conditions in market streets by the deposit of garbage and waste and were a definite obstruction to traffic, as well as a fire hazard.

11. On the basis of the above passage, the MOST accurate of the following statements is: 11.____

    A. Each peddler in the original open air markets had his own fixed location.
    B. Open air markets were originally organized by means of agreements between groups of pushcart peddlers.
    C. The locations of these markets depended upon the amount of business the vendors were able to do.
    D. There was confusion and disorder in these open air markets because the peddlers were not required to pay any fees to the city.

12. Of the following, the MOST valid implication which can be made on the basis of the above passage is that the 12.____

    A. detrimental aspect of the operations of open air markets was the probable reason for the creation of enclosed markets under the supervision of the Department of Markets
    B. open air markets could not supply any community need without proper supervision
    C. original open air markets were good examples of the operation of fair competition in business
    D. possibility of obtaining a source of revenue was probably the most important reason for the city's ultimate undertaking of the supervision of open air markets

Questions 13-14.

DIRECTIONS: Questions 13 and 14 are to be answered SOLELY on the basis of the following passage.

A person who displays on his window, door, or in his place of business words or letters in Hebraic characters other than the word *kosher,* or any sign, emblem, insignia, six-pointed star, symbol or mark in simulation of same, without displaying in conjunction there-with in English letters of at least the same size as such characters, signs, emblems, insignia or marks, the words *we sell kosher meat and food only* or *we sell non-kosher meat and food only* or *we sell both kosher and non-kosher meat and food,* as the case may be, is guilty of a misdemeanor. Possession of non-kosher meat and food in any place of business advertising the sale of kosher meat and food only is presumptive evidence that the person in possession exposes the same for sale with intent to defraud, in violation of the provisions of this section.

13. Of the following, the MOST valid implication that can be made on the basis of the above passage is that a person who 13.____

    A. displays on his window a six-pointed star in addition to the word *kosher* in Hebraic letters is guilty of intent to defraud
    B. displays on his window the word *kosher* in Hebraic characters intends to indicate that he has only kosher food for sale
    C. sells both kosher and non-kosher food in the same place of business is guilty of a misdemeanor
    D. sells only that type of food which can be characterized as neither kosher nor non-kosher, such as fruit and vegetables, without an explanatory sign in English is guilty of intent to defraud

14. Of the following, the one which would constitute a violation of the rules of the above passage is a case in which a person 14.____

    A. displays the word *kosher* on his window in Hebraic letters has only kosher meat and food in the store but has some non-kosher meat in the rear of the establishment
    B. selling both kosher and non-kosher meat and food uses words in Hebraic letters, other than the word *kosher,* on his window and a sign of the same size letters in English stating *we sell both kosher and non-kosher meat and food*
    C. selling only kosher meat and food uses words in Hebraic letters, other than the word *kosher,* on his window and a sign of the same size letters in English stating *we sell kosher meat and food only*
    D. selling only non-kosher meat and food displays a six-pointed star on his window and a sign of the same size letters in English stating *we sell only non-kosher meat and food*

Questions 15-16.

DIRECTIONS: Questions 15 and 16 are to be answered SOLELY on the basis of the following passage.

COMMODITIES IN GLASS BOTTLES OR JARS

The contents of the bottle may be stated in terms of weight or of fluid measure, the weight being indicated in terms of pounds and ounces and the fluid measure being indicated in terms of gallons, quarts, pints, half-pints, gills, or fluid ounces. When contents are liquid, the amount should not be stated in terms of weight. The marking indicating content is to be on a tag attached to the bottle or upon a label. The letters shall be in bold-faced type at least one-ninth of an inch (1/9") in height for bottles or jars having a capacity of a gill, half-pint, pint, or multiples of a pint, and letters at least three-sixteenths of an inch (3/16") in height for bottles of other capacities, on a part of the tag or label free from other printing or ornamentation, leaving a clear space around the marking which indicates the contents.

15. Of the following, the one which does NOT meet the requirements of the above passage is a 15.____

    A. bottle of cooking oil with a label stating *contents—16 fluid ounces* in appropriate sized letters
    B. bottle of vinegar with a label stating *contents—8 ounces avoir.* in appropriate sized letters
    C. glass jar filled with instant coffee with a label stating *contents—1 lb. 3 ozs. avoir.* in appropriate sized letters
    D. glass jar filled with liquid bleach with a label stating *contents—1 quart* in appropriate sized letters

16. Of the following, the one which does meet the requirements of the above passage is a 16.____

    A. bottle filled with a low-calorie liquid sweetener with a label stating *contents—3 fluid ounces* in letters 1/12" high
    B. bottle filled with ammonia solution for cleaning with a label stating *contents—1 pint* in letters 1/10" high

C. jar filled with baking powder with a label stating *contents—$\frac{1}{2}$ pint* in letters $\frac{1}{4}$" high

D. jar filled with hard candy with a label stating *contents—1 lb. avoir.* in letters $\frac{1}{2}$" high

Question 17.

DIRECTIONS: Question 17 is to be answered SOLELY on the basis of the information contained in the following passage.

DEALERS IN SECOND HAND DEVICES

1. It shall be unlawful for any person to engage in or conduct the business of dealing in, trading in, selling, receiving, or repairing condemned, rebuilt, or used weighing or measuring devices without a permit therefor.

2. Such permit shall expire on the twenty-eighth day of February next succeeding the date of issuance thereof.

3. Every person engaged in the above business, within five days after the making of a repair, or the sale and delivery of a repaired, rebuilt, or used weighing or measuring device, shall serve notice in writing on the commissioner giving the name and address of the person for whom the repair has been made or to whom a repaired, rebuilt, or used weighing or measuring device has been sold or delivered, and shall include a statement that such device has been so altered, repaired, or rebuilt as to conform to the regulations of the department.

17. According to the above passage, the MOST accurate of the following statements is: 17.____

A. A permit issued to engage in the business mentioned above, first issued on April 23, 1968, expired on February 28, 1969.
B. A rebuilt or repaired weighing or measuring device should not operate with less error than the tolerances permitted by the regulations of the department.
C. If a used scale in good condition is sold, it is not necessary for the seller to notify the commissioner of the name and address of the buyer.
D. There is a difference in the time required to notify the commissioner of a repair or of a sale of a repaired device.

Questions 18-19.

DIRECTIONS: Questions 18 and 19 are to be answered SOLELY on the basis of the following passage.

A. It shall be unlawful for any person, firm, or corporation to sell or offer for sale at retail for use in internal combustion engines in motor vehicles any gasoline unless such seller shall post and keep continuously posted on the individual pump or other dispensing device from which such gasoline is sold or offered for sale a sign or placard not less than seven inches in height and eight inches in width nor larger than twelve inches in height and twelve inches in width and stating clearly in numbers of uniform size the selling price or prices per gallon of such gasoline so sold or offered for sale from such pump or other dispensing device.

B. The amount of governmental tax to be collected in connection with the sale of such gasoline shall be stated on such sign or placard and separately and apart from such selling price or prices.

18. The one of the following price signs posted on a gasoline pump which would be in violation of the above passage is a sign _____ square inches in size and _____ inches high.

    A. 144; 12   B. 84; 7   C. 72; 12   D. 60; 8

19. According to the above passage, the LEAST accurate of the following statements is:

    A. Gasoline may be sold from a dispensing device other than a pump.
    B. If two different pumps are used to sell the same grade of gasoline, a price sign must appear on each pump.
    C. The amount of governmental tax and the price of the gasoline must not be stated on the same sign.
    D. The sizes of the numbers used on a sign to indicate the price of gasoline must be the same.

Questions 20-21.

DIRECTIONS: Questions 20 and 21 are to be answered SOLELY on the basis of the following passage.

In all systems of weights and measures based on one or more arbitrary fundamental units, the concrete representation of the unit in the form of a standard is necessary, and the construction and preservation of such a standard is a matter of primary importance. Therefore, it is essential that the standard should be so constructed as to be as nearly permanent and invariable as human ingenuity can contrive. The reference of all measures to an original standard is essential for their correctness, and such a standard must be maintained and preserved in its integrity by some responsible authority which is thus able to provide against the use of false weights and measures. Accordingly, from earliest times, standards were constructed and preserved under the direction of kings and priests, and the temples were a favorite place for their deposit. Later, this duty was assumed by the government, and today we find the integrity of standards of weights and measures safeguarded by international agreement.

20. Of the following, the MOST valid implication which can be made on the basis of the above passage is that

    A. fundamental units of systems of weights and measures should be represented by quantities so constructed that they are specific and constant
    B. in the earliest times, standards were so constructed that they were as permanent and invariable as modern ones
    C. international agreement has practically relieved the U.S. government of the necessity of preserving standards of weights and measures
    D. the preservation of standards is of less importance than the ingenuity used in their construction

21. Of the following, the MOST appropriate title for the above passage is   21._____

    A. THE CONSTRUCTION AND PRESERVATION OF STANDARDS OF WEIGHTS AND MEASURES
    B. THE FIXING OF RESPONSIBILITY FOR THE ESTABLISHMENT OF STANDARDS OF WEIGHTS AND MEASURES
    C. THE HISTORY OF SYSTEMS OF WEIGHTS AND MEASURES
    D. THE VALUE OF PROPER STANDARDS IN PROVIDING CORRECT WEIGHTS AND MEASURES

Questions 22-23.

DIRECTIONS: Questions 22 and 23 are to be answered SOLELY on the basis of the following passage.

Accurate weighing and good scales insure that excess is not given just for the sake of good measure. No more striking example of the fundamental importance of correct weighing to the business man is found than in the simple and usual relation where a charge or value is obtained by multiplying a weight by a unit price. For example, a scale may weigh *light,* that is, the actual quantity delivered is in excess by 1 percent. The actual result is that the seller taxes himself. If his profit is supposed to be 10 percent of total sales, an overweight of 1 percent represents 10 percent of that profit. Under these conditions, the situation is as though the seller were required to pay a sales tax equivalent to what he is taxing himself.

22. Of the following, the MOST valid implication which can be made on the basis of the above passage is that   22._____

    A. consistent use of scales that weigh *light* will reduce sellers' profits
    B. no good businessman would give any buyer more than the weight required even if his scale is accurate
    C. the kind of situation described in the above passage could not arise if sales were being made of merchandise sold by the yard
    D. the use of incorrect scales is one of the reasons causing governments to impose sales taxes

23. According to the above passage, the MOST accurate of the following statements is: 23._____

    A. If his scale weighs *light* by an amount of 2 percent, the seller would deliver only 98 pounds when 100 pounds was the amount agreed upon.
    B. If the seller's scale weighs *heavy,* the buyer will receive an amount in excess of what he intended to purchase.
    C. If the seller's scale weighs *light* by an amount of 1 percent, a buyer who agreed to purchase 50 pounds of merchandise would actually receive $50 \frac{1}{2}$ pounds.
    D. The use of a scale which delivers an amount which is in excess of that required is an example of deliberate fraud.

Questions 24-25.

DIRECTIONS: Questions 24 and 25 are to be answered SOLELY on the basis of the following passage.

Food shall be deemed to be misbranded:
1. If its labeling is false or misleading in any particular.

2. If any word, statement, or other information required by or under authority of this article to appear on the label or labeling is not prominently placed thereon with such conspicuousness (as compared with other words, statements, designs, or devices in the labeling) and in such terms as to render it likely to be read and understood by the ordinary individual under customary conditions of purchase and use.

3. If it purports to be or is represented as a food for which a standard of quality has been prescribed and its quality falls below such standard, unless its label bears a statement that it falls below such standard.

24. According to the above passage, the MOST accurate of the following statements is:

    A. A food may be considered misbranded if the label contains a considerable amount of information which is not required.
    B. If a consumer purchased one type of canned food, although he intended to buy another, the food is probably misbranded.
    C. If a food is used in large amounts by a group of people of certain foreign origin, it can be considered misbranded unless the label is in the foreign language with which they are familiar.
    D. The required information on a label is likely to be in larger print than other information which may appear on it.

25. According to the above passage, the one of the following foods which may be considered to be misbranded is a

    A. can of peaches with a label which carries the brand name of the packer but states *Below Standard in Quality*
    B. can of vegetables with a label on which is printed a shield which states *U.S. Grade B*
    C. package of frozen food which has some pertinent information printed on it in very small type which a customer cannot read and which the store manager cannot read when asked to do so by the customer
    D. package of margarine of the same size as the usual package of butter, kept near the butter, but clearly labeled as margarine

KEY (CORRECT ANSWERS)

1. C
2. D
3. B
4. B
5. B

6. A
7. D
8. C
9. D
10. A

11. C
12. A
13. B
14. A
15. B

16. D
17. A
18. C
19. C
20. A

21. D
22. A
23. C
24. D
25. C

BASIC MATHEMATICS
EXAMINATION SECTION
TEST 1

DIRECTIONS: Each question or incomplete statement is followed by several suggested answers or completions. Select the one that BEST answers the question or completes the statement. *PRINT THE LETTER OF THE CORRECT ANSWER IN THE SPACE AT THE RIGHT.*

1. Add: 5,796 + 6 + 243 + 24   1.____
   A. 6,069   B. 6,079   C. 6,169   D. 6,179

2. Subtract: 8,007 - 6,898   2.____
   A. 1,109   B. 1,119   C. 1,209   D. 2,109

3. Multiply: 3,876 x 904   3.____
   A. 364,344   B. 3,493,904
   C. 3,494,904   D. 3,503,904

4. Divide: $76\overline{)58,976}$ 4.____
   A. 775   B. 776   C. 786   D. 876

5. Combine: (+4) + (-3) - (-7)   5.____
   A. -6   B. +6   C. +8   D. +14

6. Simplify: [(-8) x (-6)] ÷ (-3)   6.____
   A. -16   B. -14   C. +14   D. +16

7. Add: 1 3/5 + 3 7/8   7.____
   A. 4 10/40   B. 4 10/13   C. 4 19/40   D. 5 19/40

8. Subtract: 4 3/8 - 2 2/3   8.____
   A. 1 17/24   B. 2 1/24   C. 2 1/5   D. 2 17/24

9. Multiply: 3 2/3 x 5 1/2   9.____
   A. 15 1/3   B. 16 1/3   C. 20 1/6   D. 21 1/6

10. Divide: $7\frac{1}{2} \div 2\frac{1}{4}$ 10.____
    A. 3/10   B. 3 1/3   C. 3 1/2   D. 16 7/8

11. Add: 434.7 + .04 + 7.107   11.____
    A. .441847   B. .442207   C. 441.847   D. 442.207

12. Subtract: 986.4 - 34.87

    A. 6.377   B. 63.77   C. 951.53   D. 9,515.3

13. Multiply: 5.96×87.4

    A. 51.0904   B. 52.0904   C. 510.904   D. 520.904

14. Divide: $.034 \overline{)6.698}$

    A. 19.2   B. 19.7   C. 192   D. 197

15. Add: $.7 + \frac{1}{2}$

    A. .12   B. 1.2   C. 7/2   D. 15/2

16. What is 5.5% of 75?

    A. 4.125   B. 13.65   C. 41.25   D. 412.5

17. 12 is what percent of 6?

    A. $\frac{1}{2}$%   B. 5%   C. 50%   D. 200%

18. 14 is 28% of _____.

    A. 2   B. 5   C. 50   D. 500

19. A record player sells for $92.00. It is discounted 15% for a special sale. What is the sale price?

    A. $13.80   B. $68.20   C. $77.00   D. $78.20

20.

Table A - Acme Mortgage Company
$320 Loan - 3/4 of 1% Interest

Month	Payment	Principal Paid/Month	Interest Paid/Month
1	$ 27.98	$ 25.58	$ 2.40
2	27.98	25.77	2.21
3	27.98	25.96	2.02
4	27.98	26.15	1.83
5	27.98	26.35	1.63
6	27.98	26.55	1.43
7	27.98	26.75	1.23
8	27.98	26.95	1.03
9	27.98	27.15	.83
10	27.98	27.35	.63
11	27.98	27.56	.42
12	27.93	27.77	.16
Total	$335.82	$ 320.00	$ 15.82

Acme Mortgage Company charges 3/4 of 1% (.0075) on the unpaid balance per month. Bowman Mortgage Company charges 9% per year on the total loan. Which company charges the LEAST amount of interest on a $320 loan held for one year?

    A. Acme charges the least amount.
    B. Bowman charges the least amount.
    C. Acme and Bowman charge the same.
    D. Insufficient information to determine.

21. Percent of Auto Insurance Discounts for High School Students with Certain Grade Point Averages

Policy Coverage	Grade Point Averages Percent of Discount		
	A	B	C
Liability	33 1/3%	33 1/3%	10%
Comprehensive	20%	10%	-
Collision	25%	20%	-

Frank Verna has a B average. The regular 6-month amounts to be paid for insurance before discount follow:

    Liability $18.00
    Comprehensive $20.00
    Collision $60.00
    Total $98.00

How much does Frank pay for insurance for 6 months?

    A. $20.00   B. $58.00   C. $78.00   D. $156.00

22. Mr. Martinez had a fire in his home. Repairing the damage will cost about $900. His home is valued at $14,000 and is insured for $12,000. Mr. Martinez had paid $32.00 a year for ten years for his insurance. The insurance company has agreed to pay the full amount of the claim ($900).
Which of the following statements are TRUE?
    I. The amount of the claim is more than what has been paid to the company.
    II. The insurance company should pay $14,000 for this claim.
    III. If the house had been completely burned, the insurance company would pay $14,000.
    IV. The maximum claim Mr. Martinez could collect is $12,000
The CORRECT answer is:

    A. I, II   B. I, III   C. II, III   D. I, IV

23. When two coins are tossed, what is the chance that both will be heads?
1 in

    A. 1   B. 2   C. 3   D. 4

24. If 4 teams are in a football league, how many games are necessary to allow each team to play every team one time? _____ games.

    A. 6   B. 9   C. 12   D. 16

25. Five people donated money to the Red Cross. The donations were: $52.00, $76.00, $18.00, $94.00, and $120.00.
What was the AVERAGE donation?

   A. $70   B. $72   C. $76   D. $360

26. From the following statements, determine the CORRECT conclusion.
   I. If Lauraine is a red-head, then Lauraine is hot-tempered.
   II. Lauraine is not hot-tempered.
The CORRECT answer is:

   A. Lauraine is a red-head.
   B. Lauraine is not a red-head.
   C. Lauraine could be a red-head.
   D. All red-heads are hot-tempered.

27. The graph represents the way the Jones family spends its money (budget). What is the monthly income if they are spending $4080 per year for food?
   A. $1,020
   B. $1,360
   C. $4,080
   D. $16,320

28.

	S	M	T	W	T	F	S
Charlie Simms	?	8	8	8	8	8	3
Jim Chow	2	9	8	8	9	9	4

Time and one-half is paid on Saturdays and for hours worked beyond 8 hours each day. Double-time is paid for Sunday work.
Mr. Simms would have to work how many hours on Sunday to earn as much as Mr. Chow?

   Regular time - $2.00/hour
   Time and one-half - $3.00/hour
   Double time - $4.00/hour

   _____ hours.

   A. 2   B. 5   C. 6   D. 20

29. Jane Gunther wrote checks for these items:
   $16.95 for a hair dryer
   $125.50 for a car payment
   $33.68 for television repair
   $21.59 for a dress
Jane had a beginning check balance (before she wrote the checks) of $351.76. She also deposited $41.50 into her account.
After the checks were written and the deposit made, what was her new balance?

   A. $154.04   B. $195.54   C. $196.54   D. $239.22

30. Given the formula I = PRT:
    If I = 24, R = .05, T = 3, find P.

    A. .00625   B. 1.6   C. 3.6   D. 160.0

31. Fencing is needed to enclose a piece of land 26 meters on a side.
    How much fencing is needed?
    _____ meters.
    A. 52
    B. 98
    C. 104
    D. 676

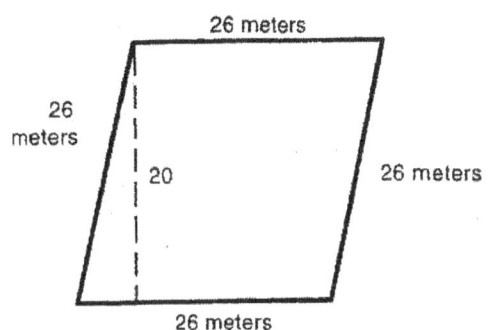

32. The area of figure A is 12 square units, and the area of B is 18 square units.
    What is the area of figure C?
    _____ square units.
    A. 16
    B. 16 1/2
    C. 17
    D. 17 1/2

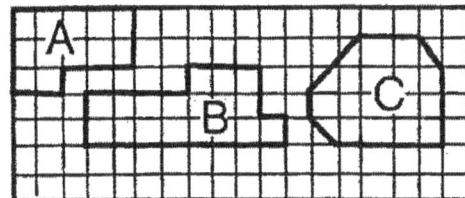

33. Using a 3 gallon spray can with a mixture rate of 1 teaspoon of insecticide per quart of water and an application rate of 1 gallon of mixture per 100 square feet, how much water and how much insecticide will be needed to spray an 85 feet by 10 feet lawn?
    _____ teaspoons of insecticide and _____ gallons of water.

    A. 34; 8 1/2   B. 34; 11   C. 17; 8 1/2   D. 24; 6

34. Bill Mata will carpet his living room which has the following dimensions. If Bill pays $6.00 per square yard for the carpet, how much will it cost to carpet his living room?
    (9 square feet = 1 square yard)
    A. $192
    B. $216
    C. $1,728
    D. $1,944

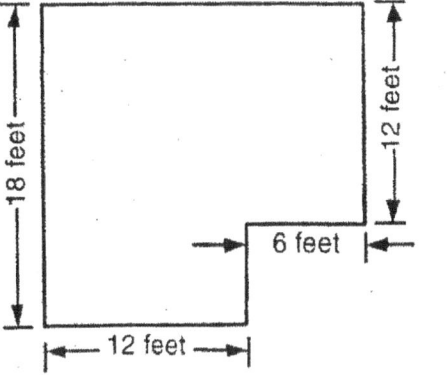

35. A cube is painted red and then divided into 27 smaller cubes.
    How many of the smaller cubes are painted on one side only?
    A. 4
    B. 6
    C. 8
    D. 10

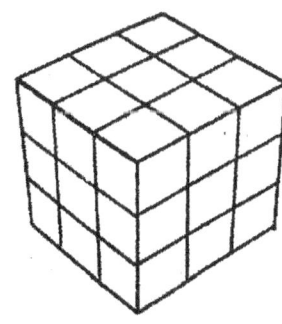

36. John and Frank wish to pour a cement walk 108 feet long, 4 feet wide, and 3 inches deep.
    If ready-mix concrete can be delivered on weekdays for $19.50 a cubic yard and on weekends for $22.50 a cubic yard, how much would they save on the complete job if they decide on Thursday rather than on the weekend? (1 cubic yard = 27 cubic feet)

    A. $3.00   B. $12.00   C. $36.00   D. $78.00

37. Antifreeze may be purchased in different size containers for different prices:
        8 oz. can - 43¢
        10 oz. can - 51¢
        12 oz. can - 62¢
    If exactly 15 pints of antifreeze are needed, how many cans of each size are needed for the cost to be minimum? (16 oz. = 1 pint)

    A. 12 - 10 oz. cans and 10 - 12 oz. cans
    B. 24 - 10 oz. cans
    C. 18 - 12 oz. cans and 3-8 oz. cans
    D. 20 - 12 oz. cans

38. From the graph, assuming the growth rate in the senior class is constant, how many students will be seniors in 2006?

    A. 225
    B. 250
    C. 300
    D. 375

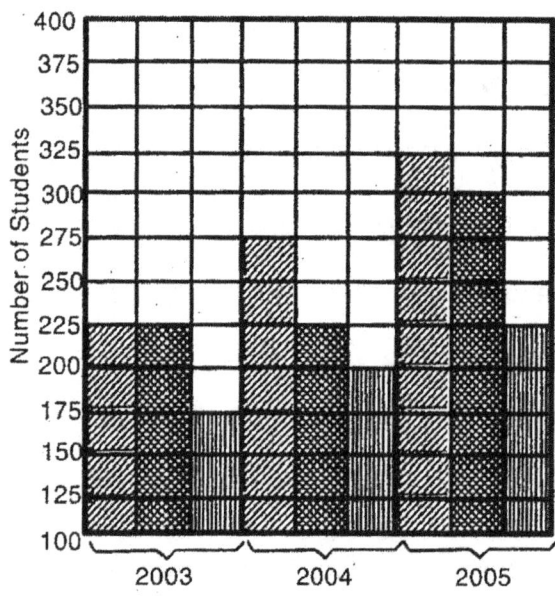

39.

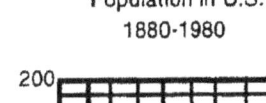
Population in U.S.
1880-1980

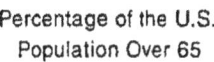
Percentage of the U.S.
Population Over 65

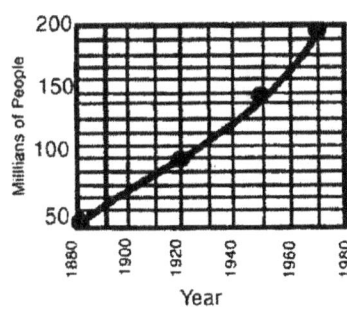

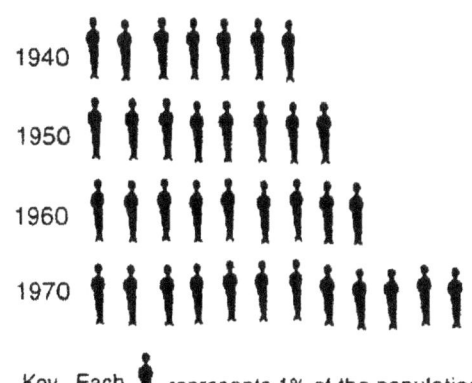

Key. Each ♟ represents 1% of the population

In looking at the two graphs, which of the following conclusions are TRUE?
- I. Both graphs show population growth.
- II. Both graphs cover exactly the same time period.
- III. The percentage of *over 65* population remains the same over the 1940 to 1970 period.
- IV. If you were in the retail business, you might expect greater sales to the *over 65* population in 1970 than in 1940.
- V. In the general population of about 200 million people in 1970, 24 million were over 65.
- VI. In 1920, there were only about 7 million people *over 65* out of about 100 million people.

The CORRECT answer is:

A. I, III, IV   B. II, IV, V
C. II, III, VI   D. I, IV, V

40. Jerry Martin owns a home with a market value of $180,000. Its assessed value is 25% of the market value. The tax rate is $5.00 per $100 of assessed value.
What is the amount of his tax?

A. $225.00   B. $2,250.00   C. $4,500.00   D. $6,750.00

41. You are governor of the state and you need an additional 500 million dollars in tax money. To raise the money, an increase in sales tax is required.
What information would be MOST helpful in determining the new tax rate?
- I. Average income per person in the state
- II. Number of people out of work
- III. Population of the state over 18 years of age
- IV. Birth rate in the state
- V. Percent of income spent on taxable goods
- VI. Percent of income spent on non-taxable goods
- VII. Number of people filing income tax returns

The CORRECT answer is:

A. I, IV, VI   B. II, III, VII
C. V, VI   D. I, V

42. Income Tax Table

If adjusted gross income is-		And the number of exemptions is -					
		1	2	3	4	5	6
At least	But less than	Your tax is -					
$24,500	$24,750	$2360	$1240	$230	$0	$0	$0
24,750	25,000	2400	1280	260	0	0	0
25,000	25,250	2440	1320	300	0	0	0
25,250	25,500	2480	1360	330	0	0	0
25,500	25,750	2530	1390	370	0	0	0
25,750	26,000	2570	1430	400	0	0	0
26,000	26,250	2610	1470	440	0	0	0
26,250	26,500	2650	1510	470	0	0	0
26,500	26,750	2700	1550	510	0	0	0
26,750	27,000	2740	1590	540	0	0	0
27,000	27,250	2780	1630	580	0	0	0
27,250	27,500	2820	1670	610	0	0	0
27,500	27,750	2870	1710	650	0	0	0
27,750	28,000	2910	1750	680	0	0	0
28,000	28,250	2950	1790	720	0	0	0
28,250	28,500	2990	1830	760	0	0	0
28,500	28,750	3040	1870	790	0	0	0

Jerry Ladd earned $28,390.00 during the year. To find his adjusted gross income, he must reduce the amount earned by the standard 10% deduction. He had only one exemption, himself.
How much tax did Jerry pay?

A. $1390 B. $1830 C. $2530 D. $2990

43.

Weight in Ounces	2 oz.	4 oz.	12 oz.	21 oz.
Price	5¢	7¢	15¢	24¢

Using the above table, predict the price if the weight is 32 ounces.

A. 27¢ B. 28¢ C. 29¢ D. 35¢

44. Given [(0,2), (1,4), (2,6),....(5,y)].
What is the value of y?

A. 8 B. 10 C. 12 D. 14

45. If the larger of two numbers is two and one-half times the smaller number, what fraction is the smaller of the larger?

A. 3/4 B. 4/5 C. 5/8 D. 2/5

46. John can save 75¢ a week. He has $3.75 in the bank now. How many weeks will it take him to have a total deposit of $12?

A. 16 B. 9 C. 11 D. 17

47. Using the approximation of 3.14 for pi, find the area of a circle whose diameter is 20 inches.
    _____ square inches.

    A. 31.4   B. 314   C. 628   D. 1256

    47.____

48. Express .045 as a percent.

    A. 45%   B. 4.5%   C. .45%   D. .045%

    48.____

49. Twenty is what percent of 50?

    A. 40   B. 60   C. 25   D. 16 2/3

    49.____

50. Two hundred twenty-five percent of 160 is

    A. 80   B. 350   C. 360   D. 440

    50.____

KEY (CORRECT ANSWERS)

1. A	11. C	21. C	31. C	41. C
2. A	12. C	22. D	32. C	42. C
3. D	13. D	23. D	33. A	43. D
4. B	14. D	24. A	34. A	44. C
5. C	15. B	25. B	35. B	45. D
6. A	16. A	26. B	36. B	46. C
7. D	17. D	27. D	37. B	47. B
8. A	18. C	28. B	38. B	48. B
9. C	19. D	29. B	39. D	49. A
10. B	20. A	30. D	40. B	50. C

10 (#1)

SOLUTIONS TO PROBLEMS

1. 5796 + 6 + 243 + 24 = 6069

2. 8007 - 6898 = 1109

3. (3876)(904) = 3,503,904

4. 58,976 76 = 776

5. (+4) + (-3) - (-7) = 4 - 3 + 7 = +8

6. [(-8)(-6)] ÷ -3 = 48 ÷ -3 = -16

7. $1\frac{3}{5} + 3\frac{7}{8} = 1\frac{24}{40} + 3\frac{35}{40} = 4\frac{59}{40} = 5\frac{19}{40}$

8. $4\frac{3}{8} - 2\frac{2}{3} = 4\frac{9}{24} - 2\frac{16}{24} = 3\frac{33}{24} - 2\frac{16}{24} = 1\frac{17}{24}$

9. $(3\frac{2}{3})(5\frac{1}{2}) = (\frac{11}{3})(\frac{11}{2}) = \frac{121}{6} = 20\frac{1}{6}$

10. $7\frac{1}{2} \div 2\frac{1}{4} = \frac{15}{2} \div \frac{9}{4} = (\frac{15}{2})(\frac{4}{9}) = \frac{60}{18} = 3\frac{1}{3}$

11. 434.7 + .04 + 7.107 = 441.847

12. 986.4 - 34.87 = 951.53

13. (5.96)(87.4) = 520.904

14. 6.698 ÷ .034 = 197

15. $.7 + \frac{1}{2} = .7 + .5 = 1.2$

16. (.055)(75) = 4.125

17. $\frac{12}{6} = 2 = 200\%$

18. 14 ÷ .28 = 50

19. $92 - (.15)($92) = $78.20

20. Acme's interest charge = $15.82, whereas Bowman's interest charge = (.09)($320) = $28.80. Thus, Acme charges less.

11 (#1)

21. ($18.00)(66$\frac{2}{3}$%) + ($20.00)(90%) + ($60.00)(80%) = $78.00

22. Statements I and IV are correct. For 10 years, he has paid $320, but collected $900 on his claim. Also, since the insured value of the home is $12,000, he could not collect more than that amount on any claim.

23. Probability of 2 heads = (1/2)(1/2) = 1/4, which means 1 in 4.

24. The number of required games = (4)(3) ÷ 2 = 6

25. Average donation = ($52.00 + $76.00 + $18.00 + $94.00 + $120.00) ÷ 5 = $72

26. The correct conclusion is B: Lauraine is not a redhead. Let p = Lauraine is a redhead, q = Lauraine is hot-tempered. The given statement says: *If p, then q.* The contrapositive, which is also true, says, *If not q, then not p.* This corresponds to statement B.

27. Let x = monthly income. Then, $4080 = Solving, x = $16,320.

28. Mr. Chow's earnings = (2)($4) + (40)($2) + (7)($3) = $109.
    For Monday through Saturday, Mr. Simms' earnings =
    (40)($2) + (3)($3) = $89. Thus, Mr. Simms would need to earn
    109 - 89 = $20 on Sunday. This means Sunday's time =
    $20 ÷ $4 = 5 hours.

29. New balance = $351.76 + $41.50 - $16.95 - $125.50 - $33.68 - $21.59 = $195.54.

30. 24 = (P)(.05)(3), 24 = .15P, so P = 160

31. Fencing: (26)(4) = 104 meters.

32. Area of C = (4)(5) - ($\frac{1}{2}$)(1)(1) - ($\frac{1}{2}$)(2)(2) - ($\frac{1}{2}$)(1)(1) = 17

33. (85)(10) = 850 sq.ft. = 8.5 gallons of water. Now, 8.5 gallons = 34 quarts, so 34 teaspoons of insecticide are needed.

34. Area = (12)(6) + (12)(18) = 288 sq.ft. = 32 sq.yds. Total cost = (32)($6) = $192

35. There are 6 cubes painted red on only one side. They are found in the center of each face of the original cube.

36. (108)(4)($\frac{1}{4}$) = 108 cu.ft. = 4 cu.yds. Savings would be ($22.50)(4) - ($19.50)(4) = $12.00

37. 15 pints = 240 oz. The costs for each selection are:
    For A: (12)(.51) + (10)(.62) = $12.32; for B: (24)(.51) = $12.24; for
    C: (18)(.62) + (3)(.43) = $12.45; for D: (20)(.62) = $12.40.
    So, selection B is the minimum cost.

38. The number of seniors in 2003, 2004, 2005 are 175, 200, and 225, respectively. If growth is constant, the number of seniors in 2006 is 250.

39. Statements I, IV, V are correct. Statement II is wrong because the 1st graph covers 1800-1970, whereas the 2nd graph covers 1940-1970. Statement III is wrong because the *over 65* population increases in percent from 7% in 1940 to 12% in 1970.

40. (25%)($180,000) = $45,000 assessed value. Amount of tax = ($5.00)($45,000 ÷ $100) = $2,250

41. For increasing sales tax, it would be helpful in knowing the respective percent of incor spent on taxable vs. non-taxable goods.

42. Adjusted gross income = ($28390)(.90) = $25551.00. On the tax chart, this figure lies between $25500 and $25750. Using the column for 1 exemption, the tax is $2530.

43. Using 2 oz. = .05, note that each additional oz. = 1 cent more. So, 32 oz. = .05 + .30 = .35.

44. (5,y) represents the sixth point in this sequence. Thus, the corresponding y value = (2)(6) = 12

45. Let x = smaller number, 2.5x = larger number.

    Then, $\dfrac{X}{2.5X} = \dfrac{1}{2.5} = \dfrac{10}{25} = \dfrac{2}{5}$

46. $12 - $3.75 = $8.25. Then, $8.25 ÷ .75 = 11 weeks

47. Radius = 10 in. Area = (3.14)(10^2) = 314 sq.in.

48. .045 = 4.5%

49. $\dfrac{20}{50} = 40\%$

50. (225%) (160) = (2.25) (160) = 360

BASIC MATHEMATICS
EXAMINATION SECTION
TEST 1

DIRECTIONS: Each question or incomplete statement is followed by several suggested answers or completions. Select the one that BEST answers the question or completes the statement. *PRINT THE LETTER OF THE CORRECT ANSWER IN THE SPACE AT THE RIGHT.*

1. 534
   18
   +1291

   A. 1733   B. 1743   C. 1833   D. 1843   E. 1853

   1.____

2. (17×23) − 16 + 20 =
   A. 459   B. 427   C. 411   D. 395   E. 355

   2.____

3. 3/7 + 5/11 =
   A. 33/35   B. 4/9   C. 8/18   D. 68/77   E. 15/77

   3.____

4. 4832 ÷ 6 =
   A. 905 1/3   B. 805 1/3   C. 95 1/3   D. 95   E. 85 1/3

   4.____

5. 62.3 − 4.9 =
   A. 5.74   B. 7.4   C. 57.4   D. 58.4   E. 67.4

   5.____

6. 3/5 × 4/9 =
   A. 4/15   B. 7/45   C. 27/20   D. 12/14   E. 15/4

   6.____

7. 14/16 − 5/16 =
   A. 8/16   B. 9/16   C. 11/16   D. 8   E. 9

   7.____

8. 5.03 + 2.7 + 40 =
   A. .570   B. 4.773   C. 5.70   D. 11.73   E. 47.73

   8.____

9. 5.37 × 21.4 =
   A. 11491.8   B. 1149.18   C. 114.918
   D. 11,4918   E. 1.14918

   9.____

10. 5 1/4 + 2 7/8 =
    A. 8 1/4   B. 8 1/8   C. 7 2/3   D. 7 1/4   E. 7 1/8

    10.____

11. −14 + 5 =
    A. −19   B. −9   C. 9   D. 19   E. 70

    11.____

12. 2/7 of 28 =
     A. 98   B. 16   C. 14   D. 8   E. 4

13. 2/5 =
     A. .10   B. .20   C. .25   D. .40   E. .52

14. 20% of _____ is 38.
     A. 7.6   B. 19   C. 76   D. 190   E. 760

15. $\frac{8.4}{400}$ =
     A. .0021   B. .021   C. .21   D. 2.1   E. 21

16. $\frac{4}{5} = \frac{?}{60}$
     A. 240   B. 48   C. 20   D. 15   E. 12

17. What is the area of the rectangle shown at the right?
     A. 47 mm²
     B. 94 mm²
     C. 240 mm²
     D. 480 mm²
     E. 960 mm²

    15 mm
    32 mm

18. What number does ▯ represent in the following equation: 25 - ▯ ▯ ▯ ▯ = 13?
     A. 13   B. 12   C. 7   D. 4   E. 3

19. Approximate lengths are given in the right triangles shown at the right.
    What does length x equal?
     A. 48
     B. 39
     C. 37
     D. 35
     E. 32

    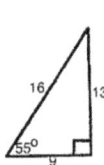
    16, 13, 55°, 9
    x, 55°, 27

20. What is the perimeter of the triangle shown at the right?
     A. 10 × 15 × 17
     B. 10 + 15 + 17
     C. 1/2 × 10 × 15
     D. 1/2 × 10 × 17
     E. 1/2(10+15+17)

    17, 15, 10

21. Which of the following expressions will give the same answer as 45 × 9?
     A. 5 × 3³   B. (4×9)+(5×9)   C. (40+9) × 5
     D. (45×3) + (45×3) E. (45×10) – (45×1)

3 (#1)

22. Find the average of 19, 21, 21, 22, and 27.
    A. 23 B. 22 C. 21 D. 20 E. 19

    22.____

23. In the triangle at the right, how many degrees is <T?
    A. 75°
    B. 85°
    C. 95°
    D. 114°
    E. 180°

    23.____

24. About how long is the paper clip?
    A. 5 cm B. 4 cm C. 3 cm D. 2 cm E. 1 cm

    24.____

25. Five stores sell the same size cans of tomato soup. Their prices are listed below.
    Which sells the soup for the LOWEST price per can? _____ cans for _____.
    A. 6; 99¢ B. 6; 90¢ C. 5; 93¢ D. 3; 56¢ E. 3; 50¢

    25.____

26. Rock star Peter Giles receives $1.97 royalty on each of his albums that is sold. 14,127 albums are sold.
    Estimate how much Peter Giles will receive.
    A. $7,000 B. $14,000 C. $20,000 D. $26,000 E. $28,000

    26.____

27. An amplifier is advertised for 20% off the list price of $430.
    What is the sale price?
    A. $516 B. $454 C. $354 D. $344 E. $215

    27.____

28. If 9 dozen eggs cost $3.60, what do 25 dozen eggs cost?
    A. $90.00 B. $10.00 C. $9.00 D. $2.54 E. $40

    28.____

29. The distance between New York State and San Antonio is 1,860 miles. If a jet averages 465 miles per hour, how many hours will it take to travel the distance?
    A. 9 B. 5 C. 4 D. 3 E. 2

    29.____

30. In a high school homeroom of 32 students, 24 are girls.
    What percent are girls?
    A. 3/4% B. 24% C. 25% D. 75% E. 80%

    30.____

31. Which problem could give the answer shown on the calculator?
    A. 2 + .3
    B. 2 × 3/10
    C. 2 × 1/3
    D. 33333 + .2
    E. 7 ÷ 3

32. Cost of Eating at Home
    (One Week)

Age	Male	Female
6-11 yrs.	$14	$14
12-19 yrs.	$19	$15
20-54 yrs.	$20	$16
55 and Up	$14	$14

    According to the above table, how much will it cost in a typical week for the 3 members of the Wright family to eat at home? Mr. Wright is 56 years old; Mrs. Wright, 52; and their son, Harry, 17.
    A. $125   B. $52   C. $49   D. $42   E. $40

33. According to the above table shown in Question 32, how much does it cost in a typical four-week month to feed a 12-year-old girl?
    A. $4   B. $16   C. $48   D. $64   E. $78

34. Reverend Whilhite jogs for 1½ hours each day, 6 days a week. If he burns 800 calories per hour of jogging, how many calories does he burn in a week?
    A. 4800   B. 5600   C. 7200   D. 8400   E. 9000

35. Ground meat costs 90¢ per pound. How much does the meat on the scale cost?
    A. $1.80
    B. $1.60
    C. $1.54
    D. $1.44
    E. $.90

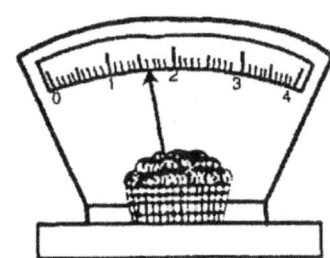

36. According to the graph at the right, about when did the weekly wages for a minimum wage worker go over $100?
  A. 2005
  B. 2010
  C. 2014
  D. 2019
  E. 2020

36.____

37. According to the bar graph at the right, what is the approximate height of the Crystal Beach Comet?
  A. 40 ft.
  B. 90 ft.
  C. 92 ft.
  D. 94 ft.
  E. 98 ft.

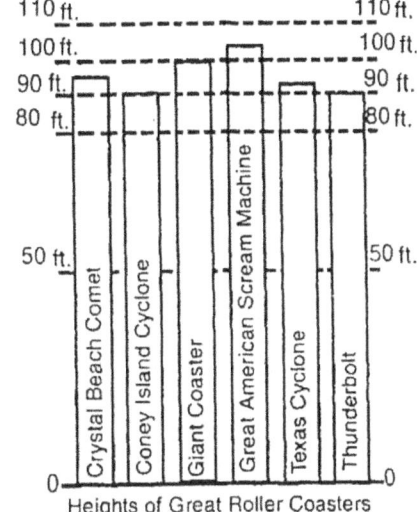

37.____

38. According to the bar graph shown in Question 37, what is the difference in height between the tallest and shortest roller coasters? _____ feet.
  A. 5   B. 10   C. 15   D. 20   E. 50

38.____

39. How much change will you receive from a $10 bill when you buy 4 grapefruits at 90¢ each and 3 apples at 40¢ each?
  A. $6.20   B. $5.20   C. $4.80   D. $4.20   E. $4.00

39.____

40. A medical supplier packages medicine in boxes. The cost of packaging is computed with the flow chart at the right.
What is the cost of packaging medicine in a box that is 30 cm long, 20 cm wide, and 20 cm high?
   A. $.20
   B. $.24
   C. $2.00
   D. $2.40
   E. $3.00

40.____

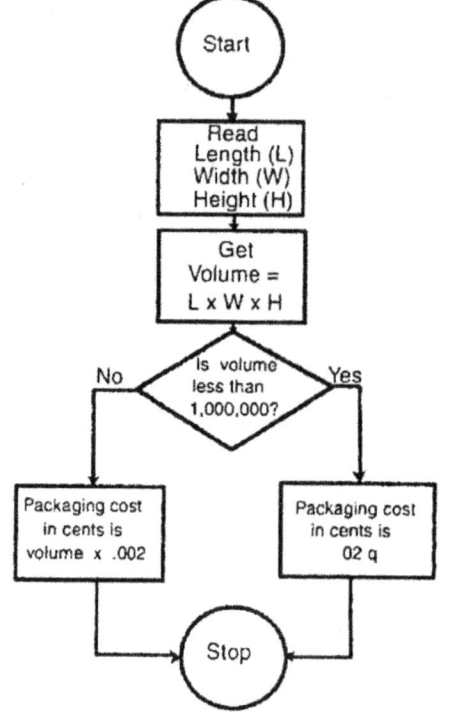

KEY (CORRECT ANSWERS)

1.	D	11.	B	21.	E	31.	E
2.	D	12.	D	22.	B	32.	C
3.	D	13.	D	23.	B	33.	D
4.	B	14.	D	24.	C	34.	C
5.	C	15.	B	25.	B	35.	D
6.	A	16.	B	26.	E	36.	C
7.	B	17.	D	27.	D	37.	D
8.	E	18.	E	28.	B	38.	C
9.	C	19.	A	29.	C	39.	B
10.	B	20.	B	30.	D	40.	A

SOLUTIONS TO PROBLEMS

1. 534 + 18 + 1291 = 1843

2. (17×23) − 16 + 20 = 391 − 16 + 20 = 395

3. $\frac{3}{7} + \frac{5}{11} = \frac{33}{77} + \frac{35}{77} = \frac{68}{77}$

4. $4832 \div 6 = 805\frac{1}{3}$

5. 62.3 − 4.9 = 57.4

6. $\frac{3}{5} \times \frac{4}{9} = \frac{12}{45} = \frac{4}{15}$

7. $\frac{14}{16} \cdot \frac{5}{16} = \frac{9}{16}$

8. 5.03 + 2.7 + 40 = 47.73

9. 5.37 × 21.4 = 114.918

10. $5\frac{1}{4} + 2\frac{7}{8} = 7\frac{9}{8} = 8\frac{1}{8}$

11. -14 + 5 = -9

12. $\frac{2}{7}$ of 28 = $(\frac{2}{7})(\frac{28}{1})$ = 8

13. $\frac{2}{5}$ = .40 as a decimal

14. Let x = missing number. Then, .20x = 38. Solving, x = 190

15. $\frac{84}{400}$ = .021

16. Let x = missing number. Then, $\frac{4}{5} = \frac{x}{60}$. 5x = 240, so x = 48

17. Area = (15)(32) = 480mm^2

18. Let x = □. Then, 25 − 4x = 13. So, -4x = -12. Solving, x = 3.

19. $\frac{9}{27} = \frac{16}{x}$. Then, 9x = 432. Solving, x = 48.

20. Perimeter = 17 + 10 + 15 = 42

21. 45 × 9 = 405 = (45×10)-(45×1)

22. 19 + 21 + 21 + 22 + 27 = 110. Then, 110 ÷ 5 = 22

23. ∠T = 180° - 50° - 45° = 85°

24. The paper clip's length is about 5 – 2 = 3 cm.

25. For A: price per can = $\frac{.99}{6}$ = .165
    For B: price per can = $\frac{.90}{6}$ = .15
    For C: price per can = $\frac{.93}{5}$ = 186
    For D: price per can = $\frac{.56}{3}$ = .18$\overline{6}$
    For E: price per can = $\frac{.50}{3}$ = .1$\overline{6}$

    Lowest price is for B.

26. $1.97 ≈ $2.00. Then, ($2.00)(14,127) = $28,254 ≈ $28,000

27. Sale price = ($430)(.80) = $344

28. Let x = cost. Then, 9x = $90, so x = $10.00

29. $\frac{1860}{465}$ = 4 hours

30. $\frac{24}{32}$ = 75%

31. $\frac{7}{3}$ = 2.$\overline{3}$ = 2.33333 on the calculator shown

32. Total cost = $14 + $16 + $19 = $49

33. Cost = ($16)(4) = $64

34. (800)(1$\frac{1}{2}$)(6) = 7200 calories

35. (.90)(1.6) = $1.44

36. Around 2015, the minimum weekly wages exceeded $100.

37. The Crystal Beach Comet's height is about 94 ft.

38. Tallest = 105 ft. and the shortest = 90 ft. Difference = 15 ft.

39. $10 – (3)(.90) – (3)(.40) = $5.20 change.

40. (30)(20)(20) = 12,000 cm³. Since 12,000 < 1,000,000, the price is 20 cents.

EXAMINATION SECTION
TEST 1

DIRECTIONS: Each question or incomplete statement is followed by several suggested answers or completions. Select the one that BEST answers the question or completes the statement. *PRINT THE LETTER OF THE CORRECT ANSWER IN THE SPACE AT THE RIGHT.*

1. In the number system with base 5, the value of the repeating decimal, .232323...., expressed as a common fraction, is   1._____

    A. 44/344   B. 14/24   C. 23/44   D. none of these

2. The number 122, base 4, is added to the number 212, base 3. Their sum, when expressed in the base 5, is written   2._____

    A. 2,314   B. 334   C. 144   D. 49

3. If 13^{62} is multiplied out, the units digit in the final product is   3._____

    A. 1   B. 3   C. 7   D. 9

4. On a $10,000 order, a merchant has a choice between three successive discounts of 20%, 20%, and 10%, and three successive discounts of 40%, 5%, and 5%. By choosing the better offer, he can save   4._____

    A. $330   B. $345   C. $360   D. $400

5. An article was sold for $21.00 more than it cost. If the marked price of this article was 150% of its cost price, and if it was sold at a discount of 30%, then its cost price was   5._____

    A. $19.09   B. $70   C. $210   D. $420

6. If the statement $202_b = (13_b).(13_b)$ is true in a number system whose base is b, and b is a natural number, then b is equal to   6._____

    A. 5   B. 6   C. 7   D. 8

7. A rope 10 yards long is divided into three lengths so that the shortest is equal to the difference in the lengths of the two others. Then the LONGEST piece is what part of the whole rope?   7._____

    A. 1/4   B. 1/2   C. 2/3   D. 3/4

8. Assume that a storekeeper reduces his profit on all merchandise in the store from 40% of the cost to 33 1/3% of the cost. If an article originally sold for $14.70, what would its new selling price be?   8._____

    A. $9.80   B. $10.78   C. $11.76   D. $14.00

9. The numbers 314 and 1011 are written in two different bases. Each number contains the largest digit available on its base. The sum of these two numbers, if written in base 3, is   9._____

    A. 10112   B. 1211002   C. 20220   D. 1011111

10. An automobile covered the first 60 miles of its journey in 1 hour 30 minutes and the next 87 miles in 2 hours. The AVERAGE speed, in miles per hour, for the total trip is

    A. 41 3/4   B. 42   C. 58 4/5   D. 73 1/2

11. If the radius of a circle is increased 50%, the area is INCREASED _____%.

    A. 50   B. 125   C. 200   D. 225

12. Assuming the use of a as a symbol for *ten* and β for *eleven,* the number 283_{ten}, when written in the duodecimal system of numeration, is represented by

    A. $1_\beta 7$ B. $1\alpha 7$ C. 21β D. 21α

13. A owns a house worth $10,000. He sells it to B at a 10% profit. B sells the house back to A at a 10% loss. Then, among the following, which is CORRECT?

    A. A comes out even.
    B. A makes $100.
    C. A makes $1,100.
    D. B loses $1,000.

14. If the length and width of a rectangle are each doubled, the area is increased by

    A. 100%   B. 200%   C. 300%   D. 400%

15. The list price of an article is $500. On this article, one dealer offers successive discounts of 10% and 20%, while another offers a single discount of 30%.
    As a result of these offers, what will the difference be in the selling price of the article be?

    A. No difference
    B. $5
    C. $10
    D. $15

16. Of a group of pupils, 1/3 walk home, 3/8 of the remaining members go home by bus, and the other 35 use bicycles to go home.
    How many pupils are there in the group?

    A. 64   B. 84   C. 120   D. 280

17. A merchant paid $90 for a desk.
    At what price should he mark it if he wishes to offer his customers a 10% discount and still make a profit of 20% on the cost?

    A. $108   B. $112   C. $116   D. $120

18. If 16 men require 24 cases of rations for 10 days, then at the same rate of consumption, the number of days that 27 cases of rations will last for 12 men is

    A. 12   B. 15   C. 18   D. 21

19. A man deposits $1,000 in a new account which earns interest at 4% compounded quarterly from the day of deposit.
    How much must he deposit in this account three months later in order that the account will contain exactly $2020 six months from the day of the initial deposit?

    A. $940   B. $980   C. $990   D. $1,000

20. The integer 5x327y, where x and y stand for missing digits, is divisible by 9. 20._____
Which of the following could the sum of x and y be?

    A. 5   B. 9   C. 10   D. 11

KEY (CORRECT ANSWERS)

1. B
2. C
3. D
4. B
5. D

6. C
7. B
8. D
9. A
10. B

11. B
12. A
13. C
14. C
15. C

16. C
17. D
18. B
19. D
20. C

SOLUTIONS TO PROBLEMS

1. $.232323..._{\text{base5}} = (\frac{2}{5} + \frac{3}{25} + \frac{2}{125} + \frac{3}{625} + \frac{2}{3125} + \frac{3}{15625}...)_{\text{base10}} =$
   $.541632.$ which approaches $\frac{13}{14}$. (Ans. B)

2. $122_{\text{,base 4}} = 26_{\text{,base 10}} \cdot 212_{\text{base 3}} = 23_{\text{base 10}}$. Sum $= 49_{\text{base 10}}$, which is $144_{\text{base 5}}$. (Ans. C)

3. $13^1 = 13$, $13^2 = 169$, $13^3 = 2197$, $13^4 = 28561$, $13^5 = 371293$, etc. The last digit is of a cyclic nature and has the pattern 3, 9, 7, 1, 3, 9, 7, 1, 3, 9, 7, 1, etc. for consecutive powers of 13.
   Now, 13^{62} would end in the same digit as 13^2 which is 9. (Ans. D)

4. Under the first option, the merchant would pay
   ($10000)(.8)(.8)(.1) = $5760; but under the second option, he would pay
   ($10000)(.6)(.95)(.95) = $5415. This represents a savings of $345. (Ans. B)

5. Let c = cost. Then, c+21 = selling price and 1.50c = marked price. Since the article was sold at a 30% discount (off the marked price), c + 21 = .70(1.50c). Solving, c = $420. (Ans. D)

6. $202_7 = (2)(7^2) + 2 = 100$ and $13_7 = 10$. Now, $202_7 = (13_7)(13_7)$. (Ans. C)

7. Let x = shortest piece, y = second piece. Then, 10 - x - y = longest piece. Now, x = (10 - x - y) - y. Thus, x + y = 5.
   Then, 10 - x - y must equal 5, and this represents 1/2 the length of the rope. (Ans. B)

8. Let x = cost. Then, 14.70 = (1.40)(x) and x = 10.50. The new selling price is (10.50)(133 1/3%) = $14.00. (Ans. D)

9. $314_{\text{base 5}} = (3)(25) + (1)(5) + 4 = 84$
   $1011_{\text{base 2}} = (1)(8) + (0)(4) + 1(2) + 1 = 11$
   The sum = 95, which is $10112_{\text{base 3}}$.
   (Ans. A)

10. Average speed = total distance/total time = 147/3.5 = 42 mph. (Ans. B)

11. If R = original radius, area = πR^2. If new radius = 1.5R, new area = $\pi(1.5R)^2 = 2.25\pi R^2$.
    The area increased $1.25\pi R^2$, which represents a 125% increase. (Ans. B)

12. ___ ___ ___ The leftmost placeholder represents $12^2 = 144$.
    Since 283 ÷ 144 = 1 with remainder of 139, the first dash = 1. The second dash represents 12, and 139 consists of 11 12's with remainder of 7. Thus, the symbol for 11, β, occupies the second dash. 7 must occupy the rightmost dash. The final answer
    $= 1\beta 7$ (Ans. A)

5 (#1)

13. A sells the house to B for ($10,000)(1.10) = $11,000. Then, B sells the house to A for ($11,000)(.90) = $9,900. A nets $1,100. (Ans. C)

14. Let L = length, w = width, so that area = Lw. The new length and width are 2L and 2w, and so the new area = 4Lw. The increase in area is 3Lw, which represents 300%. (Ans,. C)

15. Successive discounts of 10% and 20% would mean that the final price is (.80)(.90)($500) = $360. A single discount of 30% would yield a final price of (.70)($500) = $350. The difference is $10. (Ans. C)

16. Let x = number of students. Then, x - 1/3x - 3/8x = 35. 7/24x = 35. Solving, x = 120. (Ans. C)

17. Let x = marked price. Sale price = .90x, and this price will be 120% of $90. Thus, .90x = (1.20)(90) = 108. Solving, x = $120. (Ans. D)

18. For 10 days, 12 men would require x rations. 12/x = 16/24 .
Then, x = 18. Now, if 18 rations last 10 days, 27 rations will last y days. 18/10 = 27/y. Solving, y = 15. (Ans. B)

19. In three months, his account will grow to $1000(1.01)^1 = $1010. If he deposits x dollars, (1000+x)(1.01)^1 = 2020. Solving, x = $1000. (Ans. D)

20. Since the sum of all digits = a multiple of 9, 5+x+3+2+7+y = a multiple of 9. Thus, 17 + x + y = a multiple of 9, and so x+y could be 10. (Ans. C)

TEST 2

DIRECTIONS: Each question or incomplete statement is followed by several suggested answers or completions. Select the one that BEST answers the question or completes the statement. *PRINT THE LETTER OF THE CORRECT ANSWER IN THE SPACE AT THE RIGHT.*

1. Which of the following lengths: (A) 2.990 in., (B) 2.998 in., (C) 3.002 in. may be accepted for a part designed to be 3 inches long if a .003 inch tolerance is permitted?

    A. A and B *only*
    B. A and C *only*
    C. B and C *only*
    D. A, B, and C

2. The number 478 (base 10), when changed to base 5 notation, becomes

    A. 3   B. 2390   C. 3403   D. 11102

3. If an article costs $36, the price at which it should be marked to allow a discount of 10% and still make a profit of 20% on the actual selling price is

    A. $40   B. $46   C. $50   D. $54

4. Of the following pairs, the one which is composed of two equivalents is

    A. 1/2 = .5%
    B. 1.01 = 110%
    C. .0001/4 = .0025%
    D. .02/3 = .062/3%

5. A man needs $8000 for the purchase of a business. A loan is available at 6% interest, discounted in advance.
   The amount he must borrow, to the nearest dollar, to net $8000 repayable at the end of six months is

    A. $8240   B. $8247   C. $8480   D. $8511

6. Of the following, the one which is CLOSEST to the result of the computation

    of $\dfrac{(.846)^2 \sqrt[3]{18.7}}{3.42}$ is

    A. .5555   B. 5.555   C. 55.55   D. 555.5

7. Which one of the following is NOT a perfect number?

    A. 28
    B. $2^{k-1}(2^{k-1})$ (where k is prime)
    C. 15
    D. 6

8. The product of the highest common factor and the lowest common multiple of 18 and 24 is

    A. *equal* to the product of 18 and 24
    B. *equal* to the quotient of 24 and 18
    C. *greater* than the product of 18 and 24
    D. *equal* to half the product of 18 and 24

9. Which one of the following is NOT a characteristic of all *groups*?   9.____

   A. Associative law   B. Commutative law
   C. Closure   D. An inverse element

10. Of the following, the set of numbers arranged in ascending order of values is   10.____

    A. 114_{five}, 122_{three}, 10110_{two}
    B. 122_{three}, 10110_{two}, 114_{five}
    C. 10110_{two}, 122_{three}, 114_{five}
    D. 10111_{two}, 114_{five}, 122_{three}

11. All of the following numbers are congruent to -14 modulo 4, EXCEPT   11.____

    A. -8   B. -6   C. 2   D. 6

12. The product of .00000149 and .0000000006 written in scientific notation is   12.____

    A. 8.94×10^{-16} B. 8.94×10^{-17}
    C. 8.94×10^{-18} D. 8.94×10^{-19}

13. If an airplane is flying with a ground speed of 200 miles per hour, the number of seconds required for it to travel a ground mile is   13.____

    A. 1/18   B. 3 1/3   C. 18   D. 60

14. When 148, a numeral to the base 10, is expressed as a numeral to the base 7, it becomes   14.____

    A. 103   B. 231   C. 301   D. 321

15. When 231 and 332, numerals expressed to the base 4, are expressed to the base 10, the sum of the two then would be   15.____

    A. 107   B. 563
    C. 1225   D. none of these

16. The arithmetic mean of the measures 4.18, 4.23, 4.15, 4.17, 4.09 is CLOSEST to which one of the following?   16.____

    A. 4.15   B. 4.16   C. 4.17   D. 4.18

17. Of the following pairs, the one containing two equivalent values is   17.____

    A. .0375, 3 3/4%   B. 2.75, .02 3/4%
    C. .8 1/3%; 1/12   D. .0125%, .01 1/4

18. Assume that a gasoline tank was half full, and the gasoline was used until the tank is only 1/8 full. If the tank is then filled to capacity by putting in 21 gallons, the capacity of the tank, in gallons, is   18.____

    A. 24   B. 42
    C. 56   D. none of these

19. The smallest subdivision on a certain accurately calibrated instrument is .01 inch. Assuming no human errors in use, the possible error of measurement in using the above instrument is

    A. .001"   B. .005"   C. .010"   D. .050"

19.____

20. The number 1011 to the base 2, if expressed to the base 10, would be

    A. 11   B. 14   C. 22   D. 38

20.____

KEY (CORRECT ANSWERS)

1.	C	11.	A
2.	C	12.	A
3.	C	13.	C
4.	D	14.	C
5.	B	15.	A
6.	A	16.	B
7.	C	17.	A
8.	A	18.	A
9.	B	19.	B
10.	B	20.	A

SOLUTIONS TO PROBLEMS

1. $3 \pm .003$ = 2.997 to 3.003. Only choices B and C are acceptable. (Ans. C)

2. In base 5, the name of the columns are units, 5's, 25's, 125's, etc. reading from right to left. Since 478 ÷ 125 gives 3 with remainder 103, the leftmost digit = 3. Then, 103 ÷ 25 gives 4 with remainder 3; so the next digit =4. Now, 3 ÷ 5 gives 0 with remainder 3; thus the next digit = 0 and the rightmost digit = 3. The number is 3403. (Ans. C)

3. Let x = marked price. With a discount of 10%, the selling price = .90x. To realize a profit of 20% on the selling price, .90x - 36 = .20(.90x). Solving, x = $50. (Ans. C)

4. $\frac{1}{2}$ = 50% ≠ .5%, 1.01 = 101% ≠ 110%, $.000\frac{1}{4}$ = .00025 ≠ .0025%, and $.0\frac{2}{3} = .06\frac{2}{3} = .06\frac{2}{3}\%$. (Ans. D)

5. Let x = amount borrowed. Then, .97x = 8000, and x is approximately $8247. (Ans. B)

6. The expression is approximated by $\frac{(.7)(2.6)}{3.4}$, which is about .54. Thus, .5555 is the closest given approximation. (Ans. A)

7. 15 is not a perfect number since the sum of all its factors (except 15) = 1 + 3 + 5 = 9 ≠ 15. (Ans. C)

8. Highest common factor = 6, and the lowest common multiple is 72. Now, (72)(6) = 432, which equals (18)(24). (Ans. A)

9. A group need not be commutative. If it has this property, it is called Abelian. (Ans. B)

10. 122_{three} = 9 + (2)(3) + 2 = 17, 10110_{two} = 16 + 4 + 2 = 22, and 114_{five} = 25 + 5 + 4 = 34. (Ans. B)

11. -8 is NOT congruent to -14 modulo 4 since -8 -(-14) is not a multiple of 4. (Ans. A)

12. $(1.49 \times 10^{-6})(6 \times 10^{-10}) = 8.94 \times 10^{-16}$. (Ans. A)

13. 200 mi/hr = $1 mi / \frac{1}{200}$ hr. $\frac{1}{200}$ hr.=$(\frac{1}{200})(3600)$=18 seconds. (Ans. C)

14. $148_{base\ 10} = 301_{base\ 7}$, since $301_{base\ 7}$ = (3)(49)+1. (Ans. C)

15. $231_{base\ 4}$ = 2(16) + 3(4) + 1 = $45_{base\ 10}$
    $332_{base\ 4}$ = 3(16) + 3(4) + 2 = $62_{base\ 10}$
    Their sum = 107. (Ans. A)

16. The arithmetic mean of the 5 numbers = 20.82/5 = 4.164, which rounds off to 4.16. (Ans. B)

17. .0375 is equivalent to 3.75%, which equals 3 3/4%. (Ans. A)

18. 21 gallons represents 7/8 of the tank's capacity. Thus, the tank's capacity is (21)(8/7) = 24 gallons. (Ans. A)

19. The error of measurement = (1/2)(.01) = .005 inches. (Ans. B)

20. $1011_{base\ 2} = 8+2+1 = 11_{base\ 10}$. (Ans. A)

TEST 3

DIRECTIONS: Each question or incomplete statement is followed by several suggested answers or completions. Select the one that BEST answers the question or completes the statement. *PRINT THE LETTER OF THE CORRECT ANSWER IN THE SPACE AT THE RIGHT.*

1. If the integers 6 and 3 are interchanged in the number 2635 now expressed to the base seven, the quantity expressed to the base 10 by which the number is reduced is

    A. 21
    B. 30
    C. 147
    D. none of these

2. A number of the form $an^4 + bn^2 + cn + d$, where a = 4, b=2, c=2, d=1 and n = 10, is divisible by

    A. 2   B. 5   C. 7   D. 9

3. Of the following, the set in which all are units which may be used for measuring a one-dimensional object is

    A. meter, liter, decimeter, kilometer
    B. meter, kilometer, decimeter, millimeter
    C. liter, decimeter, kilometer, millimeter
    D. meter, liter, millimeter, decimeter

4. To arrange the following ruler measurements in order of increasing lengths, the CORRECT arrangement should be $A = \frac{27}{32}$ in., $B = \frac{7}{8}$ in., $C = \frac{51}{64}$ in., $D = \frac{13}{16}$ in.

    A. B, D, A, C
    B. D, C, A, B
    C. C, D, A, B
    D. C, A, D, B

5. The ratio of 3'6" to 6" is BEST expressed as

    A. 1 to 7
    B. 3.6" to 6"
    C. 6" to 42"
    D. 7 to 1

6. A layout of a rectangular foundation for a building is drawn to scale. The 72-foot length of the foundation is represented on the drawing by a line 27 inches long. The length, in inches, of the line needed to represent the 45-foot width of the foundation is

    A. 16 7/8   B. 17 1/4   C. 17 7/8   D. 18 3/8

7. A circle graph is to be made to show the parts of the total city budget allocated to each department; the total budget is 2 billion, 100 million dollars.
If 630 million dollars is allocated for education, the number of degrees on the circle graph which would represent the amount for education is CLOSEST to

    A. 30   B. 54   C. 84   D. 108

8. The screw which advances the thimble of a micrometer has 40 threads to the inch. If the thimble is turned exactly 3 threads, the micrometer will be opened by _____ inches.

    A. 0.025   B. 0.075   C. 0.340   D. 0.750

9. A voltmeter scale is divided into ten major divisions, each of which is divided into five minor divisions. Full-scale deflection occurs when 30 volts are across the meter. The number of volts indicated when the needle is on the second minor division beyond the sixth major division is

   A. 6.4   B. 16.4   C. 18.6   D. 19.2

10. The number of rectangular cards 11 inches long and 8 inches wide that can be cut from a sheet 33 inches long and 27 inches wide with a minimum of waste is

    A. 6   B. 9   C. 10   D. 12

11. Of the following four fractions, the one that is CLOSEST in value to $\sqrt{5}$ is

    A. 2 1/10   B. 2 1/5   C. 2 1/8   D. 2 1/2

12. During a transfer of oil from one tank to another, 1 1/2 gallons were lost through leaks in the hose. This represented 0.3 percent of the capacity of the first tank. The capacity of this tank, in gallons, is

    A. 50   B. 200   C. 450   D. 500

13. Using six number punches with digits 1, 2, 3, 4, 5, and 6, the number of differently numbered tags that can be made with three-digit numbers on each tag is

    A. 120   B. 216   C. 278   D. 556

14. A junior high school class studying the metric system came to the following conclusions. Of these, it is INCORRECT to conclude that a(n)

    A. basketball player can be 2 meters tall
    B. football player can weigh 100 kilograms
    C. track star can run 2 kilometers in 1 minute
    D. automobile gasoline tank can hold 80 liters of gasoline

15. The product of 32,000,000 and .000028 is

    A. 8.96×10^{-2} B. 896×10^{-2}
    C. 8.96×10^{2} D. 896×10^{2}

16. Which of the following is its own multiplicative inverse?
    I. -1   II. 0   III. +.1   IV. +1

    A. I, IV   B. II, IV   C. III, IV   D. IV only

17. If 1 inch ≈ 2.5 centimeters, then the number of yards in a kilometer can be found by computing the fraction

    A. $\dfrac{36 \times 100{,}000}{2.5}$ B. $\dfrac{1000}{2.5 \times 36}$

    C. $\dfrac{100{,}000}{2.5 \times 36}$ D. $\dfrac{2.5 \times 36 \times 100}{1000}$

18. A man invested $120,000 in a new business enterprise. The first year, he lost 37½%-of the original investment.
The next year, he made a profit of 40% of his net worth at the beginning of that year. His net worth at the end of the second year was what percent of his original investment?

    A. 62 1/2   B. 75   C. 87 1/2   D. 97 1/2

18._____

19. The arithmetic mean (average) of a set of 50 numbers is 38.
If two numbers 45 and 55 are discarded, the mean of the remaining set of numbers is

    A. 36.5   B. 37.0   C. 37.24   D. 37.5

19._____

20. Which of the following numbers is 26^9?

    A. 5,011,849,549,824   B. 5,429,503,678,976
    C. 5,847,157,808,128   D. 5,638,330,743,552

20._____

KEY (CORRECT ANSWERS)

1. D
2. D
3. B
4. C
5. D

6. A
7. D
8. B
9. D
10. B

11. B
12. D
13. B
14. C
15. C

16. A
17. C
18. C
19. D
20. B

SOLUTIONS TO PROBLEMS

1. $2635_{base\ 7} = (2)(343) + (6)(49) + (3)(7) + 5 = 1006_{base\ 10}$ and $2365_{base\ 7} = (2)(343) + (3)(49) + (6)(7) + 5 = 880_{base\ 10}$. The amount reduction is 126. (Ans. D)

2. The number's value is $4 \times 10^4 + 2 \times 10^2 + 2 \times 10 + 1 = 40{,}221$. Since the sum of the digits of this number is divisible by 9, then so must the number be divisible by 9. (Ans. D)

3. All four of the units meter, kilometer, decimeter, and millimeter are linear measurements. Thus, they can be used to measure one-dimensional objects. (Ans. B)

4. Convert all fractions to like demonimators: A = 54/64 in., B = 56/64 in., C = 51/64 in., D = 52/64 in. Thus, in increasing length, the arrangement is C, D, A, B. (Ans. C)

5. Change 3'6" to 42". Then, 42" to 6" = 7 to 1. (Ans. D)

6. Let x = required line. Then 27/X = 72/45, and x = 16 7/8 in. (Ans. A)

7. The ratio of 630 million to 2 billion, 100 million is 630 to 2100 = 3/10. (3/10)(360) = 108. (Ans. D)

8. $3 \div 40 = .075$ inches. NOTE correction of problem. (Ans. B)

9. Each major division is 30/10 = 3 volts. Each minor division is 3/5 = .6 volts. 6 major + 2 minor divisions = (6)(3) + (2)(.6) = 19.2 volts. (Ans. D)

10. $33 \div 11 = 3$ columns by $27 \div 8$ rounded down to 3 rows. (3)(3) = 9. (Ans. B)

11. $\sqrt{5} = 2.236$ approx. Finding the absolute value of the difference between 2.236 and each of 2.1, 2.2, 2.125, and 2.5 yields .136, .036, .111, and .264, respectively. Thus, 2.2 (or 2 1/5) is closest to $\sqrt{5}$. (Ans. B)

12. Use a proportion: $\dfrac{1\frac{1}{2}}{x} = \dfrac{.3\%}{100\%} = \dfrac{.003}{1}$, where x = capacity of the tank. Solving, x = 500. (Ans. D)

13. Total number of permutations = (6)(6)(6) = 216. (Ans. B)

14. 2 kilometers = 1.24 miles, which would require a MINIMUM of over 4 1/2 minutes for a superior athlete. (Ans. C)

15. $32{,}000{,}000 = 3.2 \times 10^7$ and $.000028 = 2.8 \times 10^{-5}$. Then, $(3.7 \times 10^7)(2.8 \times 10^{-5}) = 8.96 \times 10^2$. (Ans. C)

16. +1 and -1 are their own multiplicative inverses. The multiplicative inverse of 0 doesn't exist. The multiplicative inverse of +.1 is +10. (Ans. A)

5 (#3)

17. There are 100,000 centimeters in a kilometer. Since 1 inch $\approx$ 2.5 centimeters, 1 yard $\approx$ (36)(2.5) = 90 centimeters. Thus, the number of yards in 100,000 centimeters = 100,000/90 = (100,000)/[(36)(2.5)]. (Ans. C)

18. His net worth after 1 year = ($120,000)(.625) = $75,000.
    His net worth after 2 years = (75,000)(1.40) = $105,000.
    Thus, $105,000/$120,000 = .875 = 87 1/2%. (Ans. C)

19. The sum of all fifty numbers = (50)(38) = 1900. By discarding the numbers 45 and 55, the new sum is 1800 for 48 numbers. The mean is then 1800/48 = 37.5. (Ans. D)

20. Any number ending in a 6 which is raised to a positive integral value will still have 6 as its last digit. Only choice B ends in a 6. (Ans. B)

TEST 4

DIRECTIONS: Each question or incomplete statement is followed by several suggested answers or completions. Select the one that BEST answers the question or completes the statement. *PRINT THE LETTER OF THE CORRECT ANSWER IN THE SPACE AT THE RIGHT.*

1. A dealer sold two calculators for $15 each, one at a profit of 25% of its cost, the second at a loss of 25% of its cost.
   The COMBINED effect of the two transactions is

   A. no gain or loss
   B. a gain of $2
   C. a gain of $3
   D. a loss of $2

   1.___

2. One hundred dollars is invested at a rate of interest of 8% per annum compounded semi-annually.
   The TOTAL value of the investment, in dollars, at the end of one year will be

   A. 116.64   B. 108.16   C. 108.08   D. 108.00

   2.___

3. If the distance from the earth to the moon is approximately 380,000 kilometers, then this distance, in meters, is

   A. 3.8×10^8 B. 3.8×10^7 C. 3.8×10^5 D. 3.8×10^2

   3.___

4. If 14_{five} is subtracted from 123_{four}, the result, in base ten, is

   A. 18   B. 63   C. 109   D. 1299

   4.___

5. Two junior high school classes took the same test. The first class of 20 students attained an average grade of 80%. The second class of 30 students attained an average grade of 70%.
   The AVERAGE grade for all students in both classes is

   A. 75%   B. 74%   C. 73%   D. 72%

   5.___

6. In a class studying the relationship between the metric system and the English system, the following statements were made by students: a
   I. meter is a little more than a yard
   II. liter is a little more than a quart
   III. kilometer is more than a mile
   IV. kilogram is more than a pound
   Which of these statements if FALSE?

   A. I   B. II   C. III   D. IV

   6.___

7. A pupil adds his test scores and divides the sum by the number of scores.
   The result of this procedure would be the

   A. arithmetic mean
   B. median
   C. mode
   D. standard deviation

   7.___

8. If the product of two positive integers is divisible by 6, which of the following must be TRUE?

   A. One integer must be divisible by 2, and the other integer must be divisible by 3.
   B. At least one of the integers must be divisible by 6.
   C. At least one of the integers must be an even number.
   D. Neither of the integers can be a prime number.

   8.___

9. A gas tank with a capacity of 15 gallons is 5/16 full. How many gallons of fuel must be added to the tank for it to be 5/3 full?

   A. 4 11/16   B. 5 5/6   C. 9 3/8   D. 10 5/16

10. Mr. Jones bought a house for $50,000. He sold the house at a profit of 20% of his original cost. The house was resold by the new purchaser at a profit of 20% of his cost. What percent of Mr. Jones' original purchase price is the final selling price of the house?

    A. 44%   B. 122%   C. 140%   D. 144%

11. A man invested $1000 at 12% per year, compounded quarterly, for a period of 5 years. Which of the following represents the total of his investment at the end of that time?

    A. $1000 (1.03)^{20}$
    B. $1000 (1.05)^{12}$
    C. $1000 (1.12)^{5}$
    D. $1000 (1.12)^{20}$

12. The number designated by 2021_{three} can be denoted in the binary system by

    A. 111101_{two}
    B. 101011_{two}
    C. 110111_{two}
    D. 101111_{two}

13. A representation for the number .00792 in scientific notation is

    A. 7.92×10^{-3}
    B. 7.92×10^{-4}
    C. 7.92×10^{2}
    D. 7.92×10^{3}

14. An eleventh year mathematics class studying positive and negative exponents examined a number of relationships in the metric system. Which of the following is NOT a correct relationship?

    A. $1 \text{ mm} = 10^{-2} \text{ cm}$
    B. $1 \text{ cm}^3 = 10^{-3} \text{ L}$
    C. $1 \text{ kg} = 10^{6} \text{ mg}$
    D. $1 \text{ cm} = 10^{-5k} \text{ m}$

15. The last digit of 7^{253} is

    A. 1   B. 5   C. 7   D. 9

16. Of the following, the property that the set {-1,0,1} does NOT possess is

    A. closure under addition
    B. closure under multiplication
    C. an identity element for multiplication
    D. inverse elements for addition

17. A pupil is informed that his percentile rank on a test given to a certain group is 70. This means that

    A. his score is in the upper 30% of the test scores of the group
    B. his score is in the lower 30% of the test scores of the group
    C. he answered 70 of the items correctly
    D. he answered 70% of the items correctly

18. A number written in base 7 is 1231_{seven}. 18.____
    This number written in base 5 is

    A. 3323_{five} B. 3233_{five} C. 1321_{five} D. 463_{five}

19. A television console is listed in a catalog for $1000. If the set is sold with successive discounts of 20% and 10%, the ACTUAL selling price will be 19.____

    A. $700   B. $720   C. $780   D. $850

20. At a certain college, 1/3 of all applications sent to prospective students were never returned. Of those returned, 2/5 were rejected and 1/6 of those accepted decided not to attend. 20.____
    How many applications were sent out if 1,000 freshmen were admitted?

    A. 6000   B. 2000   C. 3000   D. 4500

KEY (CORRECT ANSWERS)

1.	D	11.	A
2.	B	12.	A
3.	A	13.	A
4.	A	14.	A
5.	B	15.	C
6.	C	16.	A
7.	A	17.	A
8.	C	18.	A
9.	A	19.	B
10.	D	20.	C

SOLUTIONS TO PROBLEMS

1. The first calculator's cost to the dealer = $15 ÷ 1.25 = $12. The second calculator's cost to the dealer = $15 ÷ .75 = $20. The combined effect for the dealer was ($15+$15) - ($12+$20) = -$2; thus a loss of $2. (Ans. D)

2. Total value at the end of one year = $100(1.04)^2 = $108.16. (Ans. B)

3. Since 1 kilometer = 1000 meters, 380,000 km = (380,000)(1000) = 380,000,000 or 3.8×10^8 m. (Ans. A)

4. 14_{five} = (1)(5) + 4 = 9_{ten}. 123_{four} = (1)(16) + (2)(4) + 3 = 27_{ten}. The difference is 18, base 10. (Ans. A)

5. Average = $\frac{(20)(.8Q) + (30)(.70)}{50}$ = .74 or 74%. (Ans. B)

6. A kilometer is about 5/8 of a mile. (Ans. C)

7. The arithmetic mean = sum of numbers divided by the number of numbers. (Ans. A)

8. If (A)(B)/6 is a whole number, we can conclude that either A or B or both A,B is(are) even. Furthermore, at least one of A,B must be divisible by 3. (Ans. C)

9. The required amount of fuel = $15(\frac{5}{8} - \frac{5}{16}) = 4\frac{11}{16}$. (Ans. A)

10. Mr. Jones sold his house for ($50,000)(1.20) = $60,000. The new buyer sold the house for ($60,000)(1.20) = $72,000. Now, $72,000 is (72,000/50,000) x 100 = 144% of $50,000. (Ans. D)

11. $T = P(1 + \frac{R}{n})^{nt}$, where T = total, P = principal (investment), R = annual compounded rate, n = number of times per year being compounded, t = number of years. Thus, T = 1000(1.03)^{20}. (Ans. A)

12. 2021_{three} = 2(27) + 0(9) + 2(3) + 1 = 61 in base 10. This is equivalent to 111101_{two}. (Ans. A)

13. .00792 = 7.92 x .001 = 7.92×10^{-3}. (Ans. A)

14. The CORRECT statement for A is 1 mm = 10^{-1} cm. (Ans. A)

15. 7^1 ends in 7, 7^2 ends in 9, 7^3 ends in 3, 7^4 ends in 1. This cycle is repeated, so that in order to find the last digit of 7^{253}, divide 253 by 4. The remainder of this division is 1, and thus corresponds to 7^1 which ends in 7. (Note that if there were no remainder, this would have been equivalent to a remainder of 4, corresponding to 7^4 which ends in 1.) (Ans. C)

16. Use the example 1+1=2, and 2 is not an element of {-1,0,1}. (Ans. A)

17. A percentile rank indicates the *relative* position of a score when the scores are arranged from LOWEST to HIGHEST. 70, as a percentile, means that *approximately* 70% of all the scores are LOWER and 30% of all the scores are HIGHER. (Ans. A)

18. $1231_{seven} = (1)(343) + (2)(49) + (3)(7) + 1 = 463$.
    With base 5, the rightmost column is ones, next column is fives, next column is twenty-fives, fourth column is 125's. Now, $463 = (3)(125) + (3)(25) + (2)(5) + 3(1)$, so the answer is 3323_{five}. (Ans. A)

19. Discount of 20% = ($1000)(.80) + $800, followed by a Discount of 10%= ($800)(.90) = $720 = answer. (Ans. B)

20. Let x = number of applications sent out. Then, 2/3x = number of applications returned; (3/5)(2/3x) = 2/5x = number of applicants accepted; (5/6)(3/5x) = 1/3x decided to attend. Thus, 1/3x = 1000 and so x = 3000. (Ans. C)

TEST 5

DIRECTIONS: Each question or incomplete statement is followed by several suggested answers or completions. Select the one that BEST answers the question or completes the statement. *PRINT THE LETTER OF THE CORRECT ANSWER IN THE SPACE AT THE RIGHT.*

1. In a three digit number, the units digit is two more than the tens digit. The sum of the digits is 12. The number with the digits reversed is 198 less than the original number. The original number must be between

   A. 100 and 200
   B. 200 and 300
   C. 400 and 500
   D. 600 and 700

   1._____

2. If the tenth term of an arithmetic sequence is 15 and the twentieth term is 35, then the thirtieth term is

   A. 525   B. 50   C. 55   D. 61

   2._____

3. The expressions a+bc and (a+b)(a+c) are

   A. *never* equal
   B. equal when a+b+c = 1
   C. *always* equal
   D. equal when a+b+c = 0

   3._____

4. Pour pupils answered a question. Pupil A's answer was 37.5×10^{-6}, Pupil B's answer was $3/8 \times 10^{-6}$, Pupil C's 8 answer was $15/4 \times 10^{-5}$, and Pupil D's answer was $.000037^{1/2}$. The answer that was NOT equivalent to the others was that of Pupil

   A. A   B. B   C. C   D. D

   4._____

5. If the original selling price of a certain article, including a profit of 40% of the cost, were $18.20, and if the profit were to be reduced to 30% of the cost, the selling price would become

   A. $13.39   B. $13.65   C. $16.38   D. $16.90

   5._____

6. If a 4% stock whose par value is $60.00 is purchased at a price that will make the investment yield a return of 5%, the purchase price is

   A. $30   B. $48   C. $75   D. $82

   6._____

7. If a piece of property was sold for $5,780 at a loss of 15% of the cost, the cost of the property was

   A. $4,913   B. $6,647   C. $6,800   D. $7,200

   7._____

8. If the single discount equivalent to three successive discounts is 38.8% and the first two discounts are 20% and 10%, then the third discount, in percent, is

   A. 8.8   B. 15   C. 17   D. 30

   8._____

9. The SMALLEST integral value of k (k#O) that will make 8820k the cube of a positive integer is

   A. 100   B. 150   C. 1000   D. 1050

   9._____

125

10. A wholesaler sells a certain article to the retailer at a profit of 60% of the cost. The retailer then sells this article to the consumer at a profit of 25% of his cost. The consumer pays $14.40. The cost to the wholesaler was

    A. $7.20 B. $7.78 C. $10.80 D. $12.24

11. Two bicycles start traveling from the same point at the same time. One heads due west at 8 mph and the other heads due south at 15 mph.
    They will be 51 miles apart _____ hours.

    A. 2
    C. 3
    B. approximately 2 1/4
    D. 9

12. At the end of the first two years of school, a pupil attains an average of 83% in eight majors.
    The average required in five majors in the third year at school in order to achieve an overall average of 85% is

    A. 86.5% B. 87% C. 88.2% D. 89%

13. To win an election, a candidate needs 3/4 of the votes cast.
    If after 2/3 of the votes have been counted, a candidate has 5/6 of what he needs, what part of the remaining votes does he still need?

    A. 1/8 B. 1/4 C. 3/8 D. 1/2

14. A sells an article for D dollars, less 20% and 10%. B sells the same article for D dollars less 25%.
    What additional discount should B allow in order to match A's selling price?

    A. 1.8% B. 2% C. 4% D. 5%

15. A radioactive isotope loses 1/3 of its strength during the first minute of its existence, 1/3 of its remaining strength during the second minute, 1/3 of its remaining strength during the third minute, etc.
    How long, to the nearest minute, will it be before the isotope will have lost 87% of its original activity? _____ minutes.

    A. 2 B. 3 C. 4 D. 5

16. A refrigerator was originally marked to sell at a profit of 66 2/3% of the cost. It was finally sold at a profit of 33 1/3% of the cost.
    What percent discount did the purchaser receive on the marked price?

    A. 15 B. 20 C. 25 D. 33 1/3

17. A store offers a discount of 30%. An additional discount, in percent, to make the combined discount equivalent to a single discount of 37% would be

    A. 7 B. 10 C. 23 D. 67

18. A sample of brass contained 1 3/4 pounds of copper, 1 1/2 pounds of zinc, and 2 ounces of impurities.
    The number of pounds of copper in one ton of this type of brass is

    A. 560 B. 800 C. 1080 D. 1120

19. When the temperature drops from 37°F to -8°F, the number of degrees the temperature on the Centigrade scale will fall during the same period is

    A. 7 2/9   B. 25   C. 49   D. 57

20. As part of its aircraft officer training program, the Navy sends sailors to radio school. Of those who are sent to radio school, 1/3 drop out during the course. Of those who graduate, 4/5 are assigned to aircraft carriers.
    If 3/4 of these become officers, how many sailors should the Navy send to radio school if it needs 60 aircraft officers?

    A. 120   B. 150   C. 180   D. 300

KEY (CORRECT ANSWERS)

1.	D	11.	C
2.	C	12.	C
3.	C	13.	C
4.	B	14.	C
5.	D	15.	D
6.	B	16.	B
7.	C	17.	B
8.	B	18.	D
9.	D	19.	B
10.	A	20.	B

SOLUTIONS TO PROBLEMS

1. Any three digit number can be represented as $100h + 10t + u$. From the conditions of the problem, we get three equations:
    1) $u - t = 2$
    2) $u + t + h = 12$
    3) $100h + 10t + u = 100u + 10t + h + 198$ which reduces to $-u + h = 2$

   Solving, $u = 4$, $t = 2$, $h = 6$; so the answer is 624.
   (Ans. D)

2. The nth term of an arithmetic progression with first term x and difference d is $x + (n-1)d$. Thus, $x + 9d = 15$ and $x + 19d = 35$. Solving, $x = -3$ and $d = 2$. The thirtieth term is $-3 + (29)(2) = 55$. (Ans. C)

3. $(a+b)(a+c) = a^2 + ab + ac + bc$. In order for this expression to equal $a+bc$, we need $a^2 + ab + ac = a$, which implies $a(a+b+c-1) = 0$. Now, either $a = 0$ or $a+b+c-1 = 0$; i.e., $a+b+c = 1$. Note that choice C does NOT give the FULL answer but is the BEST choice. (Ans. C)

4. Pupils A, C, and D have answers equivalent to .0000375, whereas Pupil B's answer is .000000375. (Ans. B)

5. Let C = cost. $18.20 = (1.40)(C)$, so $C = \$13.00$. Now, the new profit = $(13)(1.30) = \$16.90$. (Ans. D)

6. Let x = purchase price. Then, $(60)(.04) = (x)(.05)$. Solving, $x = \$48$. (Ans. B)

7. Let x = cost. $5780 = .85x$. Thus, $x = \$6800$. (Ans. C)

8. Let the original price = 1 (for simplicity). A single discount of 38.8% means the final sale price = .612. Two successive discounts of 20% and 10% would amount to a price of $(.8)(.9) = .72$. Letting x be the third discount, the final price = $.72(1 - x/100)$. Thus, $.612 = .72(1 - x/100)$.
   Solving, $x = 15$. (Ans. B)

9. $8820 = 2^2 \cdot 3^2 \cdot 5 \cdot 7^2$. In order to multiply this product by some factor so that the new number will be a perfect cube (and smallest non-zero perfect cube), the factor would be $2 \cdot 3 \cdot 5^2 \cdot 7 = 1050$. Note that $(8820)(1050) = 9,261,000$, which is $(210)^3$. (Ans. D)

10. Let c = wholesaler cost. The cost to the retailer = $1.6c$ and so the cost to the consumer becomes $(1.6c)(1.25) = 2c$.
    If $2c = \$14.40$, $c = 7.20$. (Ans. A)

11. Let h = number of hours. Then, $(8h)^2 + (15h)^2 = 51^2$, since the Pythagorean Theorem can be used. Solving, $h = 3$. (Ans. C)

12. An average of 83% for eight subjects means a total of 664 percentage points. Let x = average for the next five subjects, so that $5x$ = the total percentage points for these 5 subjects. To average 85% for all 13 subjects, $85\% = (664+5x)/13$. Solving, $x = 88.2\%$. (Ans. C)

13. Let V = number of votes to be cast. After 2/3V have been tallied, the candidate has 5/6 of the 3/4V he needs to win. (5/6)(3/5v) = 5/8V. From the remaining 1/3v=. votes he needs to be nominated, $\frac{3}{4}v - \frac{5}{8}v = \frac{1}{8}v$ times. Finally, $\frac{1}{8}v / \frac{1}{3}v = \frac{3}{8}$. (Ans. C)

14. Two consecutive discounts of 20% and 10% on D dollars means .90(.80D)= .72D is the selling price. If the first discount is 25%, the selling price is then .75D (B's first discount). In order to match .72D as the final selling price, a second discount of x% means (100-x)(.75D) = .72D. Then, x = 4%. (Ans. C)

15. Let x = number of minutes required. After x minutes, the isotope will retain $(\frac{2}{3})^x \cdot S$ of its strength, where S = original 3 strength. We seek x such that the retention will be $\frac{13}{100} \cdot S$.

    Solving, $(\frac{2}{3})^x = \frac{13}{100}$ by Logs yields x = 5.03 or about 5 minutes. (Ans. D)

16. Let C = cost. Then, $1\frac{2}{3}C$ = original marked price. The item was finally sold at $1\frac{2}{3}C$. The percent discount on the marked price is $[(1\frac{2}{3} - 1\frac{1}{3})/1\frac{2}{3}][100] = 20\%$. (Ans.B)

17. Let P = original price. After one discount of 30%, the price is .70P. If the second discount is x%, then the new price is $\frac{(100-x)}{100}(.70P)$. Since the combined discount is equivalent to one 37% discount, $\frac{(100-x)}{100}(.70P) = .63P$. Solving, x = 10. (Ans. B)

18. This sample contains $1\frac{3}{4} + 1\frac{1}{4} + \frac{1}{8} = 3\frac{1}{8}$ lbs Let x = number of pounds of copper in 1 ton of this brass sample.= $\frac{x}{2000} = \frac{1.75}{3.125}$. Solving by cross-multiplication, x = 1120. (Ans. D)

19. Use $C = \frac{5}{9}(F-32)$. 37°F converts to $2\frac{7}{9}$°C and -8°F converts to $-22\frac{1}{9}$°C. The drop is $24\frac{8}{9}$° or approx. 25°. (Ans. B)

20. Let x = number of sailors sent to school. Then, $\frac{2}{3}x$ graduate.

    Subsequently, $(\frac{4}{5})(\frac{2}{3}x) = \frac{8}{15}x$ are assigned to aircraft carriers.

    Finally, $(\frac{3}{4})(\frac{8}{15}x) = \frac{2}{5}x$ = number of officers = 60. Thus, x = 150. (Ans. B)

ENGLISH GRAMMAR AND USAGE

This section provides a brief review of some of the basic rules of English Usage (grammar, syntax punctuation, spelling, and organization of paragraphs in a passage).

Some *Basic English Usage Topics What is Grammar*

Grammar *is* the entire body of rules that governs the correct speaking and writing of a language. ***Syntax*** *is* that part of grammar that deals with the arrangement of words, phrases, and clauses within a sentence. ***Punctuation*** deals with the proper use of such things as commas, periods, apostrophes, and question marks which separate words into sentences, clauses, and phrases in order to clarify their meaning.

Sentence Construction

- A sentence is a grammatically independent group of words that serves as a unit of expression. It normally contains a subject and predicate.

Basic Parts of a Simple Sentence

- A simple sentence contains a subject, a verb, and an object.

Use of *Phrases in Sentences*

- A phrase is a group of related words lacking both subject and predicate. A phrase can be used as a noun, adjective, adverb, or verb. On the basis of their form, phrases are classified as *prepositional, participial, gerund, infinitive,* and *verb* phrases.

- A restrictive phrase (not set off by commas in the sentence) completes the meaning of the sentence. A nonrestrictive phrase (set off by commas in the sentence) is incidental to the meaning of the sentence.

Use of *Clauses in Sentences*

- Clauses are grammatical units containing a subject and a verb. They can be either dependent or independent. An independent clause expresses the main thought of the sentence. A dependent clause expresses an idea that is less important than the idea expressed in the main clause. Dependent clauses can be restrictive (not set off by commas in the sentence) or nonrestrictive (set off by commas in the sentence).

Verb

Definition: A word or phrase used to assert an action or state of being.

Voice of *Verb*

- The *voice* of a verb shows whether the subject performs an action (active voice) or receives it (passive voice). **Examples:** The consultant wrote a proposal. The proposal was written by the consultant.

Verb Tense

- The tense of a verb shows the time of the action of the verb. There is an active and a passive form of all tenses in English. The tenses of verbs in English are:
  a. Present (active) - she takes *or* she is taking
  b. Present (passive) -she is taken *or* she is being taken
  c. Past (active) - she took *or* she was taking
  d. Past (passive) -she was taken *or* she was being taken
  e. Future (active) -she will take *or* she will be taking
  f. Future (passive) -she will be taken
  g. Perfect (active) - she has taken *or* she has been taking
  h. Perfect (passive) - she has been taken
  i. Past perfect (active) - she had taken *or* she had been taking
  j. Past perfect (passive) -she had been taken
  k. Future perfect (active) - she will have taken *or* she will have been taking
  l. Future perfect (passive) - she will have been taken

Mood of the Verb

- The mood of a verb shows whether an action is fact (indicative mood), something other than fact, such as a possibility, wish, or supposition (subjunctive mood), or a command (imperative mood).
  Example of indicative mood: They are going to the ball game.
  Example of subjunctive mood: If they go at all, they will be late.
  Example of imperative mood: Go now!

Verb Shifts

- Unnecessary shifts in person, number, tense, or voice confuse readers and seriously weakens communication. The examples below indicate these types of errors.

- A shift in person occurs when a writer shifts back and forth among the first, second, and third persons. **Example:** If you want to pass the physical, a person has to exercise daily.

- A shift in number occurs when a plural pronoun is used to refer back to a singular antecedent or vice versa. **Example:** Anyone who shops in that department store must seriously consider their budget.

- Unnecessary shifts in tense more commonly occur within a paragraph rather than within an individual sentence. **Example:** After the historian spent several hours describing the armies' strategies, he gave a horrifying account of the attack. He points out in great detail what is going on in the minds of each of the soldiers.

- A shift in voice occurs when a writer makes unnecessary shifts between the active and the passive voice. **Example:** I wrote the journal article; the book chapter was also written by me. (The *voice* of a verb shows whether the subject performs an action (active voice) or receives it (passive voice).) In the example, the first clause is active voice and the second shifts to passive voice.

Other Rules Related to Verbs

- Transitive verbs require objects to complete their meaning. **Example:** The baseball player *signed the* autographs.

- Intransitive verbs do not require objects to complete their meaning. **Example:** The boat *has docked.*

- Linking verbs are not action verbs; rather, they express a state of being or existence. The various forms of the verb *to be* are primary linking verbs.

- Linking verbs never take objects but, instead, connect the subject to a word or idea in the predicate. **Examples:** It was he who bought the tickets. His proposal *is* unacceptable. Some dogs *are* excitable.

- The verb *to be* can also be used with another verb as a helping (auxiliary) verb to create a verb phrase. Examples: Flights *have been delayed.* The contract will *have to be reviewed*

Infinitive

Definition: An infinitive is the form of a verb which expresses action or existence without reference to person, number, or tense. **Example:** *To run* is relaxing.

- A split infinitive has a word or several words between the *to* and the *verb* following it. Splitting an infinitive is incorrect. **Example:** We will try *to successfully complete this project.* **Correct Usage:** We will try to complete this project successfully.

- An infinitive may be used as the subject of a sentence. **Example:** *To become* champion has been her lifelong dream.

- An infinitive may be used as an adjectival modifier. **Example:** She had several papers *to review* during the trip.

Gerund

Definition: A gerund is the form of a verb ending in *ing* that is used as a noun. In fact, another name for a gerund is a verbal noun.

- A gerund may be used as the subject of a sentence. **Example:** *Drawing* was his favorite personal activity.

- A gerund may be used as the object of a sentence or a prepositional phrase. **Examples:** She preferred *walking* over *bicycling. Walking* is the object and *bicycling* is the object of the preposition *over.*

Participle

Definition: A participle is a form of the verb used as an adjective. Simple participle forms end in "*_ed*" or "*_ing.*" **Examples:** The candidate felt defrayed The New Year's Eve party was *exciting.*

- When a participial phrase seems to modify a word that it cannot sensibly modify, then it is a dangling phrase. **Example:** Sailing on the open sea, many dolphins were spotted. *Sailing* does not modify dolphins. The correct use of the participle is the following: Sailing on the open sea, we spotted many dolphins.

Noun

Definition: A noun is a word that names a person, place, thing, quality, idea, or action.

- A common noun identifies one or more of a class of persons, places, things, qualities, ideas, or actions that are alike. **Examples:** The *boy* chained his *bicycle to* the *fence*.

- A proper noun identifies a particular person, place, thing, quality, idea, or action. *(Note:* needs to be capitalized.) **Examples:** *Joe Brown* drove his *Lincoln Towncar* to the *Kennedy Center.*

- A collective noun identifies a group of people or things that are related or acting as one. **Examples:** The *jury* arrives at the courthouse each day at nine in the morning. The *platoon* travels by night in order to avoid detection. *(Note:* Collective nouns are *single* in number which is reflected in the verb agreement.)

- The possessive of a singular noun is formed by adding an apostrophe and s ('s) to the noun. **Examples:** the boy's sweater; Robert's book; Alice's dress (correct) the boys' sweater; Roberts' book; Alices' dress (incorrect)

- The possessive of a plural noun ending in s is formed by adding an apostrophe only. **Examples:** wives' salaries; workers' union (correct);
    wive's salaries; worker's union (incorrect)

Pronoun

Definition: A pronoun is a word that is used in place of a noun, most frequently to eliminate monotonous repetition of the noun. There are nine types of pronouns:

- Demonstrative pronouns point out a specific person or thing. **Examples:** this, that, these, those

- Indefinite pronouns refer to people or things generally rather than specifically. Examples: all, any, anybody, anyone, anything, both, each, either, everybody, everyone, everything, few, many, most, much, neither, no one, nobody, none, nothing, one, other, several, some, somebody, someone, something, such. *(Note:* Verbs used with indefinite pronouns must agree in number. **Examples:** none *is;* much *is;* everyone *is;* many *are. None* and *much* are often used incorrectly to represent plural entities. If you think of *none* as *no one person or thing* and *much* as *a large quantity of one thing,* then it is easy to see that they are actually singular and take a singular verb.)
    Examples: None of the pencils is free (translates as: *no one pencil is free*) (correct)
       None of the books are listed (translates as: *no one book are listed*) (incorrect)

- Interrogative pronouns are used to ask questions. Examples: who, what, which

- Relative pronouns relate a subordinate part of a sentence to the main clause. **Examples:** who, whoever, whom, whomever, whose, which, whichever, what, whatever, that *(Note: Who* and *whoever are used as subjects in a sentence or phrase, while* whom and *whomever are* used as objects in a sentence or phrase.

Examples: *Who will get the tickets? Whoever is going will buy the tickets. I need to give tickets to whom? The tickets will be given to whomever.)*

- Personal pronouns refer to persons or things and change form in three different persons: first person (the person speaking), second person (the person spoken to), and third person (the person or thing spoken about). **Examples:** I, me, we, us, you, he, him, she, her, it, they, them Examples of correct use: Bill and I are going. He told Sally and me. **Example of incorrect use:** He told Sally and I to take a break.

- Possessive pronouns determine ownership or possession without using an apostrophe followed by an s. **Examples:** my, mine, our, ours, yours, his, hers, its, their, theirs (Note: *it's* is not a personal pronoun and means *it is. There* is not a personal pronoun and refers to a location.)

- Reciprocal pronouns are used together and each can be replaced by the other. **Examples:** *each other, one another*

- Reflexive pronouns refer back to the pronoun used as the subject of the sentence. **Examples:** I burned *myself.* You are deceiving *yourself.*

- Intensive pronouns are used to emphasize the first pronoun. **Examples:** You *yourself* must register. I *myself* do not understand.

Adjective and Adverb

Definitions: An adjective is a word that modifies a noun. An adverb is a word that modifies a verb, an adjective, or another adverb.

- An adjective or an adverb should be placed so that there is no doubt as to which word it modifies. Example: The *angry* boy *quickly* threw the ball. *Angry* is an adjective modifying the noun *boy. Quickly* is an adverb modifying the verb *threw.*

- Adjectives and adverbs show degrees of quality or quantity by means of their positive, comparative, and superlative forms. The positive form expresses no comparison at all. The comparative form adds an *er* to the positive form of the adjective or adverb or prefixes the positive form with the word *more* to express a greater degree or a comparison. The superlative form adds an *est* to the positive form of the adjective or adverb or prefixes the positive form with the word *most* to express the greatest degree of quantity or quality among three or more persons or things.

Examples:	**Positive**	**Comparative**	**Superlative**
	short	shorter	shortest
	beautiful	more beautiful	most beautiful
	big	bigger	biggest
	hard	harder	hardest

- Many adverbs have the characteristic *-ly* ending. **Example:** quickly, slowly, angrily

Preposition

Definition: A preposition is a word that connects a noun to some other word in the sentence. It usually establishes a relationship of time or location. The use of a preposition automatically creates a prepositional phrase. **Examples:** in a month; after a year; on the table; behind the door

- There are over 40 prepositions in English, some of which are: *about, around, before, at, below, by, for, from, in, of, on, to, through, up, upon,* and *with.*

Conjunction

Definition: A conjunction (also known as a connective) is a word that joins together sentences, clauses, phrases, or words. Conjunctions that connect two or more parts of a sentence that are of equal rank (Example: two nouns or verbs or phrases) are called coordinating conjunctions. **Examples:** *and, but, or, nor, for,* and sometimes *yet*

- Subordinating conjunctions connect dependent (subordinate) clauses to independent (main) clauses. Subordinating conjunctions include *though, as, when, while, and since.* **Example:** *Since he took the course for his own advancement,* they wouldn't pay for it.

- Conjunctions in the forms of pairs of words that connect sentence elements that are of equal rank are called correlative conjunctions. Correlative conjunctions must always appear together in the same sentence. **Examples:** *either-or, neither-nor, whether-or, both-and,* and *not only-but also* **Examples used in sentences:** His parents insisted that he *either* accept the restrictions on his use of the car *or* not drive at all. *Neither* the manager *nor* the employee had a reasonable solution to the problem. *Whether* he stayed home *or* went to school depended on a change in his symptoms. *Both* the school board *and* the PTA agreed on the increase in funding for the new equipment. He was outstanding *not only* in his studies *but also* in sports.

Sentence Organization within Paragraphs

- A paragraph presents a larger unit of thought than a sentence can contain. A paragraph must meet certain requirements:

- A paragraph should have *unity,* that is, internal consistency. It should not digress from the dominant idea expressed in the topic sentence.

- A paragraph should have *completeness.* It should present enough detailed information about the topic sentence to answer any general questions the reader may have. More specific questions would require additional paragraphs with new topic sentences.

- A paragraph should have *coherence.* Sentences should flow into each other so that the reader experiences the paragraph as an integrated unit, not as a collection of separate sentences.

- A paragraph should have *order*. Like structure in a larger work, order in a paragraph grows partly out of the material and is partly imposed by the writer. Most paragraphs and essays follow one of the two patterns that follow.

    -- *From the general to the particular:* This type of paragraph begins with a topic sentence that serves as an introductory summary of the topic. The remaining sentences explain or illustrate this statement, so that the idea becomes increasingly clear as the paragraph progresses. The topic sentence is usually at or near the beginning of the paragraph.

    -- *From the particular to the general:* This type of paragraph is the reverse of the previous pattern. It begins with a series of explanatory or illustrative statements that lead to a general statement or summary. The topic sentence is usually at or near the end of the paragraph. A paragraph can be looked upon as a microcosm, an exact parallel in miniature of the entire work:

- It has a dominant idea, usually expressed in a topic sentence.

- The dominant idea is developed by examples, comparisons, explanations, or arguments to make the meaning of the topic sentence clear.

- There is usually a concluding restatement of the topic idea, a final sentence that parallels the concluding paragraph of an essay.

Capitalization

Definition: Capitalization is the use of capital letters to place special emphasis on particular letters to set them off from lower-case letters.

- Sentences always begin with a capital letter.

- The first letter of a quotation is always capitalized.

- Proper nouns, that is, nouns that name particular persons, places, or things must be capitalized. **Examples:** Appalachian Mountains, Mississippi River, Brooklyn Bridge

- Titles that precede a proper name are capitalized; those that follow a proper name are not. Examples: Chairperson John Smith and John Smith, the chairperson

Punctuation

Definition: Punctuation is the use of periods, commas, semicolons, colons, question marks, exclamation points, dashes, apostrophes, brackets, parentheses, slashes, and quotation marks to convey the pauses and gestures that we use in speech to clarify and emphasize meaning.

- Use a period to end a sentence. **Example:** She went to the beach.

- Use a period after abbreviations. **Examples:** Mr. Ms. U.S. Corp.

- Use a comma to separate independent clauses in a compound sentence. **Example:** Suzanne made a presentation at the conference, and then she spent the remainder of the day touring the city. Restrictive dependent clauses are not required to be set off by commas. **Example:** That *he would survive* is doubtful.

- Use a comma to separate an introductory phrase or clause from the main clause of a sentence. **Example:** After completing the work, the contractor left the site.
- Place a comma after every item in a series. **Example:** The new office is furnished with a desk, a computer, two chairs, and a supply cabinet.

- Two or more adjectives that modify the noun that they precede are separated by commas. **Example:** The cold, windy morning was not a good beginning for their vacation.

- An appositive is a word or group of words that renames or identifies a noun or pronoun that it follows. Nonrestrictive appositives--those that are not essential to the meaning of a sentence--are set off by commas. **Example:** Ken Fowler, the orthopedic surgeon, was appointed Chief of Staff. Restrictive appositives--those that are essential to the meaning of the sentence--are not set off by commas. **Example:** The author Stephen King is known for his frightening stories.

- Commas are used to set off the items in a date. **Example:** Monday, August 17, 2003, he became the head of the office. Commas are not used when only the month and year are given. Example: August 2003

- A semicolon is used to separate elements in a series when some of the elements already contain commas. **Example:** Sally wishes that we attend the first, third, and fifth sessions on Wednesday; the second, fourth, and sixth sessions on Thursday; and the first only on Friday.

- Periods and commas at the end of a quote always go inside quotation marks. **Example:** Georgia said, "I do not wish to receive the award solely for the work I did on that particular project."

- Punctuation marks other than periods or commas should be placed inside the quotation marks only when they apply to the matter quoted. **Example:** As mentioned by our new director, what do you think is the "acceptable method of producing exemplary behavior"?

Spelling

- Distinguish between ie and ei. Remember that it is i before e except after c and, also, when the vowel sound in the word has the long a sound.

Examples:

i before *e*	*e* before *i* after *c*	*e* before *i* when sounded like a long *a*
believe	ceiling	sleigh
relief	deceive	weigh
shield	receive	vein

- Drop the final *e* before adding a suffix that begins with a vowel. Keep the final *e* before adding a suffix that begins with a consonant. Examples:

drive	driving	sure	surely
chime	chiming	entire	entirety
become	becoming	like	likeness
age	aging	force	forceful

Exceptions:
dye   dyeing (to distinguish from *die*   *dying*)

Final e remains to keep the soft *c* or *g* sound before a suffix beginning with *a* or *i*.

change	changeable
notice	noticeable
singe	singeing However, *practice* becomes *practicable* because the soft *c* changes to the hard *k* sound.)

Some words that take *ful* or *ly* drop the final *e*.

true	truly
due	duly
awe	awful

- A word ending in y changes the y to *i* before adding a suffix beginning with *i*. **Examples:**

forty	fortieth
rectify	rectifier
defy	defiance (However, *cry* becomes *crying* not *criing*.)

- The final consonant is doubled before adding a suffix beginning with a vowel only when the following two criteria are met:
  1) a single vowel precedes the consonant, and
  2) the consonant ends a one-syllable word an accented syllable.

  Examples:

pop	popping
drop	dropping
rip	ripping
begin	beginning

- Nouns ending in a sound that can be smoothly united with s form their plurals by adding s. **Examples:**

Singular	*Plural*
cup	cups
pencil	pencils
folder	folders
frame	frames
boat	boats

- Nouns ending in a sound that cannot be smoothly united with *s* form their plurals by adding *es*. **Examples:**

Singular	Plural
fox	foxes
pass	passes
church	churches

- Nouns ending in y preceded by a consonant form their plurals by changing y to *i* and adding es. The exceptions are proper nouns ending in y. They simply add an *s* without dropping the *y*. **Examples:**

Singular	Plural
lady	ladies
fly	flies
ruby	rubies
body	bodies

Exception: There are two Henrys assigned to my project.

- Nouns ending in y preceded by *a, e, o,* or *u* form their plurals by only adding an *s*. **Examples:**

Singular	*Plural*
bay	bays
key	keys
toy	toys
guy	guys

- Plural nouns taken from other languages retain their foreign plural spelling. **Examples:**

Singular	*Plural*
datum	data
thesis	theses
phenomenon	phenomena
alumna (fem.)	alumnae
alumnus (mas.)	alumni

- Some foreign words keep their foreign plural and an anglicized one. Both are correct. **Examples:**

Singular	Plural (foreign)	Plural (anglicized)
focus	foci	focuses
memorandum	memoranda	memorandums
radius	radii	radiuses
index	indices	indexes
appendix	appendices	appendixes

- Use a hyphen to join two or more words serving as a single adjective before a noun. But, never hyphenate the same adjectives when following the verb. Example:

a well-equipped van	no hyphen for ... The van was well equipped.
a garish-red cloak	no hyphen for ... The cloak was garish red.
the well-read scholar	no hyphen for ... The scholar was well read.

The exception is when the first word is an adverb ending in *ly*. In that case, omit the hyphen.

Examples:

    a quick-moving river   or   a quickly moving river
    a swift-running competitor   or   a swiftly running competitor

- Hyphens should be used to avoid an ambiguous or awkward union of letters. **Examples:**

    re-enter, pre-election, pre-eminence, re-address
    Exceptions: cooperation, coeducational, zoology

- Hyphens are used to form all compound numbers between twenty-one and ninety-nine, and to separate the numerator from the denominator when fractions are written.
Examples:

    thirty-three, sixty-five, one-third, two-fourths

- Always use a hyphen with the prefixes *ex, self,* and *all* and the suffix *elect.* **Examples:**
    all-American, self-composed, ex-wife, president-elect
    Note: Do not capitalize *ex* or *elect* even when used in titles. **Examples:**
    ex-Governor Riley, Mayor-elect Johnson

ENGLISH EXPRESSION
CHOICE OF EXPRESSION
COMMENTARY

One special form of the English Expression multiple-choice question in current use requires the candidate to select from among five (5) versions of a particular part of a sentence (or of an entire sentence), the one version that expresses the idea of the sentence most clearly, effectively, and accurately. Thus, the candidate is required not only to recognize errors, but also to choose the best way of phrasing a particular part of the sentence.

This is a test of choice of expression, which assays the candidate's ability to express himself correctly and effectively, including his sensitivity to the subtleties and nuances of the language.

SAMPLE QUESTIONS

DIRECTIONS: In each of the following sentences, some part of the sentence or the entire sentence is underlined. The underlined part presents a problem in the appropriate use of language. Beneath each sentence you will find five ways of writing the underlined part. The first of these indicates no change (that is, it repeats the original), but the other four are all different. If you think the original sentence is better than any of the suggested changes, you should choose answer A; otherwise you should mark one of the other choices. Select the BEST answer and print the letter in the space at the right.

This is a test of correctness and effectiveness of expression. In choosing answers, follow the requirements of standard written English; that is, pay attention to acceptable usage in grammar, diction (choice of words), sentence construction, and punctuation. Choose the answer that produces the most effective sentence—clear and exact, without awkwardness or ambiguity. Do not make a choice that changes the meaning of the original sentence.

SAMPLE QUESTION 1

Although these states now trade actively with the West, and although they are willing to exchange technological information, their arts and thoughts and social structure <u>remains substantially similar to what it has always been</u>.
  A. remains substantially similar to what it has always been
  B. remain substantially unchanged
  C. remains substantially unchanged
  D. remain substantially similar to what they have always been
  E. remain substantially without being changed

The purpose of questions of this type is to determine the candidate's ability to select the clearest and most effective means of expressing what the statement attempts to say. In this example, the phrasing in the statement, which is repeated in A, presents a problem of agreement between a subject and its verb (<u>their arts and thought and social structure</u> and <u>remains</u>), a problem of agreement between a pronoun and its antecedent (<u>their arts and thought and social structure</u> and <u>it</u>), an a problem of precise and concise phrasing (<u>remains</u>

substantially similar to what it has always been for remains substantially unchanged). Each of the four remaining choices in some way corrects one or more of the faults in the sentence, but only one deals with all three problems satisfactorily. Although C presents a more careful and concise wording of the phrasing of the statement and, in the process, eliminates the problem of agreement between pronoun and antecedent, it fails to correct the problem of agreement between the subject and its verb. In D, the subject agrees with its verb and the pronoun agrees with its antecedent, but the phrasing is not so accurate as it should be. The same difficulty persists in E. Only in B are all the problems presented corrected satisfactory. The question is not difficult.

SAMPLE QUESTION 2

Her latest novel is the largest in scope, the most accomplished in technique, and it is more significant in theme than anything she has written.
- A. it is more significant in theme than anything
- B. It is most significant in theme of anything
- C. more significant in theme than anything
- D. the most significant in theme than anything
- E. the most significant in theme of anything

This question is of greater difficulty than the preceding one. The problem posed in the sentence and repeated in A is essentially one of parallelism; Does the underlined portion of the sentence follow the pattern established by the first two elements of the series (the largest...the most accomplished)? It does not, for it introduces a pronoun and verb (it is) that the second term of the series indicates should be omitted and a degree of comparison (more significant) that is not in keeping with the superlatives used earlier in the sentence. B uses the superlative degree of significant but retains the unnecessary it is; C removes the it is, but retains the faulty comparative form of the adjective. D corrects both errors in parallelism, but introduces an error in idiom (the most...than). Only E corrects all the problems without introducing another fault.

SAMPLE QUESTION 3

Desiring to insure the continuity of their knowledge, magical lore is transmitted by the chiefs to their descendants.
- A. magical lore is transmitted by the chiefs
- B. transmission of magical lore is made by the chiefs
- C. the chiefs' magical lore is transmitted
- D. the chiefs transmit magical lore
- E. the chiefs make transmission of magical lore

The CORRECT answer is D.

SAMPLE QUESTION 4

As Malcolm walks quickly and confident into the purser's office, the rest of the crew wondered whether he would be charged with the theft.
- A. As Malcolm walks quickly and confident
- B. As Malcolm was walking quick and confident
- C. As Malcom walked quickly and confident

D. As Malcolm walked quickly and confidently
E. As Malcolm walks quickly and confidently
The CORRECT answer is D.

SAMPLE QUESTION 5

The chairman, <u>granted the power to assign any duties to whoever he</u> wished, was still unable to prevent bickering.
  A. granted the power to assign any duties to whoever he wished
  B. granting the power to assign any duties to whoever he wished
  C. being granted the power to assign any duties to whoever he wished
  D. having been granted the power to assign any duties to whosoever he wished
  E. granted the power to assign any duties to whomever he wished
The CORRECT answer is E.

SAMPLE QUESTION 6

Certainly, well-seasoned products are more expensive, <u>but those kinds prove chaper</u> in the end.
  A. but those kinds prove cheaper
  B. but these kinds prove cheaper
  C. but that kind proves cheaper
  D. but those kind prove cheaper
  E. but this kind proves cheaper
The CORRECT answer is A.

SAMPLE QUESTION 7

"We shall not," he shouted, "whatever the <u>difficulties." "lose faith in the success of our plan!!</u>"
  A. difficulties," "lose faith in the success of our plan!"
  B. difficulties, "lose faith in the success of our plan"!
  C. "difficulties, lose faith in the success of our plan!"
  D. difficulties, lose faith in the success of our plan"!
  E. difficulties, lose faith in the success of our plan!"

SAMPLE QUESTION 8

<u>Climb up the tree</u>, the lush foliage obscured the chattering monkeys.
  A. Climbing up the tree
  B. Having climbed up the tree
  C. Clambering up the tree
  D. After we had climbed up the tree
  E. As we climbed up the tree
The CORRECT answer is E.

EXAMINATION SECTION

TEST 1

DIRECTIONS: See DIRECTIONS for Sample Questions on Page 1. *PRINT THE LETTER OF THE CORRECT ANSWER IN THE SPACE AT THE RIGHT.*

1. At the opening of the story, Charles Gilbert <u>has just come</u> to make his home with his two unmarried aunts.
   A. No change
   B. hadn't hardly come
   C. has just came
   D. had just come
   E. has hardly came

   1.____

2. The sisters, who are no longer young, <u>are use to living</u> quiet lives.
   A. No change
   B. are used to live
   C. are use'd to living
   D. are used to living
   E. are use to live

   2.____

3. They <u>willingly except</u> the child.
   A. No change
   B. willingly eccepted
   C. willingly accepted
   D. willingly acepted
   E. willingly accept

   3.____

4. As the months pass, Charles' presence <u>affects many changes</u> in their household.
   A. No change
   B. affect many changes
   C. effects many changes
   D. effect many changes
   E. affected many changes

   4.____

5. These changes <u>is not all together</u> to their liking.
   A. No change
   B. is not altogether
   C. are not all together
   D. are not altogether
   E. is not alltogether

   5.____

6. In fact, they have some difficulty in adapting <u>theirselves</u> to these changes
   A. No change
   B. in adopting theirselves
   C. in adopting themselves
   D. in adapting theirselves
   E. in adapting themselves

   6.____

7. That is the man <u>whom I believe</u> was the driver of the car.
   A. No change
   B. who I believed
   C. whom I believed
   D. who to believe
   E. who I believe

   7.____

8. John's climb to fame was more rapid <u>than his brother's</u>.
   A. No change
   B. than his brother
   C. than that of his brother's
   D. than for his brother
   E. than the brother

   8.____

147

9. We knew that he had formerly swam on an Olympic team.
   A. No change
   B. has formerly swum
   C. did formerly swum
   D. had formerly swum
   E. has formerly swam

10. Not one of us loyal supporters ever get a pass to a game.
    A. No change
    B. ever did got a pass
    C. ever has get a pass
    D. ever had get a pass
    E. ever gets a pass

11. He was complemented on having done a fine job.
    A. No change
    B. was compliminted
    C. was compleminted
    D. was complimented
    E. did get complimented

12. This play is different from the one we had seen last night.
    A. No change
    B. have seen
    C. had saw
    D. have saw
    E. saw

13. A row of trees was planted in front of the house.
    A. No change
    B. was to be planted
    C. were planted
    D. were to be planted
    E. are planted

14. The house looked its age in spite of our attempts to beautify it.
    A. No change
    B. looks its age
    C. looked its' age
    D. looked it's age
    E. looked it age

15. I do not know what to council in this case.
    A. No change
    B. where to council
    C. when to councel
    D. what to counsel
    E. what to counsil

16. She is more capable than any other girl in the office.
    A. No change
    B. than any girl
    C. than any other girls
    D. than other girl
    E. than other girls

17. At the picnic the young children behaved very good.
    A. No change
    B. behave very good
    C. behaved better
    D. behave very well
    E. behaved very well

18. I resolved to go irregardless of the consequences.
    A. No change
    B. to depart irregardless of
    C. to go regarding of
    D. to go regardingly of
    E. to go regardless of

19. The new movie has a number of actors which have been famous on Broadway. 19.____
    A. No change
    B. which had been famous
    C. who had been famous
    D. that are famous
    E. who have been famous

20. I am certain that these books are not our's. 20.____
    A. No change
    B. have not been ours'
    C. have not been our's
    D. are not ours
    E. are not ours'

21. Each of your papers is filed for future reference. 21.____
    A. No change
    B. Each of your papers are filed
    C. Each of your papers have been filed
    D. Each of your papers are to be filed
    E. Each of your paper is filed

22. I wish that he would take his work more serious. 22.____
    A. No change
    B. he took his work more serious
    C. he will take his work more serious
    D. he shall take his work more seriously
    E. he would take his work more seriously

23. After the treasurer report had been read, the chairman called for the reports of the committees. 23.____
    A. No change
    B. After the treasure's report had been read
    C. After the treasurers' report had been read
    D. After the treasurerer's report had been read
    E. After the treasurer's report had been read

24. Last night the stranger lead us down the mountain. 24.____
    A. No change
    B. leaded us down the mountain
    C. let us down the mountain
    D. led us down the mountain
    E. had led us down the mountain

25. It would not be safe for either you or I to travel in Viet Nam. 25.____
    A. No change
    B. for either you or me
    C. for either I or you
    D. for either of you or I
    E. for either of I or you

KEY (CORRECT ANSWERS)

1.	A	11.	D
2.	D	12.	E
3.	E	13.	A
4.	C	14.	A
5.	D	15.	D
6.	E	16.	A
7.	E	17.	E
8.	A	18.	E
9.	D	19.	E
10.	E	20.	D

21.	A
22.	E
23.	E
24.	D
25.	B

TEST 2

DIRECTIONS: See DIRECTIONS for Sample Questions on Page 1. *PRINT THE LETTER OF THE CORRECT ANSWER IN THE SPACE AT THE RIGHT.*

1. Both the body and the mind <u>needs exercise</u>.
   - A. No change
   - B. have needs of exercise
   - C. is needful of exercise
   - D. needed exercise
   - E. need exercise

   1.____

2. <u>It's paw injured</u>, the animal limped down the road.
   - A. No change
   - B. It's paw injured
   - C. Its paw injured
   - D. Its' paw injured
   - E. Its paw injure

   2.____

3. The butter <u>tastes rancidly</u>.
   - A. No change
   - B. tastes rancid
   - C. tasted rancidly
   - D. taste rancidly
   - E. taste rancid

   3.____

4. <u>Who do you think</u> has sent me a letter?
   - A. No change
   - B. Whom do you think
   - C. Whome do you think
   - D. Who did you think
   - E. Whom can you think

   4.____

5. If more nations <u>would have fought</u> against tyranny, the course of history would have been different.
   - A. No change
   - B. would fight
   - C. could have fought
   - D. fought
   - E. had fought

   5.____

6. Radio and television programs, along with other media of communication, <u>helps us to appreciate the arts and to keep informed</u>.
   - A. No change
   - B. helps us to appreciate the arts and to be informed
   - C. helps us to be appreciative of the arts and to keep informed
   - D. helps us to be appreciative of the arts and to be informed
   - E. help us to appreciate the arts and to keep informed

   6.____

7. Music, <u>for example most always</u> has listening and viewing audiences numbering in the hundreds of thousands.
   - A. No change
   - B. for example, most always
   - C. for example, almost always
   - D. for example nearly always
   - E. for example, near always

   7.____

8. When operas are performed on radio or television, <u>they effect the listener</u>.
   - A. No change
   - B. they inflict the listener
   - C. these effect the listeners
   - D. they affects the listeners
   - E. they affect the listener

   8.____

9. After hearing then the listener wants to buy recordings of the music. 9.____
   A. No change
   B. After hearing them, the listener wants
   C. After hearing them, the listener want
   D. By hearing them the listener wants
   E. By hearing them, the listener wants

10. To we Americans the daily news program has become important. 10.____
    A. No change
    B. To we the Americans
    C. To us Americans
    D. To us the Americans
    E. To we and us Americans

11. This has resulted from it's coverage of a days' events. 11.____
    A. No change
    B. from its coverage of a days' events
    C. from it's coverage of a day's events
    D. from its' coverage of a day's events
    E. from its coverage of a day's events

12. In schools, teachers advice their students to listen to or to view certain programs. 12.____
    A. No change
    B. teachers advise there students
    C. teachers advise their students
    D. the teacher advises their students
    E. teachers advise his students

13. In these ways we are preceding toward the goal of an educated and an informed public. 13.____
    A. No change
    B. we are preeceding toward the goal
    C. we are proceeding toward the goal
    D. we are preceding toward the goal
    E. we are proceeding toward the goal

14. The cost of living is raising again. 14.____
    A. No change
    B. are raising again
    C. is rising again
    D. are rising again
    E. is risen again

15. We did not realize that the boys' father had forbidden them to keep there puppy. 15.____
    A. No change
    B. had forbade them to keep there puppy
    C. had forbade them to keep their puppy
    D. has forbidden them to keep their puppy
    E. had forbidden them to keep their puppy

16. Her willingness to help others' was her outstanding characteristic. 16.____
    A. No change
    B. Her willingness to help other's,
    C. Her willingness to help others's
    D. Her willingness to help others
    E. Her willingness to help each other

17. Because he did not have an invitation, the girls objected to him going. 17.____
    A. No change
    B. the girls object to him going
    C. the girls objected to him's going
    D. the girls objected to his going
    E. the girls object to his going

18. Weekly dances have become a popular accepted feature of the summer schedule. 18.____
    A. No change
    B. have become a popular accepted feature
    C. have become a popular excepted feature
    D. have become a popularly excepted feature
    E. have become a popularly accepted feature

19. I couldn't hardly believe that he would desert our party. 19.____
    A. No change
    B. would hardly believe
    C. didn't hardly believe
    D. should hardly believe
    E. could hardly believe

20. I found the place in the book more readily than she. 20.____
    A. No change
    B. more readily than her
    C. more ready than she
    D. more quickly than her
    E. more ready than her

21. A good example of American outdoor activities are sports. 21.____
    A. No change
    B. is sports
    C. are sport
    D. are sports events
    E. are to be found in sports

22. My point of view is much different from your's. 22.____
    A. No change
    B. much different from your's
    C. much different than yours
    D. much different from yours
    E. much different than yours'

23. The cook was suppose to use two spoonfuls of dressing for each serving. 23.____
    A. No change
    B. was supposed to use two spoonful
    C. was suppose to use two spoonsful
    D. was supposed to use two spoonsfuls
    E. was supposed to use two spoonfuls

4 (#2)

24. If anyone has any doubt about the values of the tour, <u>refer him to me</u>.　　24.____
  A. No change　　　　　　　　B. refer him to I
  C. refer me to he　　　　　　　D. refer them to me
  E. refer he to I

25. We expect that the affects of <u>the trip will be neneficial</u>.　　25.____
  A. No change
  B. the effects of the trip will be beneficial
  C. the effects of the trip should be beneficial
  D. the affects of the trip would be beneficial
  E. the effects of the trip will be benificial

KEY (CORRECT ANSWERS)

1.	E	11.	E
2.	C	12.	C
3.	B	13.	E
4.	A	14.	C
5.	E	15.	E
6.	E	16.	D
7.	C	17.	D
8.	E	18.	E
9.	B	19.	E
10.	C	20.	A

21.	B
22.	D
23.	E
24.	A
25.	B

TEST 3

DIRECTIONS: See DIRECTIONS for Sample Questions on Page 1. *PRINT THE LETTER OF THE CORRECT ANSWER IN THE SPACE AT THE RIGHT.*

1. That, my friend is not the proper attitude.
   A. No change
   B. That my friend
   C. That my fried,
   D. That—my friend
   E. That, my friend,

   1.____

2. The girl refused to admit that the note was her's.
   A. No change
   B. that the note were her's
   C. that the note was hers'
   D. that the note was hers
   E. that the note might be hers

   2.____

3. There were fewer candidates that we had been lead to expect
   A. No change
   B. was fewer candidates than we had been lead
   C. were fewer candidates than we had been lead
   D. was fewer candidates than we had been led
   E. were fewer candidates than we had been led

   3.____

4. When I first saw the car, its steering wheel was broke.
   A. No change
   B. its' steering wheel was broken
   C. it's steering wheel had been broken
   D. its steering wheel were broken
   E. its steering wheel was broken

   4.____

5. I find that the essential spirit for we beginners is missing.
   A. No change
   B. we who begin are missing
   C. us beginners are missing
   D. us beginners is missing
   E. we beginners are missing

   5.____

6. I believe that you had ought to study harder.
   A. No change
   B. you should have ought
   C. you had better
   D. you ought to have
   E. you ought

   6.____

7. This is Tom, whom I am sure, will be glad to help you.
   A. No change
   B. Tom whom, I am sure,
   C. Tom, whom I am sure
   D. Tom who I am sure,
   E. Tom, who, I am sure,

   7.____

8. His father or his mother has read to him every night since he was very small.
   A. No change
   B. did read to him
   C. have been reading to him
   D. had read to him
   E. have read to him

   8.____

155

9. He become an authority
   A. No change
   B. becomed an authority
   C. become the authority
   D. became an authority
   E. becamed an authority

10. I know of no other reason in the club who is more kind-hearted than her.
    A. No change
    B. who are more kind-hearted than they
    C. who are more kind-hearted than them
    D. whom are more kind-hearted than she
    E. who is more kind-hearted than she

11. After Bill had ran the mile, he was breathless.
    A. No change
    B. had runned the mile
    C. has ran the mile
    D. had ranned the mile
    E. had run the mile

12. Wilson has scarcely no equal as a pitcher.
    A. No change
    B. has scarcely an equal
    C. has hardly no equal
    D. had scarcely no equal
    E. has scarcely any equals

13. It was the worse storm that the inhabitants of the island could remember.
    A. No change
    B. were the worse storm
    C. was the worst storm
    D. was the worsest storm
    E. was the most worse storm

14. If only we had began before it was too late.
    A. No change
    B. we had began
    C. we would have begun
    D. we had begun
    E. we had beginned

15. Lets evaluate our year's work.
    A. No change
    B. Let us' evaluate
    C. Lets' evaluate
    D. Lets' us evaluate
    E. Let's evaluate

16. This is an organization with which I wouldn't want to be associated with.
    A. No change
    B. with whom I wouldn't want to be associated with
    C. that I wouldn't want to be associated
    D. with which I would want not to be associated with
    E. with which I wouldn't want to be associated

17. The enemy fled in many directions, leaving there weapons on the field.
    A. No change
    B. leaving its weapons
    C. letting their weapons
    D. leaving alone there weapons
    E. leaving their weapons

18. I hoped that John could effect a compromise between the approved forces.   18.____
    A. No change
    B. could accept a compromise between
    C. could except a compromise between
    D. would have effected a compromise among
    E. could effect a compromise among

19. I was surprised to learn that he has not always spoke English fluently.   19.____
    A. No change
    B. that he had not always spoke English
    C. that he did not always speak English
    D. that he has not always spoken English
    E. that he could not always speak English

20. The lawyer promised to notify my father and I of his plans for a new trial.   20.____
    A. No change   B. to notify I and my father
    C. to notify me and our father D. to notify my father and me
    E. to notify mine father and me

21. The most important feature of the series of tennis lessons were the large   21.____
    amount of strokes taught.
    A. No change   B. were the large number
    C. was the large amount   D. was the largeness of the amount
    E. was the large number

22. That the prize proved to be beyond her reach did not surprise him.   22.____
    A. No change
    B. has not surprised him
    C. had not ought to have surprised him
    D. should not surprise him
    E. would not have surprised him

23. I am not all together in agreement with the author's point of view.   23.____
    A. No change   B. all together of agreement
    C. all together for agreement   D. altogether with agreement
    E. altogether in agreement

24. Windstorms have recently established a record which meteorologists hope   24.____
    will not be equal for many years to come.
    A. No change   B. will be equal
    C. will not be equalized   D. will be equaled
    E. will not be equaled

25. A large number of Shakespeare's soliloquies must be considered <u>as representing thought</u>, not speech. 25.____
    A. No change
    B. as representative of speech, not thought
    C. as represented by thought, not speech
    D. as indicating thought, not speech
    E. as representative of thought, more than speech

KEY (CORRECT ANSWERS)

1.	E		11.	E
2.	D		12.	B
3.	E		13.	C
4.	E		14.	D
5.	D		15.	E
6.	E		16.	E
7.	E		17.	E
8.	A		18.	A
9.	D		19.	D
10.	E		20.	D

21.	E
22.	A
23.	E
24.	E
25.	A

TEST 4

DIRECTIONS: See DIRECTIONS for Sample Questions on Page 1. *PRINT THE LETTER OF THE CORRECT ANSWER IN THE SPACE AT THE RIGHT.*

1. A sight to inspire fear <u>are wild animals on the lose</u>.
   A. No change
   B. are wild animals on the loose
   C. is wild animals on the loose
   D. is wild animals on the lose
   E. are wild animals loose

   1.____

2. For many years, the settlers <u>had been seeking to workship as they please</u>.
   A. No change
   B. had seeked to workship as they pleased
   C. sought to workship as they please
   D. sought to have worshiped as they pleased
   E. had been seeking to worship as they pleased

   2.____

3. The girls stated that the dresses were <u>their's</u>.
   A. No change
   B. there's
   C. theirs
   D. theirs'
   E. there own

   3.____

4. <u>Please fellows</u> don't drop the ball.
   A. No change
   B. Please, fellows
   C. Please fellows;
   D. Please, fellows,
   E. Please! fellows

   4.____

5. Your sweater <u>has laid</u> on the floor for a week.
   A. No change
   B. has been laying
   C. has been lying
   D. laid
   E. has been lain

   5.____

6. I wonder whether <u>you're sure that scheme of yours'</u> will work.
   A. No change
   B. your sure that scheme of your's
   C. you're sure that scheme of yours
   D. your sure that scheme of yours
   E. you're sure that your scheme's

   6.____

7. Please let <u>her and me</u> do it.
   A. No change
   B. she and I
   C. she and me
   D. her and I
   E. her and him

   7.____

8. I expected him to be angry <u>and to scold</u> her.
   A. No change
   B. and that he would scold
   C. and that he might scold
   D. and that he should scold
   E. , scolding

   8.____

159

9. Knowing little about algebra, it was difficult to solve the equation.
   A. No change
   B. the equation was difficult to solve
   C. the solution to the equation was difficult to find
   D. I found it difficult to solve the equation
   E. it being difficult to solve the equation

10. He worked more diligent now that he had become vice president of the company.
    A. No change
    B. works more diligent
    C. works more diligently
    D. began to work more diligent
    E. worked more diligently

11. Flinging himself at the barricade he pounded on it furiously.
    A. No change
    B. Flinging himself at the barricade: he
    C. Flinging himself at the barricade—he
    D. Flinging himself at the barricade; he
    E. Flinging himself at the barricade, he

12. When he begun to give us advise, we stopped listening.
    A. No change
    B. began to give us advise
    C. begun to give us advice
    D. began to give us advice
    E. begin to give us advice

13. John was only one of the boys whom as you know was not eligible.
    A. No change
    B. who as you know were
    C. whom as you know were
    D. who as you know was
    E. who as you know is

14. Why was Jane and he permitted to go?
    A. No change
    B. was Jane and him
    C. were Jane and he
    D. were Jane and him
    E. weren't Jane and he

15. Take courage Tom: we all make mistakes.
    A. No change
    B. Take courage Tom—we
    C. Take courage, Tom; we
    D. Take courage, Tom we
    E. Take courage! Tom: we

16. Henderson, the president of the class and who is also captain of the team, will lead the rally.
    A. No change
    B. since he is captain of the team
    C. captain of the team
    D. also being captain of the team
    E. who be also captain of the team

17. Our car has always run good on that kind of gasoline.
    A. No change
    B. run well
    C. ran good
    D. ran well
    E. done good

18. There was a serious difference of opinion among her and I. 18.____
    A. No change   B. among she and I
    C. between her and I D. between her and me
    E. among her and me

19. "This is most unusual," said Helen, "the mailman has never been this late before." 19.____
    A. No change   B. Helen, "The
    C. Helen—"The   D. Helen; "The
    E. Helen." The

20. The three main characters in the story are Johnny Hobart a teenager, his mother a widow, and the local druggist. 20.____
    A. No change
    B. teenager; his mother, a widow; and
    C. teenager; his mother a widow; and
    D. teenager, his mother, a widow and
    E. teenager, his mother, a widow; and

21. How much has food costs raised during the past year? 21.____
    A. No change   B. have food costs rose
    C. have food costs risen D. has food costs risen
    E. have food costs been raised

22. "Will you come too" she pleaded? 22.____
    A. No change   B. too,?"she pleaded
    C. too?" she pleaded   D. too," she pleaded?
    E. too, she pleaded?"

23. If he would have drank more milk, his health would have been better. 23.____
    A. No change   B. would drink
    C. had drank   D. had he drunk
    E. had drunk

24. Jack had no sooner laid down and fallen asleep when the alarm sounded. 24.____
    A. No change
    B. no sooner lain down and fallen asleep than
    C. no sooner lay down and fell asleep when
    D. no sooner laid down and fell asleep than
    E. no sooner lain down than he fell asleep when

25. Jackson is one of the few Sophomores, who has ever made the varsity team. 25.____
    A. No change
    B. one of the few Sophomores, who have
    C. one of the few sophomores, who has
    D. one of the few sophomores who have
    E. one of the few sophomores who has

KEY (CORRECT ANSWERS)

1. C
2. E
3. C
4. D
5. C

6. C
7. A
8. A
9. D
10. E

11. E
12. D
13. B
14. C
15. C

16. C
17. B
18. D
19. E
20. B

21. C
22. C
23. E
24. B
25. D

TEST 5

DIRECTIONS: See DIRECTIONS for Sample Questions on Page 1. *PRINT THE LETTER OF THE CORRECT ANSWER IN THE SPACE AT THE RIGHT.*

1. The lieutenant had ridden almost a kilometer when the scattering shells <u>begin landing</u> uncomfortably close.
   A. No change
   B. beginning to land
   C. began to land
   D. having begun to land
   E. begin to land

   1.____

2. <u>Having studied eight weeks</u>, he now feels sufficiently prepared for the examination.
   A. No change
   B. For eight weeks he studies so
   C. Due to eight weeks of study
   D. After eight weeks of studying
   E. Since he's been spending the last eight weeks in study

   2.____

3. <u>Coming from the Greek, and the word "democracy" means government by the people</u>.
   A. No change
   B. "Democracy," the word which comes from the Greek, means government by the people.
   C. Meaning government by the people, the word "democracy" comes from the Greek.
   D. Its meaning being government by the people in Greek, the word is "democracy."
   E. The word "democracy" comes from the Greek and means government by the people.

   3.____

4. Moslem universities were one of the chief agencies <u>in the development</u> and spreading Arabic civilization.
   A. No change
   B. in the development of
   C. to develop
   D. in developing
   E. for the developing of

   4.____

5. The water of Bering Strait <u>were closing</u> to navigation by ice early in the fall.
   A. No change
   B. has closed
   C. have closed
   D. had been closed
   E. closed

   5.____

6. The man, <u>since he grew up</u> on the block, felt sentimental when returning to it.
   A. No change
   B. having grown up
   C. growing up
   D. since he had grown up
   E. whose growth had been

   6.____

163

7. <u>Jack and Jill watched the canoe to take their parents out of sight round the bend of the creek</u>.
   A. No change
   B. The canoe, taking their parents out of sight, rounds the bend as Jack and Jill watch.
   C. Jack and Jill watched the canoe round the bend of the creek, taking their parents out of sight,
   D. The canoe rounded the bend of the creek as it took their parents out of sight, Jack and Jill watching.
   E. Jack and Jill watching, the canoe is rounding the bend of the creek to take their parents out of sight.

8. Chaucer's best-known work is THE CANTERBURY TALES, a collection of stories <u>which he tells</u> with a group of pilgrims as they travel to the town of Canterbury.
   A. No change
   B. which he tells through
   C. who tell
   D. told by
   E. told through

9. The Estates-General, the old feudal assembly of France, <u>had not met</u> for one hundred and seventy-five years when it convened in 1789.
   A. No change
   B. has not met
   C. has not been meeting
   D. had no meeting
   E. has no meeting

10. Just forty years ago, <u>there had been</u> fewer than one hundred symphony orchestras in the United States.
    A. No change
    B. there had
    C. there were
    D. there was
    E. there existed

11. Mrs. Smith complained that her son's temper tantrums <u>aggravated her</u> and caused her to have a headache.
    A. No change
    B. gave her aggravation
    C. were aggravating to her
    D. aggravated her condition
    E. instigated

12. A girl <u>like I</u> would never be seen in a place like that.
    A. No change   B. as I   C. as me
    D. like I am   E. like me

13. <u>Between you and me,</u> my opinion is that this room is certainly nicer than the first one we saw.
    A. No change
    B. between you and I
    C. among you and me
    D. betwixt you and I
    E. between we

14. It is important to know for <u>what kind of a person you are working</u>. 14._____
    A. No change
    B. what kind of a person for whom you are working
    C. what kind of person you are working
    D. what kind of person you are working for
    E. what kind of a person you are working for

15. I had <u>all ready</u> finished the book before you came in. 15._____
    A. No change   B. already   C. previously
    D. allready   E. all

16. <u>Ask not for who the bell tolls, it tolls for thee.</u> 16._____
    A. No change
    B. Ask not for whom the bell tolls, it tolls for thee.
    C. Ask not whom the bell tolls for; it tolls for thee.
    D. Ask not for whom the bell tolls; it tolls for thee.
    E. As not who the bell tolls for: It tolls for thee.

17. It is a far better thing I do, than <u>ever I did</u> before. 17._____
    A. No change   B. never I did
    C. I have ever did   D. I have ever been done
    E. ever have I done

18. <u>Ending a sentence with a preposition is something up with which I will not put.</u> 18._____
    A. No change
    B. Ending a sentence with a preposition is something with which I will not put up.
    C. To end a sentence with a preposition is that which I will not put up with.
    D. Ending a sentence with a preposition is something of which I will not put up.
    E. Something I will not put up with is ending a sentence with a preposition.

19. Everyone <u>took off their hats and stand up</u> to sing the national anthem. 19._____
    A. No change
    B. took off their hats and stood up
    C. take off their hats and stand up
    D. took off his hat and stood up
    E. have taken off their hats and standing up

20. <u>She promised me that if she had the opportunity she would have came irregardless of the weather.</u> 20._____
    A. No change
    B. She promised me that if she had the opportunity she would have come regardless of the weather.
    C. She assured me that had she had the opportunity he would have come regardless of the weather.
    D. She assured me that if she would have had the opportunity she would have come regardless of the weather.

4 (#5)

    E. She promised me that if she had had the opportunity she would have came irregardless of the weather.

21. The man decided it would be advisable to marry a girl <u>somewhat younger than him</u>.
    A. No change
    B. somehow younger than him
    C. some younger than him
    D. somewhat younger from him
    E. somewhat younger than he

21.____

22. Sitting near the campfire, the old man told <u>John and I about many exciting adventures he had had</u>.
    A. No change
    B. John and me about many exciting adventures he had,
    C. John and I about much exciting adventure which he'd had
    D. John and me about many exciting adventures he had had
    E. John and me about many exciting adventures he has had.

22.____

23. <u>If you had stood at home and done your homework</u>, you would not have failed the course.
    A. No change
    B. If you had stood at home and done you're homework,
    C. If you had staid at home and done your homework,
    D. Had you stayed at home and done your homework,
    E. Had you stood at home and done your homework,

23.____

24. The children didn't, as a rule, <u>do anything beyond</u> what they were told to do.
    A. No change
    B. do hardly anything beyond
    C. do anything except
    D. do hardly anything except for
    E. do nothing beyond

24.____

25. <u>Either the girls or him is</u> right.
    A. No change
    B Either the girls or he is
    C. Either the girls or him are
    D. Either the girls or he are
    E. Either the girls nor he is

25.____

KEY (CORRECT ANSWERS)

1.	C	11.	D
2.	A	12.	E
3.	E	13.	A
4.	D	14.	C
5.	D	15.	B
6.	B	16.	D
7.	C	17.	E
8.	D	18.	E
9.	A	19.	D
10.	C	20.	C

21. E
22. D
23. D
24. A
25. B

WRITTEN ENGLISH EXPRESSION
EXAMINATION SECTION
TEST 1

DIRECTIONS: In each of the sentences below, four portions are underlined and lettered. Read each sentence and decide whether any of the UNDERLINED parts contains an error in spelling, punctuation, or capitalization, or employs grammatical usage which would be inappropriate for carefully written English. If so, note the letter printed under the unacceptable form and indicate this choice in the space at the right. If all four of the underlined portions are acceptable as they stand, select the answer E. (No sentence contains more than ONE unacceptable form.)

1. The revised <u>procedure</u> was <u>quite</u> different <u>than</u> the one which <u>was</u> employed up
     A   B   C   D
to that time. <u>No error</u>
      E

1.____

2. <u>Blinded</u> by the storm that <u>surrounded</u> him, his plane <u>kept going</u> in <u>circles</u>.
 A   B   C   D
<u>No error</u>
E

2.____

3. They <u>should</u> give the book to <u>whoever</u> <u>they</u> think deserves <u>it</u>. <u>No error</u>
    A   B C   D E

3.____

4. The <u>government</u> will not consent to your <u>firm</u> <u>sending</u> that package as
   A   B C
<u>second class</u> matter. <u>No error</u>
  D   E

4.____

5. She <u>would have</u> avoided all the trouble <u>that</u> followed if she <u>would have</u> waited
   A   B   C
ten minutes <u>longer</u>. <u>No error</u>
    D   E

5.____

6. <u>His</u> poetry, <u>when</u> it was carefully examined, showed <u>characteristics</u> not unlike
 A   B   C
<u>Wordsworth</u>. <u>No error</u>
  D   E

6.____

7. <u>In my opinion</u>, based upon long years of research, <u>I think</u> the plan offered by
   A   B
my opponent is <u>unsound</u>, because it is not <u>founded</u> on true facts. <u>No error</u>
      C   D   E

7.____

8. The soldiers of Washington's army at Valley Forge were men ragged in
                          A   B
   appearance but who were noble in character. No error
        C   D   E
   8.____

9. Rabbits have a distrust of man due to the fact that they are so often shot.
              A   B   C   D
   No error
      E
   9.____

10. This is the man who I believe is best qualified for the position. No error
     A   B   C   D   E
   10.____

11. Her voice was not only good, but she also very clearly enunciated.
                    A   B   C   D
    No error
       E
   11.____

12. Today he is wearing a different suit than the one he wore yesterday. No error
     A   B   C   D   E
   12.____

13. Our work is to improve the club; if anybody must resign, let it not be you or I.
              A   B   C   D
    No error
       E
   13.____

14. There was so much talking in back of me as I could not enjoy the music.
                                 A   B   C   D
    No error
       E
   14.____

15. Being that he is that kind of boy, he cannot be blamed for the mistake.
        A   B   C   D
    No error
       E
   15.____

16. The king, having read the speech, he and the queen departed. No error
              A   B   C   D   E
   16.____

17. I am so tired I can't scarcely stand. No error
      A B   C   D   E
   17.____

18. We are mailing bills to our customers in Canada, and, being eager to
              A   B   C
    clear our books before the new season opens, it is to be hoped they will
                                                      D
    send their remittances promptly. No error
                                        E
   18.____

19. I reluctantly acquiesced to the proposal. No error   19.____
    A   B   C   D   E

20. It had lain out in the rain all night. No error   20.____
    A   B   C   D   E

21. If he would have gone there, he would have seen a marvelous sight.   21.____
          A   B   C   D
    No error
       E

22. The climate of Asia Minor is somewhat like Utah. No error   22.____
                 A   B   C   D   E

23. If everybody did unto others as they would wish others to do unto them, this   23.____
          A   B   C   D
    world would be a paradise. No error
                                    E

24. This was the jockey whom I saw was most likely to win the race. No error   24.____
        A   B   C   D   E

25. The only food the general demanded was potatoes. No error   25.____
         A   B   C   D   E

KEY (CORRECT ANSWERS)

1.	C	11.	C
2.	A	12.	C
3.	B	13.	D
4.	B	14.	B
5.	C	15.	A
6.	D	16.	A
7.	B	17.	C
8.	D	18.	C
9.	B	19.	E
10.	E	20.	E

21. A
22. D
23. D
24. B
25. E

TEST 2

DIRECTIONS: In each of the sentences below, four portions are underlined and lettered. Read each sentence and decide whether any of the UNDERLINED parts contains an error in spelling, punctuation, or capitalization, or employs grammatical usage which would be inappropriate for carefully written English. If so, note the letter printed under the unacceptable form and indicate this choice in the space at the right. If all four of the underlined portions are acceptable as they stand, select the answer E. (No sentence contains more than ONE unacceptable form.)

1. A party <u>like</u> <u>that</u> <u>only</u> <u>comes</u> once a year. <u>No error</u>
       A   B   C   D   E

    1.____

2. <u>Our's</u> <u>is</u> <u>a</u> <u>swift moving</u> age. <u>No error</u>
    A   B C   D   E

    2.____

3. The <u>healthy</u> climate soon <u>restored</u> him <u>to</u> his <u>accustomed</u> vigor. <u>No error</u>
          A   B   C   D   E

    3.____

4. <u>They</u> needed six typists and hoped that <u>only</u> that <u>many</u> <u>would</u> apply for the
    A   B   C   D
position. <u>No error</u>
           E

    4.____

5. He <u>interviewed</u> people <u>whom</u> he thought had <u>something</u> <u>to impart</u>. <u>No error</u>
        A   B   C   D   E

    5.____

6. <u>Neither</u> of his three sisters <u>is</u> older <u>than</u> <u>he</u>. <u>No error</u>
    A   B   C D   E

    6.____

7. <u>Since</u> he is <u>that</u> <u>kind</u> of <u>a</u> boy, he cannot be expected to cooperate with us.
    A   B   C   D
<u>No error</u>
 E

    7.____

8. When <u>passing</u> <u>through</u> the tunnel, the air pressure <u>affected</u> <u>our</u> years. <u>No error</u>
         A   B   C   D   E

    8,____

9. <u>The story having</u> a sad ending, <u>it</u> never <u>achieved</u> popularity <u>among</u> the
    A   B   C   D
students. <u>No error</u>
           E

    9.____

10. <u>Since</u> we are both hungry, <u>shall</u> we go <u>somewhere</u> for <u>lunch?</u> <u>No error</u>
     A   B   C   D   E

    10.____

2 (#2)

11. Will you please bring this book down to the library and give it to my friend, 11.____
    A   B   C   D
    who is waiting for it? No error
                            E

12. You may have the book; I am finished with it. No error   12.____
        A   B   C   D   E

13. I don't know if I should mention it to her or not. No error   13.____
      A   B   C   D   E

14. Philosophy is not a subject which has to do with philosophers and   14.____
                      A   B   C
    mathematics only. No error
                D   E

15. The thoughts of the scholar in his library are little different than the old woman   15.____
                                A   B
    who first said, "It's no use crying over spilt milk." No error
        C   D   E

16. A complete system of philosophical ideas are implied in many simple   16.____
                 A   B   C
    utterances. No error
        D   E

17. Even if one has never put them into words, his ideas compose a kind of a   17.____
         A   B   C   D
    philosophy. No error
                 E

18. Perhaps it is well enough that most people do not attempt this formulation.   18.____
               A   B   C   D
    No error
      E

19. Leading their ordered lives, this confused body of ideas and feelings is   19.____
        A   B   C   D
    sufficient. No error
                 E

20. Why should we insist upon them formulating it? No error   20.____
         A   B   C   D   E

21. Since it includes something of the wisdom of the ages, it is adequate for the   21.____
      A   B   C
    purposes of ordinary life. No error
        D   E

173

3 (#2)

22. Therefore, I have sought to make a pattern of mine, and so there were, early
         A   B   C
moments of my trying to find out what were the elements with which I had to
            D
deal. No error
       E

23. I wanted to get what knowledge I could about the general structure of the
       A   B   C   D
universe. No error
          E

24. I wanted to know if life per se had any meaning or whether I must strive to give
                  A B   C   D
it one. No error
        E

25. So, in a desultory way, I began to read. No error
    A   B   C   D   E

KEY (CORRECT ANSWERS)

1.	C		11.	B
2.	A		12.	C
3.	A		13.	B
4.	C		14.	D
5.	B		15.	B
6.	A		16.	B
7.	D		17.	A
8.	A		18.	C
9.	A		19.	A
10.	E		20.	D

21. E
22. C
23. C
24. B
25. E

WRITTEN ENGLISH EXPRESSION
EXAMINATION SECTION
TEST 1

DIRECTIONS: The questions that follow the paragraph below are designed to test your appreciation of correctness and effectiveness of expression in English. The paragraph is presented first in full so that you may read it through for sense. Disregard the errors you find, as you will be asked to correct them in the questions that follow. The paragraph is then presented sentence by sentence with portions underlined and numbered. At the end of this material, you will find numbers corresponding to those below the underlined portions, each followed by five alternatives lettered A to E. In every case, the usage in the alternative lettered A is the same as that in the original paragraph and is followed by four possible usages. Choose the usage you consider BEST in each case. *PRINT THE LETTER OF THE CORRECT ANSWER IN THE SPACE AT THE RIGHT.*

   When this war is over, no nation will either be isolated in war or peace. Each will be within trading distance of all the others and will be able to strike them. Every nation will be most as dependent on the rest for the maintainance of peace as is any of our own American states on all the others. The world that we have known was a world made up of individual nations, each of which has the priviledge of doing about as they pleased without being embarassed by outside interference. The world has dissolved before the impact of an invention, the airplane has done to our world what gunpowder did to the feudal world. Whether the coming century will be a period of further tragedy or one of peace and progress depend very largely on the wisdom and skill with which the present generation adjusts their thinking to the problems immediately at hand. Examining the principal movements sweeping through the world, it can be seen that they are being accelerated by the war. There is undoubtedly many of these whose courses will be affected for good or ill by the settlement that will follow the war. The United States will share the responsibility of these settlements with Russia, England and China. The influence of the United States, however, will be great. This country is likely to emerge from the war stronger than any other nation. Having benefitted by the absence of actual hostilities on our own soil, we shall probably be less exhausted than our allies and better able to help restore the devastated areas. However many mistakes have been made in our past, the tradition of America, not only the champion of freedom but also fair play, still lives among millions who can see light and hope scarcely nowhere else.

1. When this war is over, no nation will <u>either be isolated in war or peace</u>. 1.____
   A. either be isolated in war or peace
   B. be either isolated in war or peace
   C. be isolated in neither war nor peace
   D. be isolated either in war or in peace
   E. be isolated neither in war or peace

2. <u>Each</u> 2.____
   A. Each   B. It   C. Some   D. They   E. A nation

3. within trading distance of all the others and will be able to strike them.
   A. within trading distance of all the others and will be able to strike them.
   B. near enough to trade with and strike all the others.
   C. trading and striking the others.
   D. within trading and striking distance of all the others.
   E. able to strike and trade with all the others,

4. Every nation will be most as dependent on
   A. most   B. wholly   C. much   D. mostly   E. almost

5. the rest for the maintainance of peace as is
   A. maintainance   B. maintainence   C. maintenence
   D. maintenance   E. maintanence

6. any of our own American states on all the others. The world that we have known was a world made up of individual nations, each
   A. nations, each   B. nations. Each   C. nations: each
   D. nations; each   E. nations each

7. of which had the priviledge of doing about as
   A. priviledge   B. priveledge   C. privelege
   D. privalege   E. privilege

8. they pleased without being
   A. they   B. it   C. they individually
   D. he   E. the nations

9. embarassed by outside interference. That
   A. embarassed   B. embarrassed   C. embaressed
   D. embarrased   E. embarressed

10. world has dissolved before the impact of an invention, the airplane has done to our world what gunpowder did to the feudal world. Whether the coming century will be a period of further tragedy or one of peace and
    A. invention, the   B. invention but the   C. invention: the
    D. invention. The   E. invention and the

11. progress depend very largely on the wisdom and skill with which the present generation
    A. depend   B. will have depended   C. depends
    D. depended   E. shall depend

12. adjusts their thinking to the problems immediately at hand.
    A. adjusts their   B. adjusts there   C. adjusts its
    D. adjust our   E. adjust it's

13. Examining the principal movements sweeping through the world, it can be seen
    A. Examining the principal movements sweeping through the world, it can be seen
    B. Having examined the principal movements sweeping through the world, it can be seen
    C. Examining the principal movements sweeping through the world can be seen
    D. Examining the principal movements sweeping through the world, we can see
    E. It can be seen examining the principal movements sweeping through the world

13.____

14. that they are being accelerated by the war.
    A. accelerated   B. acelerated   C. accelerated
    D. acellerated   E. acelerrated

14.____

15. There is undoubtedly many of these whose courses will be affected for good or ill by the settlements that will follow the war. The United States will share the responsibility of these settlements with Russia, England and China. The influence of the United
    A. is   B. were   C. was   D. are   E. might be

15.____

16. States, however, will be great. This country is likely to emerge from the war stronger than any other nation.
    A. , however,   B. however,   C. , however
    D. however   E. ; however

16.____

17. Having benefitted by the absence of actual hostilities on our own soil, we shall probably be less exhausted
    A. benefitted   B. benifitted   C. benefited
    D. benifited   E. benafitted

17.____

18. than our allies and better able than them to help restore the devastated areas. However many mistakes have been made in our past, the tradition of American,
    A. them   B. themselves   C. they
    D. the world   E. the nations

18.____

19. not only the champion of freedom but also fair play, still lives among millions who can
    A. not only the champion of freedom but also fair play,
    B. the champion of not only freedom but also of fair play,
    C. the champion not only of freedom but also of fair play,
    D. not only the champion but also freedom and fair play,
    E. not the champion of freedom only, but also fair play,

19.____

20. see light and hope <u>scarcely nowhere else.</u> 20._____
    A. scarcely nowhere else
    B. elsewhere
    C. nowhere
    D. scarcely anywhere else
    E. anywhere

KEY (CORRECT ANSWERS)

1.	D	11.	C
2.	A	12.	C
3.	D	13.	D
4.	E	14.	A
5.	D	15.	D
6.	A	16.	A
7.	E	17.	C
8.	B	18.	C
9.	B	19.	C
10.	D	20.	D

TEST 2

DIRECTIONS: The questions that follow the paragraph below are designed to test your appreciation of correctness and effectiveness of expression in English. The paragraph is presented first in full so that you may read it through for sense. Disregard the errors you find, as you will be asked to correct them in the questions that follow. The paragraph is then presented sentence by sentence with portions underlined and numbered. At the end of this material, you will find numbers corresponding to those below the underlined portions, each followed by five alternatives lettered A to E. In every case, the usage in the alternative lettered A is the same as that in the original paragraph and is followed by four possible usages. Choose the usage you consider BEST in each case. *PRINT THE LETTER OF THE CORRECT ANSWER IN THE SPACE AT THE RIGHT.*

    The use of the machine produced up to the present time outstanding changes in our modern world. One of the most significant of these changes have been the marked decreases in the length of the working day and the working week. The fourteen-hour day not only has been reduced to one of ten hours but also, in some lines of work, to one of eight or even six. The trend toward a decrease is further evidenced in the longer weekend already given to employees in many business establishments. There seems also to be a trend toward shorter working weeks and longer summer vacations. An important feature of this development is that leisure is no longer the privilege of the wealthy few,—it has become the common right of most people. Using it wisely, leisure promotes health, efficiency, and happiness, for there is time for each individual to live their own "more abundant life" and having opportunities for needed recreation.

    Recreation, like the name implies, is a process of revitalization. In giving expression to the play instincts of the human race, new vigor and effectiveness are afforded by recreation to the body and to the mind. Of course not all forms of amusement, by no means, constitute recreation. Furthermore, an activity that provides recreation for one person may prove exhausting for another. Today, however, play among adults, as well as children, is regarded as a vital necessity of modern life. Play being recognized as an important factor in improving mental and physical health and thereby reducing human misery and poverty,

    Among the most important forms of amusement available at the present time are the automobile, the moving picture, the radio, television, and organized sports. The automobile, especially, has been a boon to the American people, since it has been the chief means of them getting out into the open. The motion picture, the radio and television have tremendous opportunities to supply wholesome recreation and to promote cultural advancement. A criticism often leveled against organized sports as a means of recreation is because they make passive spectators of too many people. It has been said "that the American public is afflicted with "spectatoritis," but there is some recreational advantages to be gained even from being a spectator at organized games. Such sports afford a release from the monotony of daily toil, get people outdoors and also provide an exhilaration that is tonic in its effect.

    The chief concern, of course, should be to eliminate those forms of amusement that are socially undesirable. There are, however, far too many people who, we know, do not use their leisure to the best advantage. Sometimes leisure leads to idleness, and idleness may lead to demoralization. The value of leisure both to the individual and to society will depend on the uses made of it.

2 (#2)

1. The use of the machine <u>produced</u> up to the
   A. produced
   B. produces
   C. has produced
   D. had produced
   E. will have produced

2. present time many outstanding changes in our modern world. One of the most significant of these changes <u>have been</u> the marked
   A. have been
   B. was
   C. were
   D. has been
   E. will be

3. decreases in the length of the working day and the working week. <u>The fourteen-hour day not only has been reduced</u> to one of ten hour but also, in some line of work, to one of eight or even six.
   A. The fourteen-hour day not only has been reduced
   B. Not only the fourteen-hour day has been reduced
   C. Not the fourteen-hour day only has been reduced
   D. The fourteen-hour day has not only been reduced
   E. The fourteen-hour day has been reduced not only

4. The trend toward a decrease is further evidenced in the longer week end <u>already</u> given
   A. already   B. all ready   C. allready   D. ready   E. all in all

5. to employees in many business establishments. There seems also to be a trend toward shorter working weeks and longer summer vacations. An important feature of this development is that leisure is no longer the privilege of the wealthy few,<u>—it</u> has become the common right of people.
   A. ,—it
   B. : it
   C. ; it
   D. …it
   E. omit punctuation

6. <u>Using it wisely,</u> leisure promotes health, efficiency, and happiness, for there is time for
   A. Using it wisely
   B. If used wisely
   C. Having used it widely
   D. Because of its wise use
   E. Because of usefulness

7. each individual to live <u>their</u> own "more abundant life"
   A. their   B. his   C. its   D. our   E. your

8. and <u>having</u> opportunities for needed recreation.
   A. having
   B. having had
   C. to have
   D. to have had
   E. had

9. Recreation, <u>like</u> the name implies, is a
   A. like   B. since   C. through   D. for   E. as

180

10. process of revitalization. In giving expression to the play instincts of the human race, <u>new vigor and effectiveness are afforded by recreation to the body and to the mind.</u>
    A. new vigor and effectiveness are afforded by recreation to the body and to the mind.
    B. recreation affords new vigor and effectiveness to the body and to the mind.
    C. there are afforded new vigor and effectiveness to the body and to the mind.
    D. by recreation the body and mind are afforded new vigor and effectiveness.
    E. the body and the mind afford new vigor and effectiveness to themselves by recreation.

10.____

11. Of course not all forms of amusement, <u>by no means,</u> constitute recreation. Furthermore, an activity that provides recreation for one person may prove exhausting for another. Today, however, play among adults, as well as children, is regarded as a vital necessity of modern life.
    A. by no means   B. by those means   C. by some means
    D. by every means E. by any means

11.____

12. <u>Play being recognized</u> as an important factor in improving mental and physical health and thereby reducing human misery and poverty.
    A. . Play being recognized as   B. . by their recognizing play as
    C. . They recognizing play as   D. . Recognition of it being
    E. , for play is recognized as

12.____

13. Among the most important forms of amusement available at the present time are the automobile, the moving picture, the radio, television, and organized sports. The automobile, especially, has been a boon to the American people, since it has been the chief means of <u>them</u> getting out into the open. The motion picture, the radio, and television have tremendous opportunities to supply wholesome recreation and to promote cultural advancement. A criticism often leveled against organized
    A. them   B. their   C. his   D. our   E. the people

13.____

14. sports as a means of recreation is <u>because</u> they make passive spectators of too many people
    A. because   B. since   C. as   D. that   E. why

14.____

15. It has been said "<u>that</u> the American public is afflicted with "spectatoritis,"
    A. "that   B. "that"   C. that"   D. 'that   E. that

15.____

16. but there <u>is</u> some recreational advantages to be gained even from being a spectator at organized games
    A. is   B. was   C. are   D. were   E. will be

16.____

17. Such sports afford a release from the monotony of daily toil, get people outdoors and also provide an exhilaration that is tonic in its effect. The chief concern, of course, should be to eliminate those forms of amusement that are socially undesirable. There are, however, far too many people who, we know, do not use their leisure to the best advantage. Sometimes leisure leads to idleness, and idleness may lead to demoralization. The value of leisure both to the individual and to society will depend on the uses made of it.
    A. who   B. whom   C. which   D. such as   E. that which

17.____

KEY (CORRECT ANSWERS)

1.	C	11.	E
2.	D	12.	E
3.	E	13.	B
4.	A	14.	D
5.	C	15.	E
6.	B	16.	C
7.	B	17.	A
8.	C		
9.	E		
10.	B		

TEST 3

DIRECTIONS: The questions that follow the paragraph below are designed to test your appreciation of correctness and effectiveness of expression in English. The paragraph is presented first in full so that you may read it through for sense. Disregard the errors you find, as you will be asked to correct them in the questions that follow. The paragraph is then presented sentence by sentence with portions underlined and numbered. At the end of this material, you will find numbers corresponding to those below the underlined portions, each followed by five alternatives lettered A to E. In every case, the usage in the alternative lettered A is the same as that in the original paragraph and is followed by four possible usages. Choose the usage you consider BEST in each case. *PRINT THE LETTER OF THE CORRECT ANSWER IN THE SPACE AT THE RIGHT.*

    The process by which the community influence the actions of its members is known as social control. Imitation which takes place when the action of one individual awakens the impulse in each other to attempt the same thing, is one of the means by which society gains this control. When the child acts as other members of his group acts, he receives their approval. There is also adults who seem almost equally imitative. Advertisers of luxuries are careful to convey the idea that important persons use and indorse the merchandise concerned, for most folk will do their utmost to follow the example of those whom they think are the best people.

    Akin to imitation as a means of social control is suggestion. The child is taught to think and feel as do the adults of his community. He is neither encouraged to be critical or to examine all the evidence for his opinion. To be sure, there would be scarcely no time left for other things if school children would have been expected to have considered all sides of every matter on which they hold opinions. It is possible, however and probably very desirable, for pupils of high school age to learn that the point of view accepted in their community is not the only one, and that many widely held opinions may be mistaken. The way in which suggestion operates is illustrated by advertising methods. Depending on skillful suggestion, argument is seldom used in advertising. The words accompanying the picture do not seek to convince the reason but only to intensify the suggestion.

    Some persons are more susceptible to suggestion than others. The ignorant person is more easily moved to action by suggestion than he who is well educated, education developing the habit of criticizing what is read and heard. Whoever would think clearly, freeing himself from emotion and prejudice, must beware of the influence of the crowd or mob. A crowd is a group of people in a highly suggestible condition, each stimulating the feelings of the others until an intense uniform emotion has control of the group. Such a crowd may become irresponsible and anonymous, and whose activity may lead in any direction. The educated person ought to be beyond reach of this kind of appeal, no one may be said to have a real individuality who, at the mercy of the suggestions of others, allow themselves to succumb to "crowd-mindedness."

1. The process by which the community <u>influence the action of its members</u> is known as social control.
    A. influence the actions of its members
    B. influences the actions of its members
    C. had influenced the actions of its members
    D. influences the actions of their members
    E. will influence the actions of its members

1.____

2. Imitation which takes place when the action
   A. which   B. , which   C. —which   D. that   E. what

3. of one individual awakens the impulse in each other to attempt the same thing, is one of the means by which society gains this control.
   A. each other   B. some other   C. one other
   D. another   E. one another

4. When the child acts as other members of his group acts, he receives their approval
   A. acts   B. act   C. has acted
   D. will act   E. will have acted

5. There is also adults who seem almost equally imitative.
   A. is   B. are   C. was   D. were   E. will be

6. Advertisers of luxuries are careful to convey the idea that important persons use and indorse the merchandise concerned, for most folk will do their utmost to follow the example of those whom they think are the best people.
   A. whom   B. what   C. which
   D. who   E. that which

7. Akin to imitation as a means of social control is suggestion. The child is taught to think and feel as do the adults of his community.
   A. do   B. does   C. had   D. may   E. might

8. He is neither encouraged to be critical or to examine all the evidence for his opinions.
   A. neither encouraged to be critical or to examine
   B. neither encouraged to be critical nor to examine
   C. either encouraged to be critical or to examine
   D. encouraged either to be critical nor to examine
   E. not encouraged either to be critical or to examine

9. To be sure, there would be scarcely no time left for other things.
   A. scarcely no   B. hardly no   C. scarcely any
   D. enough   E. but only

10. if school children would have been expected
    A. would have been   B. should have been   C. would have
    D. were   E. will be

11. to have considered all sides of every matter on which they hold opinions
    A. to have considered   B. to be considered
    C. to consider   D. to have been considered
    E. and have considered

12. It is possible, however and probably very desirable, for pupils of high school age to learn that the point of view accepted in their community is not the only one, and that many widely held opinions may be mistaken. The way in which suggestion operates is illustrated by advertising methods.   12.____
    A. , however   B. however,   C. ; however,
    D. however   E. , however,

13. Depending on skillful suggestion, argument is seldom used in advertising. The words accompanying the picture do not seek to convince the reason but only to intensify the suggestion.   13.____
    A. Depending on skillful suggestion, argument is seldom used in advertising.
    B. Argument is seldom used by advertisers, who depend instead on skillful suggestion.
    C. Skillful suggestion is depended on by advertisers instead of argument.
    D. Suggestion, which is more skillful, is used in place of argument by advertisers.
    E. Instead of suggestion, depending on argument is used by skillful advertisers.

14. Some persons are more susceptible to suggestion than others. The ignorant person is more easily moved to action by suggestion than he who is well educated, education developing the habit of criticizing what is read and heard. Whoever would think clearly, freeing himself from emotion and prejudice, must beware of the influence of the crowd or mob.   14.____
    A. , education developing   B. , education developed by
    C. , for education develops   D. . Education will develop
    E. . Education developing

15. A crowd is a group of people in a highly suggestible condition, each stimulating the feelings of the others until an intense uniform emotion has control of the group. Such a crowd may become irresponsible and anonymous, and whose activity may lead in any direction. The educated person ought to be beyond reach of this kind of appeal,   15.____
    A. and whose   B. whose   C. and its
    D. and the   E. and the crowd's

16. no one may be said to have a real individuality who,   16.____
    A. , no   B. : no   C. —no
    D. . No   E. omit punctuation

17. at the mercy of the suggestions of others, allow themselves to succumb to "crowd-mindedness."   17.____
    A. allow themselves   B. allows themselves   C. allow himself
    D. allows himself   E. allow ourselves

KEY (CORRECT ANSWERS)

1. B   11. C
2. B   12. E
3. D   13. B
4. B   14. C
5. B   15. C

6. D   16. D
7. A   17. D
8. E
9. C
10. D

TEST 4

DIRECTIONS: The questions that follow are designed to test your appreciation of correctness and effectiveness of expression in English. In each statement, you will find underlined portions. In some cases, the usage in the underlined portion is correct. In other cases, it requires correction. Five (5) alternatives lettered A to E are presented. In every case, the usage in the alternative lettered A (No Change) is the same as that in the original statement and is followed by four (4) other possible usages. Choose the usage you consider BEST in each case. *PRINT THE LETTER OF THE CORRECT ANSWER IN THE SPACE AT THE RIGHT.*

Sample Questions and Answers

Questions
1. John ran home.
    A. No change
    B. run
    C. runned
    D. runed
    E. None right

2. John aint here.
    A. No change
    B. ain't
    C. am not
    D. arre'nt
    E. None right

Answers
1. A
    (The sentence is obviously correctly written. Therefore, the correct answer is A. No change.)

2. E
    (word aint is unacceptable in usage today. The correct answer should be is not or isn't. Since the alternatives offered in A, B, C, and D are all incorrect, the correct answer is, therefore, E. None right.)

1. It takes study to become a lawyer.
    A. No change
    B. before you can become
    C. in becoming
    D. for becoming
    E. None right

2. His novels never concern old people who wished to be young.
    A. No change
    B. concerned old people who wish
    C. concerned old people who had wished
    D. concern old people who wish
    E. None right

3. You people like we boys as much as we. boys like you.
    A. No change
    B. we boys as much as us
    C. us boys as much as us
    D. us boys as much as we
    E. None right

187

4. Jane and Mary are <u>more poised than he, but Bill is the brighter</u> of all three. 4.____
   A. No change
   B. more poised than he, but Bill is the brightest
   C. more poised than him, but Bill is the brightest
   D. more poised than him, but Bill is the brighter
   E. None right

5. It is a thing of joy, beauty, <u>and containing</u> terror. 5.____
   A. No change   B. and abounding in   C. and of
   D. and contains   E. None right

6. If he <u>was able, he would demand that she return</u> home. 6.____
   A. No change
   B. were able, he would demand that she return
   C. was able, he would demand that she returns
   D. were able, he would demand that she returns
   E. None right

7. He <u>use to visit when he was supposed to.</u> 7.____
   A. No change
   B. use to visit when he was suppose to.
   C. used to visit when he was suppose to.
   D. used to visit when he was supposed to.
   E. None right

8. I saw the <u>seamstress and asked her for a needle, hook and eye,</u> and thimble. 8.____
   A. No change
   B. seamstress, and asked her for a needle, hook and eye
   C. seamstress and asked her for a needle, hook and eye
   D. seamstress, and asked her for a needle, hook and eye
   E. None right

9. A tall, young<u>, man threw the heavy, soggy,</u> ball. 9.____
   A. No change
   B. , young man threw the heavy, soggy
   C. young man threw the heavy, soggy
   D. , young man threw the heavy soggy
   E. None right

10. The week <u>before my sister, thinking of other matters,</u> thrust her hand into the fire. 10.____
    A. No change
    B. before, my sister thinking of other matters
    C. before my sister thinking of other matters
    D. before my sister, thinking of other matters
    E. None right

11. We seldom eat a roast at our house. <u>My</u> wife being a vegetarian. 11.____
    A. No change   B. my   C. , my
    D. ; my   E. None right

3 (#4)

12. I have only one request. That you leave at once. 12.____
    A. No change   B. that   C. ; that
    D. : that   E. None right

13. I admire stimulating conversation and appreciative listening, therefore I talk 13.____
    to myself.
    A. No change   B. , therefore,   C. therefore
    D. therefore,   E. None right

14. The battle-scarred veteran was as bald as a newlaid egg. 14.____
    A. No change
    B. battlescarred veteran was as bald as a new-laid egg.
    C. battle-scarred veteran was as bald as a new-laid egg.
    D. battle scarred veteran was as bald as a new laid egg.
    E. None right

15. The President's proclamation opened with the following statement: "The 15.____
    intention of the government is, to make the people aware of one of the greatest
    dangers to the safety of the country."
    A. No change
    B. , "The intention of the government is
    C. : "The intention of the government is:
    D. : "The intention of the government is
    E. None right

16. I get only a week vacation after two years work. 16.____
    A. No change
    B. week's vacation after two years work.
    C. week's vacation after two years' work.
    D. weeks vacation after two years work.
    E. None right

17. You first wash your brush in turpentine. Then hang it up to dry. 17.____
    A. No change   B. First you   C. First you should
    D. First   E. None right

18. The teacher insisted that you and he were responsible for the mistakes of 18.____
    Joe and me.
    A. No change
    B. him were responsible for the mistakes of Joe and me.
    C. he were responsible for the mistakes of Joe and I.
    D. him were responsible for the mistakes of Joe and I.
    E. None right

19. He sometimes in a generous mood gave the flowers to others that he had grown 19.____
    in his garden.
    A. No change
    B. He in a generous mood sometimes gave to others the flowers
    C. In a generous mood he sometimes gave the flowers to others

189

D. Sometimes in a generous mood he gave to others the flowers
E. None right

20. He is attending college since September.
    A. No change
    B. has attended
    C. was attending
    D. attended
    E. None right

21. He enjoys me hearing him singing.
    A. No change
    B. my hearing him sing
    C. me hearing him sing
    D. me hearing his singing
    E. None right

22. Even patients of anxious temperament occasionally feel an element of primitive pleasure.
    A. No change
    B. temperament occassionally feel an element of primitive
    C. temperment occasionally feel an element of primitive
    D. temperament occasionally feel an element of primitive
    E. None right

23. Undoubtedly even the loneliest patient feels tranquill.
    A. No change
    B. Undoubtably even the loneliest patient feels tranquill.
    C. Undoubtedly even the loneliest patient feels tranquil.
    D. Undouvtably even the loneliest patient feels tranquil.
    E. None right

24. Sophmores taking behavioral psychology must pay a labratory fee.
    A. No change
    B. Sophmores taking behavioral psychology must pay a laboratory
    C. Sophmores taking behavioral psychology must pay a laboratory
    D. Sophomores taking behavioral psychology must pay a laboratory
    E. None right

25. Atheletic heroes often find their studies an unnecessary hinderance.
    A. No change
    B. Athletic heroes often find their studies an unnecessary hinderance.
    C. Athletic heros often find their studies an unnecessary hindrance.
    D. Athletic heroes often find their studies an unnecessary hindrance.
    E. None right

KEY (CORRECT ANSWERS)

1. A
2. D
3. D
4. B
5. E

6. B
7. D
8. D
9. C
10. E

11. C
12. D
13. E
14. C
15. D

16. C
17. D
18. A
19. D
20. B

21. B
22. A
23. E
24. C
25. D

TEST 5

DIRECTIONS: The questions that follow are designed to test your appreciation of correctness and effectiveness of expression in English. In each statement, you will find underlined portions. In some cases, the usage in the underlined portion is correct. In other cases, it requires correction. Five (5) alternatives lettered A to E are presented. In every case, the usage in the alternative lettered A (No Change) is the same as that in the original statement and is followed by four (4) other possible usages. Choose the usage you consider BEST in each case. *PRINT THE LETTER OF THE CORRECT ANSWER IN THE SPACE AT THE RIGHT.*

1. Many of the <u>childrens' games were supervised by students who's</u> interests lay in teaching.
   A. No change
   B. children's games were supervised by students who's
   C. childrens' games were supervised by students whose
   D. children's games were supervised by students whose
   E. None right

2. I told <u>father that a college president</u> was invited to speak.
   A. No change
   B. Father that a college president
   C. father that a College President
   D. Father that a College president
   E. None right

3. One should either <u>be able to read</u> German or French.
   A. No change
   B. be able either to read
   C. be able to either read
   D. be able to read either
   E. None right

4. <u>Twirling around on my piano stool, my head begins to swim.</u>
   A. No change
   B. My head begins to swim, twirling around on my piano stool.
   C. Twirling around on my piano stool, a dizzy spell ensues.
   D. Twirling around on my piano stool, I begin to feel dizzy.
   E. None right

5. As the reverberations of my deep bass voice <u>increase, one of my dogs starts</u> to howl.
   A. No change
   B. increase, one of my dogs start
   C. increases, one of my dogs start
   D. increases, one of my dogs starts
   E. None right

6. Roy bellows at Eve that it is <u>her, not he</u> who shouts.
   A. No change
   B. her, not him
   C. she, not him
   D. she, not he
   E. None right

2 (#5)

7. The only man who I think will knock out whoever he fights is Roy.   7.____
   A. No change
   B. who I think will knock out whomever
   C. whom I think will knock out whomever
   D. whom I think will knock out whoever
   E. None right

8. The more prettier of my eyes is the glass one.   8.____
   A. No change   B. most pretty   C. prettier
   D. prettiest   E. None right

9. When a good actress cries, she feels real sad.   9.____
   A. No change   B. feels real sadly
   C. feels really sadly   D. really feels sad
   E. None right

10. I asked the instructor what I should do with this examina-paper. Can you   10.____
    imagine what he said?
    A. No change   B. ? Can you imagine what he said.
    C. ? Can you imagine what he said? D. . Can you imagine what he said.
    E. None right

11. Not wishing to hurt my friend's feeling, I tell him that I am leaving, because   11.____
    I have a previous engagement.
    A. No change   B. I tell him that I am leaving
    C. , I tell him that I am leaving   D. I tell him that I am leaving,
    E. None right

12. I remember Utopia College where I studied, while I lived abroad, when the   12.____
    world was at peace.
    A. No change
    B. College where I studied, while I lived abroad
    C. College, where I studied while I lived abroad
    D. College, where I studied, while I lived abroad
    E. None right

13. Would Robinson Crusoe have survived if he was less unimaginative?   13.____
    A. No change   B. were   C. had been
    D. would have been E. None right

14. Neither time nor tide delay either the traveler or the stay-at-home from his   14.____
    pastime.
    A. No change
    B. delays either the traveler or the stay-at-home from his
    C. delay either the traveler or the stay-at-home from their
    D. delays either the traveler or the stay-at-home from their
    E. None right

15. When the committee reports <u>its findings somebody will lose their</u> composure. 15.____
    A. No change
    B. their findings somebody will lose their
    C. their findings somebody will lose his
    D. its findings somebody will lose his
    E. None right

16. The worst one of the problems which <u>is confronting me concern</u> money. 16.____
    A. No change
    B. are confronting me concern
    C. is confronting me concerns
    D. are confronting me concerns
    E. None right

17. Far in the distance <u>rumble the motors of the convoy, but there's</u> no signs of it yet. 17.____
    A. No change
    B. rumbles the motors of the convoy, but there is
    C. rumbles the motors of the convoy, but there are
    D. rumble the motors of the convoy, but there are
    E. None right

18. Neither of the patients <u>believe that Hansel or Gretel are</u> alive. 18.____
    A. No change
    B. believes that Hansel or Gretel are
    C. believe that Hansel or Gretel is
    D. believes that Hansel or Gretel is
    E. None right

19. <u>Its in untried emergencies that a man's native metal receives its</u> ultimate test. 19.____
    A. No change
    B. It's in untried emergencies that a man's native metal receives its
    C. It's in untried emergencies that a man's native metal receives its
    D. It's in untried emergencies that a man's native metal receives its'
    E. None right

20. Expecting my friends to be on time, <u>their tardiness seemed almost an insult.</u> 20.____
    A. No change
    B. it seemed that their tardiness was almost an insult.
    C. resentment at their tardiness grew in my mind.
    D. only an accident on the way could account for their tardiness.
    E. None right

21. <u>On first reading "The Wasteland" seems obscure.</u> 21.____
    A. No change
    B. On first reading it, "The Wasteland" seems obscure.
    C. "The Wasteland" seems an obscure poem on first reading it.
    D. On first reading "The Wasteland," it seems an obscure poem.
    E. None right

4 (#5)

22. <u>A special light will be required to inspect the engine.</u>   22.____
    A. No change
    B. To inspect the engine, a special light will be required.
    C. To inspect the engine, you will require a special light.
    D. To inspect the engine, your light must be special.
    E. None right

23. When <u>mixing it,</u> the cake batter must be thoroughly beaten.   23.____
    A. No change   B. mixing   C. being mixed
    D. being mix   E. None right

24. What you say may be different <u>from me.</u>   24.____
    A. No change   B. from what I say   C. than me
    D. than mine   E. None right

25. Trumping is <u>playing</u> a trump when another suit has been led.   25.____
    A. No change   B. to play   C. if you play
    D. where one plays   E. None right

KEY (CORRECT ANSWERS)

1.	D	11.	C
2.	A	12.	C
3.	D	13.	C
4.	D	14.	B
5.	A	15.	D
6.	D	16.	D
7.	B	17.	D
8.	C	18.	D
9.	D	19.	B
10.	A	20.	E

21.	B
22.	B
23.	C
24.	B
25.	A

WRITTEN ENGLISH EXPRESSION
EXAMINATION SECTION
TEST 1

DIRECTIONS: The following questions are designed to test your knowledge of grammar, sentence structure, correct usage, and punctuation. In each group, there is one sentence that contains an error. Select the letter of the INCORRECT sentence. *PRINT THE LETTER OF THE CORRECT ANSWER IN THE SPACE AT THE RIGHT.*

1. A. All things considered, he did unusually well.
    B. The poor boy takes everything too seriously.
    C. Our club sent two delegates, Ruth and I, to Oswego.
    D. I like him better than her.
    E. His eccentricities continually made good newspaper copy.

    1.____

2. A. If we except Benton, no one in the club foresaw the changes.
    B. The two-year-old rosebushes are loaded with buds—and beetles!
    C. Though the pitcher had been broken by the cat, Teena was furious.
    D. Virginia got the cake recipe off of her grandmother.
    E. Neither one of the twins was able to get a summer vacation.

    2.____

3. A. "What do you wish?" he asked, "may I help you?"
    B. Whose gloves are these?
    C. Has he drink all the orange juice?
    D. It was he who spoke to the manager of the store.
    E. Mary prefers this kind of evening dress.

    3.____

4. A. Charles himself said it before the assembled peers of the realm.
    B. The wind stirred the rose petals laying on the floor.
    C. The storm beat hard on the frozen windowpanes.
    D. Worn out by the days of exposure and storm, the sailor clung pitifully to the puny raft.
    E. The day afterward he thought more kindly of the matter.

    4.____

5. A. Between you and me, I think Henry is wrong.
    B. This is the more interesting of the two books.
    C. This is the most carefully written letter of all.
    D. During the opening course I read not only four plays but also three historical novels.
    E. This assortment of candies, nuts, and fruits are excellent.

    5.____

6. A. According to your report card, you are not so clever as he.
    B. If he had kept his eyes open, he would not have fallen into that trap.
    C. We were certain that the horse had broken it's leg.
    D. The troop of scouts and the leader are headed for the North Woods.
    E. I knew it to be him by the knock at the door.

    6.____

7. A. Being one of the earliest spring flowers, we welcome the crocus.
    B. The cold running water became colder as time sped on.
    C. Those boys need not have stood in line for lunch.
    D. Can you, my friend, donate ten dollars to the cause?
    E. Because it's a borrowed umbrella, return it in the morning.

    7.____

8. A. If Walter would have planted earlier in the spring, the rosebushes would have survived.
    B. The flowers smell overpoweringly sweet.
    C. There are three *e*'s in dependent.
    D. May I be excused at the end of the test?
    E. Carl has three brothers-in-law.

    8.____

9. A. We have bought neither the lumber nor the tools for the job.
    B. Jefferson was re-elected despite certain powerful opposition.
    C. The Misses Jackson were invited to the dance.
    D. The letter is neither theirs nor yours.
    E. The retail price for those items are far beyond the wholesale quotations.

    9.____

10. A. To find peace of mind is to gain treasure beyond price.
    B. Fred is cheerful, carefree; his brother is morose.
    C. Whoever fails to understand the strategic importance of the Arctic fails to understand modern geography.
    D. They came promptly at 8 o'clock on August 7, 2020, without prior notification.
    E. Every one tried their best to guess the answer, but no one succeeded.

    10.____

11. A. Is this hers or theirs?
    B. Having been recognized, Frank took the floor.
    C. Alex invited Sue; Paul, Marion; and Dan, Helen.
    D. If I were able to do the task, you can be sure that I'd do it.
    E. Stamp collecting, or philately as it is otherwise called is truly an international hobby.

    11.____

12. A. He has proved himself to be reliable.
    B. The fisherman had arisen before the sun.
    C. By the time the truck arrived, I had put out the blaze.
    D. The doctor with his colleagues were engaged in consultation.
    E. I chose to try out a new method, but in spite of my efforts it failed.

    12.____

13. A. He has drunk too much iced tea.
    B. I appreciated him doing that job for me.
    C. The royal family fled, but they were retaken.
    D. The secretary and the treasurer were both present on Friday,
    E. Iago protested his honesty, yet he continued to plot against Desdemona.

    13.____

14. A. The family were all together at Easter.
    B. It is altogether too fine a day for us to stay indoors.
    C. However much you dislike him, you should treat him fairly.
    D. The judges were already there when the contestants arrived.
    E. The boy's mother reported that he was alright again after the accident.

    14.____

15. A. Ham and eggs is a substantial breakfast.
    B. By the end of the week the pond had frozen.
    C. I should appreciate any assistance you could offer me.
    D. Being that tomorrow is Sunday, we expect to close early.
    E. If he were to win the medal, I for one would be disturbed.

    15.____

16. A. Give the letter to whoever comes for it.
    B. He feels bad, but his sister is the one who looks sicker.
    C. He had an unbelievable large capacity for hard physical work.
    D. Earth has nothing more beautiful to offer than the autumn colors of this section of the country.
    E. Happily we all have hopes that the future will soon bring forth fruits of a lasting peace.

    16.____

17. A. This kind of apples is my favorite.
    B. Either of the players is capable of performing ably.
    C. Though trying my best to be calm, the choice was not an easy one for me.
    D. The nearest star is not several light years away; it is only 93,000,000 miles away.
    E. There were two things I still wished to do—to see the Lincoln Memorial and to climb up the Washington Monument.

    17.____

18. A. It is I who is to blame.
    B. That dress looks very good on Jane.
    C. People often take my brother to be me.
    D. I could but think she had deceived me.
    E. He himself told us that the story was true,

    18.____

19. A. They all went but Mabel and me.
    B. Has he ever swum across the river?
    C. We have a dozen other suggestions besides these.
    D. The Jones's are going to visit their friends in Chicago.
    E. The ideal that Arthur and his knights were in quest of was a better world order.

    19.____

20. A. Would I were able to be there with you!
    B. Whomever he desires to see should be admitted.
    C. It is not for such as we to follow fashion blindly.
    D. His causing the confusion seemed to affect him not at all.
    E. Please notify all those whom you think should have this information.

    20.____

21. A. She was not only competent but also friendly in nature. 21.____
    B. Not only must we visualize the play we are reading; we must actually hear it.
    C. The firm was not only acquiring a bad reputation but also indulging in illegal practices.
    D. The bank was not only uncooperative but also was indifferent to new business offered them.
    E. I know that a conscious effort was made not only to guard the material but also to keep it from being used.

22. A. How old shall you be on your next birthday? 22.____
    B. I am sure that he has been here and did what was expected of him.
    C. Near to the bank of the river, stood, secluded and still, the house of the hermit.
    D. Because of its efficacy in treating many ailments, penicillin has become an important addition to the druggist's stock.
    E. ROBINSON CRUSOE, which is a fairy tale to the child, is a work of social philosophy to the mature thinker.

23. A. We had no sooner started than it rained. 23.____
    B. The fact that the prisoner is a minor will be taken into consideration.
    C. Many parents think more of their older children than of their younger ones.
    D. The boy laid a book, a knife and a fishing line on the table.
    E. John is the tallest of any boy in his class.

24. A. Although we have been friend for many years, I must admit that May is most inconsiderate. 24.____
    B. He is not able to run, not even to walk.
    C. You will bear this pain as you have so many greater ones.
    D. The harder the work, the more studious she became.
    E. Too many "and's" in a sentence produce an immature style.

25. A. It would be preferable to have you submit questions after, not before, the lecture. 25.____
    B. Plan your work; then work your plan.
    C. At last John met his brother, who had been waiting two hours for him.
    D. Should one penalize ones self for not trying?
    E. There are other considerations besides this one.

KEY (CORRECT ANSWERS)

1.	C	11.	E
2.	D	12.	D
3.	A	13.	B
4.	B	14.	E
5.	E	15.	D
6.	C	16.	C
7.	A	17.	C
8.	A	18.	A
9.	E	19.	D
10.	E	20.	E

21. D
22. B
23. E
24. C
25. D

TEST 2

DIRECTIONS: The following questions are designed to test your knowledge of grammar, sentence structure, correct usage, and punctuation. In each group, there is one sentence that contains an error. Select the letter of the INCORRECT sentence. *PRINT THE LETTER OF THE CORRECT ANSWER IN THE SPACE AT THE RIGHT.*

1.
   A. "Halt!" cried the sentry, "Who goes there?"
   B. "It is in talk alone," said Robert Louis Stevenson, "that we can learn our period and ourselves."
   C. The world will long remember the "culture" of the Nazis.
   D. When duty says, "You must," the youth replies, "I can."
   E. Who said, "Give me liberty or give me death?"

   1.____

2.
   A. Why are you so quiet, Martha?
   B. Edward Jones, a banker who lives near us, expects to retire very soon.
   C. I picked up the solid-gold chain.
   D. Any boy, who refuses to tell the truth, will be punished.
   E. Yes, honey tastes sweet.

   2.____

3.
   A. I knew it to be him by the style of his clothes.
   B. No one saw him doing it.
   C. Her going away is a loss to the community.
   D. Mary objected to her being there.
   E. Illness prevented him graduating in June.

   3.____

4.
   A. Being tired, I stretched out on a grassy knoll.
   B. While we were rowing on the lake, a sudden squall almost capsized the boat.
   C. Entering the room, a strange mark on the floor attracted my attention.
   D. Mounting the curb, the empty car crossed the sidewalk and came to rest against a building.
   E. Sitting down, they watched him demonstrate his skill.

   4.____

5.
   A. The coming of peace effected a change in her way of life.
   B. Spain is as weak, if not weaker than, she was in 1900.
   C. In regard to that, I am not certain what my attitude will be.
   D. That unfortunate family faces the problem of adjusting itself to a new way of life.
   E. Fred Eastman states in his essay that one of the joys of reading lies in discovering courage.

   5.____

6.
   A. Not one in a thousand readers take the matter seriously.
   B. Let it lie there.
   C. You are not as tall as he.
   D. The people began to realize how much she had done.
   E. He was able partially to accomplish his purpose.

   6.____

7. A. In the case of members who are absent, a special letter will be sent.
   B. The visitors were all ready to see it.
   C. I like Burns's poem "To a Mountain Daisy."
   D. John told William that he was sure he had seen it.
   E. Both men are Yale alumni.

   7._____

8. A. The audience took their seats promptly.
   B. Each boy and girl must finish his examination this morning.
   C. Every person turned their eyes toward the door.
   D. Everyone has his own opinion.
   E. The club nominated its officers by secret ballot.

   8._____

9. A. I can do that more easily than you.
   B. This kind of weather is more healthful.
   C. Pick out the really important points.
   D. Because of his aggressive nature, he only plays the hardest games.
   E. He pleaded with me to let him go.

   9._____

10. A. It is I who am mistaken.
    B. Is it John or Susie who stand at the head of the class?
    C. He is one of those who always do their lessons.
    D. He is a man on whom I can depend in time of trouble.
    E. Had he known who it was, he would have come.

    10._____

11. A. Somebody has forgotten his umbrella.
    B. Please let Joe and me use the car.
    C. We thought the author to be he.
    D. Whoever they send will be welcome.
    E. They thought the intruders were we.

    11._____

12. A. If I had known that you were coming, I should have met you.
    B. All the girls but her were at the game.
    C. I expected to have heard the concert before the present time.
    D. Walter would not have said it if he had thought it would make her unhappy.
    E. I have always believed that cork is the best material for insulation.

    12._____

13. A. Their contributions amounted to the no insignificant sum of ten thousand dollars.
    B. None of them was there.
    C. Ten dollars is the amount I agreed to pay.
    D. Fewer than one hundred persons assembled.
    E. Exactly what many others have done and are doing, Frank did.

    13._____

14. A. Neither Jane or her sister has arrived.
    B. Either Richard or his brother is going to drive.
    C. Refilling storage batteries is the work of the youngest employee.
    D. Helen has to lie still for two weeks.
    E. Mother lay down for an hour yesterday.

    14._____

15. A. He is not the man whom you saw entering the house.
    B. He asked why I wouldn't come.
    C. This is the cow whose horns are the longest.
    D. Helen, this is a man I met on the train one day last February.
    E. He greeted every foreign representative which came to the conference.

16. A. You, but not I, are invited.
    B. Guy's technique of service and return is masterly.
    C. Please pass me one of the books that are lying on the table.
    D. Mathematics is my most difficult subject.
    E. Unable to agree on a plan of organization, the class has departed in several directions.

17. A. He spoke to Gertrude and to me of the seriousness of the occasion.
    B. They seem to have decided to invite everyone except you and I.
    C. Your attitude is insulting to me who am your friend.
    D. He wished to know who our representative was.
    E. You may tell whomsoever you wish.

18. A. My favorite studies were Latin and science.
    B. The committee made its report.
    C. To get your work done promptly is better than leaving it until the last minute.
    D. That's what he would do if he were governor.
    E. He said that his chosen colors were red and blue.

19. A. Punish whoever disobeys orders.
    B. Come here, Henry; and sit with me.
    C. Has either of them his notebook?
    D. He talked as if he meant it.
    E. You did well; therefore you should be rewarded.

20. A. Many of us students were called to work.
    B. He shot the albatross with a crossbow.
    C. A house that is set on a hill is conspicuous.
    D. The wooden beams had raised slowly about a foot and then had settled back into place.
    E. Whom do you want to go with you?

21. A. He does not drive as he should.
    B. I can't hardly wait for the holidays.
    C. I like it less well than last week's.
    D. You were troubled by his coming.
    E. I don't know but that you are correct.

22. A. He was angry at both of us, her and me.
    B. When one enters the town, they see big crowds.
    C. They laid the tools on the ground every night.
    D. He is the only one of my friends who has written.
    E. He asked for a raise in wages.

23. A. None came with his excuse.
    B. Walking down the street, a house comes into view.
    C. "Never!" shouted the boy.
    D. Both are masters of their subject.
    E. His advice was to drive slowly.

    23._____

24. A. There is both beef and lamb on the market.
    B. Either beans or beets are enough with potatoes.
    C. Where does your mother buy bananas?
    D. Dinners at the new restaurant are excellent.
    E. Each was rewarded according to his deeds.

    24._____

25. A. Accordingly, we must prepare the food.
    B. The work, moreover, must be done today.
    C. Nevertheless, we must first have dinner.
    D. I always chose the most liveliest of the ponies.
    E. At six o'clock tomorrow the job will have been completed,

    25._____

KEY (CORRECT ANSWERS)

1.	E		11.	C
2.	D		12.	C
3.	E		13.	A
4.	C		14.	A
5.	B		15.	E
6.	A		16.	E
7.	C		17.	B
8.	C		18.	C
9.	D		19.	B
10.	B		20.	D

21.	B
22.	B
23.	B
24.	A
25.	D

TEST 3

DIRECTIONS: In each group of five sentences below, one or more sentences contain an error in usage. Choose the lettered answer which indicates ALL the sentences containing errors in usage. *PRINT THE LETTER OF THE CORRECT ANSWER IN THE SPACE AT THE RIGHT.*

1. I. Shortly after the terms of the contract for the new road transpired, an aroused constituency showed its disapproval by voting the senator out of office.
    II. Neither father nor sons work for a living but spend their days in drinking and gambling at the pub.
    III. Like his Italian predecessor, Boccaccio, whose DECAMERON was used as a model, a company of people of various occupations and stations in life, brought together for a pilgrimage, are called upon to relate stories to help relieve the tedium of their journey,
    IV. Sarah hurried into the kitchen and after a half hour emerged with a nauseous brew which she called coffee.
    V. It was to the major that the people applied for redress and by his armed guards that they were driven away.
    The CORRECT answer is:
    A. I B. III C. I, II, III D. IV, III E. II, III

    1.____

2. I. As we approached the castle, which was illuminated suddenly by the full moon breaking through the clouds, we described a rider coming to meet us.
    II. The reason for his loss of interest in boxing, as far as I can see, was due to the pressure of his work and the distance of the local "Y" from his home.
    III. Accompanied by a handsome member of the British legation, Elsie was about to enter the luxuriously furnished salon to meet the countess.
    IV. In spite of all of John's gifts and attentions, little Rosalie, upon being asked to make a choice, said she liked me better than him.
    V. The scar of the clearing for the power line extended for a hundred miles over the mountains, and the great poles with fifty feet between each carried cable from Niagara to Albany.
    The CORRECT answer is:
    A. II, III B. I, IV, III C. I, II, IV, III
    D. II, V   E. III, V

    2.____

3. I. The high wind had blown the roofs of several houses; the water supply had been contaminated by the floods; transportation to the business center had ground to a half; but the mayor said there was no reason for alarm!
    II. Because there is a need to soften tragic or painful news, we resort to such euphuisms for the simple "to die" as "to pass away," "to go to a better world," or "to join the great majority."
    III. Hardly had the salient on the western shore of the river been obliterated than one on the eastern bank crossed on a pontoon bridge and in boats of all sorts.
    IV. The distinction between the man who gives in a spirit of charity and him who gives for social recognition is often to be seen in the nature of the gift.
    V. After a few months in office, the new superintendent effected many changes, not all of them for the good, in the administration of the plant.

    3.____

The CORRECT answer is:
A. II, III   B. II, III, IV   C. III, IV   D. I, II, V   E. I, II, III

4. I. The defendants published an advertisement and notice giving information, directly and indirectly, stating where, how, and when, and by what means and what purports to be the said book can be purchased.
    II. In common with most Eskimos of her time, she had long spells of silence; and nature, while endowing her with immense sagacity, had thrust on her a compelling reticence.
    III. The entire report was read in less than half an hour to the full committee, giving no time for comment or question, and offered for vote.
    IV. Students going through this course almost always find themselves becoming critical of their own writing.
    V. In his report of 1968, Mr. Jones states that his chief problem is the rapid turnover of personnel which has prevailed to the moment of writing.
    The CORRECT answer is:
    A. I, IV   B. II, III   C. III, IV, V   D. I, IV, V   E. I, III

5. I. The material was destroyed after it had served our purposes, and after portions of it had been excluded and portions included in our report.
    II. We checked our results very carefully, too carefully perhaps, for we spent several hours on our task.
    III. We should keep constantly in mind the fact that writing has no purpose save to meet the needs of the reader.
    IV. Not even discussed in October, when Lathrop flew in from the Coast, the problem of expense was settled at the June meeting.
    V. Whether our facts were right or not, it was not necessary for you to rebuke him in such a discourteous manner.
    The CORRECT answer is:
    A. I only   B. I, IV   C. II, III   D. V only   E. I, V

6. I. At first the novel was interesting and liked by members of the class; but later the long reading assignments dampened the pupils' enthusiasm.
    II. Donnie had no love or confidence in his mother, who, when abandoned by her husband, put the boy in an orphanage and seldom went to visit him.
    III. Built during the Civil War, the house has a delicate air, supported as it is by iron columns and rimmed by an iron railing.
    IV. Recently a newspaper editor from the South returned from an eight-week trip through the Caribbean and made a number of recommendations on what we should do to counter the lack of accurate information about the United States.
    V. The need is to be candid about our problems, to be informed on what we are going about them, and to resolve them as expeditiously as possible.
    The CORRECT answer is:
    A. I, II   B. II, III   C. III, IV   D. I, V   E. I, III

7. I. "Man is flying too fast for a world that is round," he said. "Soon he will catch up with himself in a great rear-end collision."
    II. After the raid on the club, each of the men suspected of accepting racetrack bets, along with the owner of the club, were held for questioning at police headquarters.
    III. It seems to me that at the opening performance of the play the audience were of different opinions about its merit and about its chances for a long run.
    IV. Oak from the forests of Vermont and steel from the mills of Pittsburgh are the material of this magnificent modern structure.
    V. The machine is subjected to severe strains which it must withstand and at the same time work easily and rapidly.
    The CORRECT answer is:
    A. I, II   B. II, III   C. IV, V   D. I, V   E. II, V

8. I. We don't have to worry about cutting down on expenses; money is no object in this venture.
    II. And now, my dear, let you and I tell our guests of the plans we have for the future.
    III. For all his errors of the past, no one can or has said that he did not turn out on this occasion a perfectpiece of work.
    IV. Hercule Poirot, when looking for a suspect in the murder case never thought of its being me.
    V. During the interpellation the minister refused to answer any questions concerning his predecessor's conduct of the war.
    The CORRECT answer is:
    A. I, III   B. I, IV, V   C. II, III, IV   D. III, IV   E. II, III

9. I. John Steinbeck received the Nobel Prize only a few years ago for his work of the thirties, work, which now, according to some critics, has lost its timeliness and which never had timelessness.
    II. Respect is shown the flag by no matter when it is displayed, whether it be in the window of a private home or on the pole of a public building.
    III. When dinner was over we strolled through the garden and exclaimed at the beauty of the red gladioluses, the pride of the Jenkinses' gardener.
    IV. Mrs. Cosgrove's gift of $100,000 to the hospitals is only the latest of the many acts of generosity by which she has before now benefited her fellow men.
    V. Am I repeating your question exactly when I say, "How many of you are willing to join me in my attempt to rid America of the traitors who are threatening its freedom"?
    The CORRECT answer is:
    A. I, II, III, IV   B. II, IV   C. II, III, IV
    D. I, IV, V   E. I, II, IV

10. I. Slashing the original 73 projects to 20 with little loss of subject matter in the consolidated schedule, a stalemate was avoided and the work of the Council speeded up.

II. I was particularly struck by the unselfishness of the American school children, many of whom willingly donating their allowances, because they felt that they should help the refugees.
III. As a result of Henry VIII's defiance of the Church of Rome, the ecclesiastical principle of government was substituted by the national.
IV. I wish you had invited me to the concert, for I should have liked particularly to hear Piatigorsky.
V. John will be in the best possible position for getting the most out of his vacation and of making business contacts in new markets.

The CORRECT answer is:
A. I, II, III, IV   B. I, II, III, V   C. I, II, III
D. III, IV, V   E. I, II, III, IV, V

11. I. They took him to be me despite ever so many differences in our appearance and despite his addiction to loquacity.
II. They may have more money, they may have more possessions, but they are not any happier than us, as we and they all know.
III. Either Betty or Bob must have thought the teacher's remarks were addressed to him.
IV. There was present at today's conference—and at next week's conference the same group is expected—representatives of many foreign countries, including Italy, France, England, and Germany.
V. The most important criteria in judging the performance of a pianist is not virtuosity but maturity of interpretation.

The CORRECT answer is:
A. I, IV   B. II, III, V   C. II, IV, V   D. I, III   E. I, IV, V

12. I. Thoroughly exhausted after we had swum for six hours, we lay breathless on the sand and oblivious of anything but our utter fatigue.
II. The jury seems in violent disagreement about the culpability of the defendant; such shouting as we hear from the jury room is most unusual among these halls.
III. The difference between the class' average grades for the first week and those for the eighth week, on alternate forms of the same test, were quite insignificant, indicating, we thought, that instruction had been ineffective.
IV. Each tree and each bush give forth a flaming hue such as we have not seen for many seasons in these climes.
V. We met a man whom we thought we had met many years since, when we lived in South Africa.

The CORRECT answer is:
A. III, IV, V   B. I, II, V   C. III, IV   D. I, II   E. I, III, IV

13. I. That old friend, whom I met again last night after a lapse of many a year, stands head and shoulders above any person I have ever known.
II. This is one of the finest pictures which have ever been put on canvas, bringing out rare qualities of tone-color, mature interpretation, and virtuosity in execution.
III. Which of them would you prefer to have working for you, considering the inordinate physical and mental demands of the work, him or his brother?

IV. Throughout Saturday and Sunday, the townsfolk took scarcely any notice of the absence of Jed Gorman, believing him to be off on a drunken spree; but on Monday a body was discovered in the river obviously that of the missing handyman.
V. Things being so pleasant as they were, we could not fathom the reason for John leaving so soon after he had started what we considered an excellent job with unlimited opportunities.

The CORRECT answer is:
A. I, V   B. II, III, V   C. II, III   D. II, IV, V   E. I, IV, V

14.
I. He is unfailingly polite not only to his superiors and his colleagues but even to those who are in subordinate positions, and, in general, to whoever else he thinks is deserving of kindly consideration.
II. Without more ado, he took the books off the radiator, where they had lain quite neglected for several days and where their bindings were beginning to grow loose.
III. We can still include a discussion of the lunchroom situation among the topics, for the agenda have not yet been printed and will not be for another hour or two.
IV. We knew who would be at the party and who would take us home, but we didn't know who to expect to meet us at the station upon our arrival.
V. Despite his protestations, we know that the true reason why he was suffering such obvious anguish and failing to do his work was because of marital trouble.

The CORRECT answer is:
A. I, III, IV   B. II, III, V   C. I, IV, V   D. I, II   E. IV, V

14.____

15.
I. A difficult stretch of bad road in addition to a long detour which caused a series of minor motor mishaps, have much delayed our visitor's arrival and have created an awkward situation for us all.
II. To make the campaign effective, there is posted in every building, in full view of all entrants, one notice of the location of the shelter, and a second notice intended to boost morale and win cooperation.
III. One day while leading sheep in the desert and musing upon his people's future, the angel of the Lord appeared to Moses.
IV. Though he plead with the tongue of an angel, he will not ever alter her cold eyes nor trouble her calm fount of speech.
V. Despite continuous and well-advised and well-directed efforts by each of us, neither he nor I am able to improve the situation.

The CORRECT answer is:
A. I, V   B. III, IV, V   C. I, II, III   D. II, III, IV   E. I, III

15.____

16.
I. Though business has been brisk of late, this kind of appliances have not sold well at all, despite our continuous and concentrated efforts.
II. The return trip was a desperate one, with time of the essence; and partly blinded by the unexpected snowstorm, the trip was doubly hazardous.
III. I started on my journey by foot through forest and mountain, after a last warning to be careful about snake bites by my parents—a warning I knew I must heed on that dangerous terrain.

16.____

IV. That he was losing to a better man, a man who had worked diligently and a man of impeccable virtue, was a consideration of but small import to him.
V. The precarious state of affairs was aggravated by a new hazard, notwithstanding all our cautions to avoid any change in the situation.
The CORRECT answer is:
A. I, III, V   B. II, IV   C. IV, V   D. I, II, III   E. II, III

17.
I. Who's responsible for the feeding of his cat and its young, I'd like to know, we or they? If we, let's feed them.
II. The books that had lain on the desk for many weeks were laid in the bookcase, where they lay until picked up by the messenger from the second-handbook shop.
III. You say I merit the award for competence in my duties; but he deserves an award as well as I, for he is as good, without doubt, or even better than I.
IV. The Joneses' car was more luxurious than, but not necessarily as expensive as, the Browns'.
V. Slowly they tiptoed into the living room hoping not to be heard, but we were fully aware of it being they.
The CORRECT answer is:
A. II, IV   B. I, III, IV   C. I, V   D. I, II, V   E. III, V

17.____

18.
I. I shall lay the rug in the sun, where it has laid many times before; and I shall lie in the sun, too, as always I have lain at leisure while the rug has been drying.
II. Though he knew a great deal about printing machinery, he thought, mistakenly, that the new machine could be made to cast type as well as setting it up.
III. Knowledge in several major fields with sympathy for varied points of view make him an excellent choice for student adviser.
IV. You will find the girls' equipment in the teachers' lounge where the boy's father left it at Professor Wills's suggestion.
V. I know that the Burnses have worked for the mill for generations, and that the Smiths have but recently removed from town, but does either of the Norton boys work here?
The CORRECT answer is:
A. I, II, III   B. II, III, IV   C. I, IV, V   D. III, V   E. I, II, IV

18.____

19.
I. I can put two and two together as quick as most mean; but understanding how he, a slow-witted dolt, could achieve so notable a victory over his opponent is one of the things that puzzle and, forevermore, will puzzle me.
II. Besides my two brothers, my sister, and I, there are a cousin and my father's nephew living at home with us,
III. He has lived in the Reno for many years; previously he lived in Chicago for a short space, after he had come from Los Angeles.
IV. Researchers have been baffled for a long time by this statistic, for it contradicts many of their most highly cherished hypotheses.
V. So intense was the heat near the furnace that all the men at work could not carry on; consequently, production came to a halt,

19.____

The CORRECT answer is:
A. I, II, IV   B. III, V   C. I, III, IV   D. I, II, V   E. II, V

20. I. If we can escape from our desks for a brief interval, let's you, Henry, and I put in an appearance at the party.
    II. If you persevere in your ambitions, you are likely to achieve at least a modicum of success; if you malinger, you are liable to court failure.
    III. You may find conditions here congenial, but since I neither like he work nor the salary, it is to no avail for you to attempt to persuade me to stay.
    IV. He has never deigned to take a drink with us, his office colleagues, though we know him now for over fifteen years; and he takes an occasional drink, we know, at home and at his golf club,
    V. Though the results of your investigation are at variance with the hypothesis we advanced, I believe you have interpreted these data in the only ways that have scientific validity.
    The CORRECT answer is:
    A. I, II, IV   B. I, II   C. IV, V   D. II, III, V   E. I, III, IV

21. I. He can't hardly hear anything unless the room is completely quiet.
    II. His attitude seemed perfectly alright to me.
    III. One can't be too careful, can one?
    IV. He is one of those people who believe in the perfectability of man.
    V. His uneasiness is reflected in his unwillingness to compromise on even the smallest point.
    The CORRECT answer is:
    A. II, III, V   B. I, III   C. I, IV, V   D. I, II, IV   E. III, IV

22. I. "Have you found what you were looking for?" he asked.
    II. "I have never," she insisted, "Seen such careless disregard for the rights of others."
    III. "I found this ticket on the step," he said. "Did you lose it?"
    IV. "In one way I'd like to enter the contest," said Anne; "in another way I'm not too eager."
    V. "Did he say, 'I'm coming?'"
    The CORRECT answer is:
    A. I, III, IV   B. II, V   C. III, V   D. II, IV   E. I, II, IV

23. I. Were I the owner of the dog, I'd keep him muzzled.
    II. In the tennis match Don was paired with Bill; Ed, with Al.
    III. He was given an excellent trade-in allowance on his old car.
    IV. Why doesn't this window raise?
    V. The prow of the vessel had almost completely sank by the time the rescuers arrived on the scene.
    The CORRECT answer is:
    A. I, II, V   B. I, IV, V   C. I, II, III   D. II, V   E. IV, V

24. I. Turning the pages rapidly, his glance fell upon a peculiarly worded advertisement.
    II. Turning the pages rapidly, his eyes noticed a peculiarly worded advertisement.
    III. Turning the pages rapidly, he noticed a peculiarly worded advertisement.
    IV. Turning the pages rapidly made him more attentive to the unusual.
    V. Turning the pages rapidly does not guarantee rapid comprehension.
    The CORRECT answer is:
        A. III, IV, V   B. I, II, IV   C. III, V   D. I, II   E. I, II, III

25. I. They told us how they had suffered.
    II. It is interesting (a) to the student, (b) to the parent, and (c) to the teacher.
    III. There were blue, green and red banners.
    IV. "Will you help", he asked?
    V. In addition to reproducibility, an attitude scale must meet various other requirements characteristic of scale analysis procedures.
    The CORRECT answer is:
        A. I, II   B. II, III   C. I only   D. IV only   E. IV, V

KEY (CORRECT ANSWERS)

1.	C		11.	C
2.	D		12.	C
3.	A		13.	D
4.	E		14.	E
5.	A		15.	C
6.	A		16.	D
7.	E		17.	C
8.	A		18.	A
9.	B		19.	E
10.	B		20.	F

21.	D
22.	B
23.	E
24.	D
25.	D

WRITTEN ENGLISH EXPRESSION EXAMINATION SECTION
TEST 1

DIRECTIONS: The following questions are designed to test your knowledge of grammar, sentence structure, correct usage, and punctuation. In each group there is one sentence that contains no errors. Select the letter of the CORRECT sentence. *PRINT THE LETTER OF THE CORRECT ANSWER IN THE SPACE AT THE RIGHT.*

1. A. A low ceiling is when the atmospheric conditions make flying inadvisable.
   B. They couldn't tell who the card was from.
   C. No one but you and I are to help him.
   D. What kind of a teacher would you like to be?
   E. To him fall the duties of foster parent.

   1.____

2. A. They couldn't tell whom the cable was from.
   B. We like these better than those kind.
   C. It is a test of you more than I.
   D. The person in charge being him, there can be no change in policy.
   E. Chicago is larger than any city in Illinois.

   2.____

3. A. Do as we do for the celebration.
   B. Do either of you care to join us?
   C. A child's food requirements differ from the adult.
   D. A large family including two uncles and four grandparents live at the hotel.
   E. Due to bad weather, the game was postponed.

   3.____

4. A. If they would have done that they might have succeeded.
   B. Neither the hot days or the humid nights annoy our Southern visitor.
   C. Some people do not gain favor because they are kind of tactless.
   D. No sooner had the turning point come than a new issue arose.
   E. I wish that I was in Florida now.

   4.____

5. A. We haven't hardly enough tine.
   B. Immigration is when people come into a foreign country to live.
   C. After each side gave their version, the affair was over with.
   D. Every one of the cars were tagged by the police.
   E. He either will fail in his attempt or will seek other employment.

   5.____

6. A. They can't seem to see it when I explain the theory.
   B. It is difficult to find the genuine signature between all those submitted.
   C. She can't understand why they don't remember who to give the letter to
   D. Every man and woman in America is interested in his tax bill.
   E. Honor as well as profit are to be gained by these studies.

   6.____

215

7. A. He arrived safe.
    B. I do not have any faith in John running for office.
    C. The musicians began to play tunefully and keeping the proper tempo indicated for the selection.
    D. Mary's maid of honor bought the kind of an outfit suitable for an afternoon wedding.
    E. If you would have studied the problem carefully you would have found the solution more quickly.

8. A. The new plant is to be electric lighted.
    B. The reason the speaker was offended was that the audience was inattentive.
    C. There appears to be conditions that govern his behavior.
    D. Either of the men are influential enough to control the situation.
    E. The gallery with all its pictures were destroyed.

9. A. If you would have listened more carefully, you would have heard your name called.
    B. Did you inquire if your brother were returning soon?
    C. We are likely to have rain before nightfall.
    D. Let's you and I plan next summer's vacation together.
    E. The man whom I thought was my friend deceived me.

10. A. There's a man and his wife waiting for the doctor since early this morning.
    B. The owner of the market with his assistants is applying the most modern principles of merchandise display.
    C. Every one of the players on both of the competing teams were awarded a gold watch.
    D. The records of the trial indicated that, even before attaining manhood, the murderer's parents were both dead.
    E. We had no sooner entered the room when the bell rang.

11. A. Why don't you start the play like I told you?
    B. I didn't find the construction of the second house much different from that of the first one I saw.
    C. "When", inquired the child, "Will we begin celebrating my birthday?"
    D. There isn't nothing left to do but not to see him anymore.
    E. There goes the last piece of cake and the last spoonful of ice cream.

12. A. The child could find neither the shoe or the stocking.
    B. The musicians began to play tunefully and keeping the proper tempo indicated for the selection.
    C. The amount of curious people who turned out for Opening Night was beyond calculation.
    D. I fully expected that the children would be at their desks and to find them ready to begin work,
    E. "Indeed," mused the poll-taker, "the winning candidate is much happier than I."

13. A. Just as you said, I find myself gaining weight.
     B. A teacher should leave the capable pupils engage in creative activities.
     C. The teacher spoke continually during the entire lesson, which, of course, was poor procedure.
     D. We saw him steal into the room, pick up the letter, and tear it's contents to shreds.
     E. It is so dark that I can't hardly see.

14. A. The new schedule of working hours and rates was satisfactory to both employees and employer.
     B. Many common people feel keenly about the injustices of Power Politics.
     C. Mr. and Mrs. Burns felt that their grandchild was awfully cute when he waved good-bye.
     D. The tallest of the twins was also the most intelligent,
     E. Please come here and try and help me finish this piece of work.

15. A. My younger brother insists that he is as tall as me.
     B. Suffering from a severe headache all day, one dose of the prescribed medicine relieved me,
     C. "Please let my brothers and I help you with your packages," said Frank to Mrs. Powers.
     D. Every one of the rooms we visited had displays of pupils' work in them.
     E. Do you intend bringing most of the refreshments yourself?

16. A. The telephone linesmen, working steadily at their task during the severe storm, the telephones soon began to ring again.
     B. Meat, as well as fruits and vegetables, is considered essential to a proper diet.
     C. He looked like a real good boxer that night in the ring.
     D. The man has worked steadily for fifteen years before he decided to open his own business.
     E. The winters were hard and dreary, nothing could live without shelter.

17. A. No one can foretell when I will have another opportunity like that one again.
     B. The last group of paintings shown appear really to have captured the most modern techniques,
     C. We searched high and low, both in the attic and cellar, but were unsuccessful in locating mementos.
     D. None of the guests was able to give the rules of the game accurately.
     E. When you go to the library tomorrow, please bring this book to the librarian in the reference room.

18. A. After the debate, every one of the speakers realized that, given another chance, he could have done better.
     B. The reason given by the physician for the patient's trouble was because of his poor eating habits.
     C. The fog was so thick that the driver couldn't hardly see more than ten feet ahead.
     D. I suggest that you present the medal to who you think best.
     E. I don't approve of him going along.

19. A. A decision made by a man without much deliberation is sometimes no different than a slow one.
    B. By the time Mr. Brown's son will graduate Dental School, he will be twenty-six years of age.
    C. Who did you predict would win the election?
    D. The auctioneer had less stamps to sell this year than last year.
    E. Being that he is occupied, I shall not disturb him.

20. A. Having pranced into the arena with little grace and unsteady hoof for the jumps ahead, the driver reined his horse.
    B. Once the dog wagged it's tail, you knew it was a friendly animal.
    C. Like a great many artists, his life was a tragedy.
    D. When asked to choose corn, cabbage, or potatoes, the diner selected the latter.
    E. The record of the winning team was among the most noteworthy of the season.

21. A. The maid wasn't so small that she couldn't reach the top window for cleaning.
    B. Many people feel that powdered coffee produces a really good flavor.
    C. Would you mind me trying that coat on for size?
    D. This chair looks much different than the chair we selected in the store.
    E. I wish that he would have talked to me about the lesson before he presented it.

22. A. After trying unsuccessfully to land a job in the city, Will located in the country on a farm.
    B. On the last attempt, the pole-vaulter came nearly to getting hurt.
    C. The observance of Armistice Day throughout the world offers an opportunity to reflect on the horrors of war.
    D. Outside of the mistakes in spelling, the child's letter was a very good one.
    E. The annual income of New York is far greater than Florida.

23. A. Scissors is always dangerous for a child to handle.
    B. I assure you that I will not yield to pressure to sell my interest.
    C. Ask him if he has recall of the incident which took place at our first meeting.
    D. The manager felt like as not to order his usher-captain to surrender his uniform.
    E. Everyone on the boat said their prayers when the storm grew worse.

24. A. The mother of the bride climaxed the occasion by exclaiming, "I want my children should be happy forever."
    B. We read in the papers where the prospects for peace are improving.
    C. "Can I share the cab with you?" was frequently heard during the period of gas rationing.
    D. The man was enamored with his friend"s sister.
    E. Had the police suspected the ruse, they would have taken proper precautions.

25. A. The teacher admonished the other students neither to speak to John, nor should they annoy him.
    B. Fortunately we had been told that there was but one service station in that area.
    C. An usher seldom rises above a theatre manager.
    D. The epic, "Gone With the Wind," is supposed to have taken place during the Civil War Era.
    E. Now that she has been graduated she should be encouraged to make her own choice as to the career she is to follow.

KEY (CORRECT ANSWERS)

1.	E	11.	B
2.	A	12.	E
3.	A	13.	A
4.	D	14.	A
5.	E	15.	E
6.	D	16.	B
7.	A	17.	D
8.	B	18.	A
9.	C	19.	C
10.	B	20.	E

21. B
22. C
23. B
24. E
25. B

TEST 2

DIRECTIONS: The following questions are designed to test your knowledge of grammar, sentence structure, correct usage, and punctuation. In each group, there is one sentence that contains no errors. Select the letter of the CORRECT sentence. *PRINT THE LETTER OF THE CORRECT ANSWER IN THE SPACE AT THE RIGHT.*

1. A. Shall you be at home, let us say, on Sunday at two o'clock?
    B. We see Mr. Lewis take his car out of the garage daily, newly polished always.
    C. We have no place to keep our rubbers, only in the hall closet.
    D. Isn't it true what you told me about the best way to prepare for an examination?
    E. Mathematics is among my favorite subjects.

    1._____

2. A. The host thought the guests were of the hungry kinds so he prepared much food.
    B. The museum is often visited by students who are fond of early inventions, and especially patent attorneys.
    C. I rose to nominate the man who most of us felt was the most diligent worker in the group.
    D. The child was sent to the store to purchase a bottle of milk, and brought home fresh rolls, too.
    E. Hidden away in the closet, I found the long-lost purse.

    2._____

3. A. The garden tool was sent to be sharpened, and a new handle to be put on.
    B. At the end of her vacation, Joan came home with little money, but which systematic thrift soon overcame.
    C. We people have opportunities to show the rest of the world how real democracy functions.
    D. The guide paddled along, then fell in a reverie which he related the history of the region.
    E. No sooner had the curtain dropped when the audience shouted its approval in chorus.

    3._____

4. A. The data you need is to be made available shortly.
    B. The first few strokes of the brush were enough to convince me that Tom could paint much better than me.
    C. We inquired if we could see the owner of the store, after we waited for one hour.
    D. The highly-strung parent was aggravated by the slightest noise that the baby made.
    E. We should have investigated the cause of the noise by bringing the car to a halt.

    4._____

5. A. The police, investigating the crime, were successful in discovering only one possibly valuable clue.
    B. Due to an unexpected change in plans, the violin soloist did not perform.
    C. Besides being awarded a Bachelor's degree at college, the scientist has since received many honorary degrees.
    D. The data offered in advance of the recent Presidential election seems to have possessed elements of inaccuracy.
    E. I don't believe your the only one who has been asked to come here.

    5._____

2 (#2)

6. A. I don't quite see that I will be able to completely finish the job in time.   6.____
   B. By my statement, I infer that you are guilty of the offense as charged.
   C. Wasn't it strange that they wouldn't let no one see the body?
   D. I hope that this is the kind of rolls you requested me to buy.
   E. The storekeeper distributed cigars as bonuses between his many customers.

7. A. He said he preferred the climate of Florida to California.   7.____
   B. Because of the excessive heat, a great amount of fruit juice was drunk by the guests.
   C. This week's dramatic presentation was neither as lively nor as entertaining as last week.
   D. The fashion expert believed that no one could develop new creations more successfully than him.
   E. A collection of Dicken's works is a "must" for every library.

8. A. There was such a large amount of books on the floor that I couldn't find a place for my rocking chair.   8.____
   B. Walking up the rickety stairs, the bottle slipped from his hands and smashed.
   C. The reason they granted his request was because he had a good record.
   D. Little Tommy was proud that the teacher always asked him to bring messages to the office.
   E. That kind of orange is grown only in Florida.

9. A. The new mayor is a resident of this city for thirty years.   9.____
   B. Do you mean to imply that had he not missed that shot he would have won?
   C. Next term I shall be studying French and history.
   D. I read in last night's paper where the sales tax is going to be abolished.
   E. In order to prevent breakage, she placed a sheet of paper between each of the plates when she packed them.

10. A. To have children vie against one another is psychologically unsound.   10.____
    B. Would anyone else care to discuss his baby?
    C. He was interested and aware of the problem.
    D. I sure would like to discover if he is motivating the lesson properly.
    E. The cloth was first lain on a flat surface; then it was pressed with a hot iron.

11. A. She graduated Barnard College twenty-five years ago.   11.____
    B. He studied the violin since he was seven.
    C. She is not so diligent a researcher as her classmate.
    D. He discovered that the new data corresponds with the facts disclosed by Werner.
    E. How could he enjoy the television program; the dog was barking and the baby was crying.

12. A. You have three alternatives: law, dentistry, or teaching.   12.____
    B. If I would have worked harder, I would have accomplished my purpose.
    C. He affected a rapid change of pace and his opponents were outdistanced.
    D. He looked prosperous, although he had been unemployed for a year.
    E. The engine not only furnishes power but light and heat as well.

13. A. The children shared one anothers toys and seemed quite happy.
    B. They lay in the sun for many hours, getting tanned.
    C. The reproduction arrived, and had been hung in the living room.
    D. First begin by calling the roll.
    E. Tell me where you hid it; no one shall ever find it.

    13.___

14. A. Deliver these things to whomever arrives first.
    B. Everybody but she and me is going to the conference.
    C. If the number of patrons is small, we can serve them.
    D. When each of the contestants find their book, the debate may begin.
    E. Some people, farmers in particular, lament the substitution of butter by margarine.

    14.___

15. A. After his illness, he stood in the country three weeks.
    B. If you wish to effect a change, submit your suggestions.
    C. It is silly to leave children play with knives.
    D. Play a trick on her by spilling water down her neck.
    E. There was such a crowd of people at the crossing we couldn't hardly get on the bus.

    15.___

16. A. This is a time when all of us must show our faith and devotion to our country.
    B. Either you or I are certain to be elected president of the new club.
    C. The interpellation of the Minister of Finance forced him to explain his policies.
    D. After hoisting the anchor and removing the binnacle, the ship was ready to set sail.
    E. Please bring me a drink of cold water from the refrigerator.

    16.___

17. A. Mistakes in English, when due to carelessness or haste, can easily be rectified.
    B. Mr. Jones is one of those persons who will try to keep a promise and usually does.
    C. Being very disturbed by what he had heard, Fred decided to postpone his decision.
    D. There is a telephone at the other end of the corridor which is constantly in use.
    E. In his teaching, he always kept the childrens' interests and needs in mind.

    17.___

18. A. The lazy pupil, of course, will tend to write the minimum amount of words acceptable.
    B. His success as a political leader consisted mainly of his ability to utter platitudes in a firm and convincing manner.
    C. To be cognizant of current affairs, a person must not only read newspapers and magazines but also recent books by recognized authorities.
    D. Although we intended to have gone fishing, the sudden outbreak of a storm caused us to change our plans.
    E. It is the colleges that must take the responsibility for encouraging greater flexibility in the high-school curriculum.

    18.___

19. A. "I am sorry," he said, "but John's answer was 'No'."   19._____
    B. A spirited argument followed between those who favored and opposed Marie's expulsion from the club.
    C. Whether a forward child should be humored or punished often depends upon the circumstances.
    D. Excessive alcoholism is certainly not conducive with efficient performance of one's work.
    E. Stroking his beard thoughtfully, an idea suddenly came to him.

20. A. "Take care, my children," he said sadly, "lest you not be deceived."   20._____
    B. Those continuous telephone calls are preventing Betty from completing her homework.
    C. They dug deep into the earth at the spot indicated on the map, but they found nothing.
    D. We petted and cozened the little girl until she finally stopped weeping.
    E. There was, in the mail, an inquiry for a house by a young couple with two or three bedrooms.

21. A. Please fill in the required information on the application form and return same by April 15.   21._____
    B. Tom was sitting there idly, watching the clouds scud across the sky.
    C. We started for home so that our parents would not suspect that anything out of the ordinary took place.
    D. The sudden abatement from the storm enabled the ladies to resume their journey.
    E. Each of the twelve members were agreed that the accused man was innocent.

22. A. The number of gifted students not continuing their education beyond secondary school present a nationwide problem.   22._____
    B. A man's animadversions against those he considers his enemies are usually reflections of his own inadequacies.
    C. The alembic of his fevered imagination produced some of the greatest romantic poetry of his era.
    D. The first case of smallpox dates back more than 3000 years and has gone unchecked until recently.
    E. He promised to go irregardless of the rain or snow.

23. A. The child picked up several of the coracles, which he had seen glittering in the sand, and brought them to his mother.   23._____
    B. He muttered in dejected tones – and no one contradicted him – "We have failed."
    C. A girl whom I believed to be she waved cheerily to me from a passing automobile.
    D. We discovered that she was a former resident of our own neighborhood who eloped some years ago with a milkman.
    E. It looks now like he will not be promoted after all.

24. A. Mary is the kind of a person on whom you can depend in any emergency.
    B. I am sure that either applicant can fill the job you offer competently and efficiently.
    C. Although we searched the entire room, the scissors was not to be found.
    D. Being that you are here, we can proceed with the discussion.
    E. In spite of our warning whistle, the huge ship continued to sail athwart our course.

24.____

25. A. The salaries earned by college graduates vary as much if not more than those earned by high school graduates.
    B. The apothegms that he felt to be so witty were all too often either trite or platitudinous.
    C. She read the letter carefully, took out one of the pages, and tore it into small pieces.
    D. A young man, who hopes to succeed, must be diligent in his work and alert to his opportunities.
    E. No one should plan a long journey for pleasure in these days.

25.____

KEY (CORRECT ANSWERS)

1.	A	11.	C
2.	C	12.	D
3.	C	13.	E
4.	E	14.	C
5.	A	15.	B
6.	D	16.	C
7.	B	17.	A
8.	E	18.	E
9.	B	19.	C
10.	B	20.	C

21. B
22. C
23. B
24. E
25. B

ENGLISH EXPRESSION

EXAMINATION SECTION

TEST 1

DIRECTIONS: Each question or incomplete statement is followed by several suggested answers or completions. Select the one that BEST answers the question or completes the statement. *PRINT THE LETTER OF THE CORRECT ANSWER IN THE SPACE AT THE RIGHT.*

Questions 1-9.

DIRECTIONS: The following sentences contain problems in grammar, usage diction (choice of words), and idiom. Some sentences are correct. No sentence contains more than one error. You will find that the error, if there is one, is underlined and lettered. Assume that all other elements of the sentence are correct and cannot be changed. In choosing answers, follow the requirements of standard written English. If there is an error, select the *one underlined* part that must be changed in order to make the sentence correct. If there is no error, mark E.

1. <u>In planning</u> your future, <u>one must be</u> as honest with yourself as possible, make careful 1.____
       A   B

   decisions about the best course <u>to follow to achieve</u> a particular purpose, and, above all,
                                             C

   have the courage <u>to stand by those</u> decisions. <u>No error</u>
                       D   E

2. <u>Even though</u> history does not actually repeat itself, knowledge <u>of</u> history <u>can give</u> 2.____
       A   B   C

   current problems a familiar, <u>less</u> formidable look. <u>No error</u>
                               D   E

3. The Curies <u>had almost exhausted</u> their resources, and <u>for a time it seemed</u> 3.____
                 A   B

   unlikely that <u>they ever</u> would find the <u>solvent to their financial problems</u>. <u>No error</u>
               C   D   E

4. <u>If the rumors are</u> correct, Deane <u>will not be convicted</u>, for each of the officers 4.____
          A   B

   on the court realizes that Colson and Holdman may be <u>the real culprit and</u> that
                                                                  C

   <u>their</u> testimony is not completely trustworthy. <u>No error</u>
    D   E

5. The citizens of Washington, <u>like Los Angeles</u>, prefer to commute by automobile,
      A
   even though motor vehicles contribute <u>nearly as many</u> contaminants to the air
                                              B
   <u>as do all other</u> sources <u>combined</u>. <u>No error</u>
           C   D   E

6. <u>By the time Robert Vasco completes</u> his testimony, every major executive of our
      A
   company but Ray Ashurst <u>and I</u> <u>will have been</u> <u>accused of</u> complicity in the stock
                              B   C   D
   swindle. <u>No error</u>
                 E

7. <u>Within six months</u> the store was operating <u>profitably and efficient</u>; shelves
        A   B
   <u>were well stocked</u>, goods were selling rapidly, and the cash register
           C
   <u>was ringing constantly</u>. <u>No error</u>
           D   E

8. Shakespeare's comedies have an advantage <u>over Shaw</u> <u>in that Shakespeare's</u> were
                                                 A   B
   <u>written primarily</u> to entertain and <u>not to</u> argue for a cause. <u>No error</u>
           C   D   E

9. Any true insomniac <u>is well aware of</u> the futility of <u>such measures as</u> drinking
                              A   B
   hot milk, <u>regular hours, deep breathing</u>, counting sheep, and <u>concentrating on</u>
                        C   D
   black velvet. <u>No error</u>
                       E

Questions 10-15.

DIRECTIONS: In each of the following sentences, some part of the sentence or the entire sentence is underlined. Beneath each sentence you will find five ways of phrasing the underlined part. The first of these repeats the original; the other four are different. If you think the original is better than any of the alternatives, choose answer A; otherwise choose one of the others. In choosing answers, follow the requirements of standard written English; that is, pay attention to grammar, choice of words, sentence construction, and punctuation. Choose the answer that produces the most effective sentence—clear and exact, without awkwardness or ambiguity. Do not make a choice that changes the meaning of the original sentence.

10. The tribe of warriors believed that boys and girls should be <u>reared separate, and, as soon as he was weaned, the boys were taken from their mothers.</u>
    A. reared separate, and, as soon as he was weaned, the boys were taken from their mothers

B. reared separate, and, as soon as he was weaned, a boy was taken from his mother
C. reared separate, and, as soon as he was weaned, the boys were taken from their mothers
D. reared separately, and, as soon as a boy was weaned, they were taken from their mothers
E. reared separately, and, as soon as a boy was weaned, he was taken from his mother

11. <u>Despite Vesta being only the third largest, it is by far the brightest of the known asteroids.</u>
    A. Despite Vesta being only the third largest, it is by far the brightest of the known asteroids.
    B. Vesta, though only the third largest asteroid, is by far the brightest of the known ones.
    C. Being only the third largest, yet Vesta is by far the brightest of the known asteroids.
    D. Vesta, though only the third largest of the known asteroids, is by far the brightest.
    E. Vesta is only the third largest of the asteroids, it being, however, the brightest one.

12. As a result of the discovery of the Dead Sea Scrolls, our understanding of the roots of Christianity <u>has had to be revised considerably.</u>
    A. has had to be revised considerably
    B. have had to be revised considerably
    C. has had to undergo revision to a considerable degree
    D. have had to be subjected to considerable revision
    E. has had to be revised in a considerable way

13. Because <u>it is imminently suitable to</u> dry climates, adobe has been a traditional building material throughout the southwestern states.
    A. it is imminently suitable to
    B. it is eminently suitable for
    C. It is eminently suitable when in
    D. of its eminent suitability with
    E. of being imminently suitable in

14. <u>Martell is more concerned with demonstrating that racial prejudice exists than preventing it from doing harm, which explains</u> why his work is not always highly regarded.
    A. Martell is more concerned with demonstrating that racial prejudice exists than preventing it from doing harm, which explains
    B. Martell is more concerned with demonstrating that racial prejudice exists than with preventing it from doing harm, and this explains
    C. Martell is more concerned with demonstrating that racial prejudice exists than with preventing it from doing harm, an explanation of
    D. Martell's greater concern for demonstrating that racial prejudice exists than preventing it from doing harm—this explains
    E. Martell's greater concern for demonstrating that racial prejudice exists than for preventing it from doing harm explains

15. Throughout this history of the American West there runs a steady commentary on the deception and mistreatment of the Indians.
   A. Throughout this history of the American West there runs a steady commentary on the deception and mistreatment of the Indians.
   B. There is a steady commentary provided on the deception and mistreatment of the Indians and it runs throughout this history of the American West.
   C. The deception and mistreatment of the Indians provide a steady comment that runs throughout this history of the American West.
   D. Comment on the deception and mistreatment of the Indians is steadily provided and runs throughout this history of the American West.
   E. Running throughout this history of the American West is a steady commentary that is provided on the deception and mistreatment of the Indians.

15.____

Questions 16-20.

DIRECTIONS: In each of the following questions you are given a complete sentence to be rephrased according to the directions which follow it. You should rephrase the sentence mentally to save time, although you may make notes in your test book if you wish. Below each sentence and its directions are listed words or phrases that may occur in your revised sentence. When you have thought out a good sentence, look in the choices A through E for the word or entire phrase that is included in your revised sentence, and print the letter of the correct answer in the space at the right. The word or phrase you choose should be the most accurate and most nearly complete of all the choices given, and should be part of a sentence that meets the requirements of standard written English. Of course, a number of different sentences can be obtained if the sentence is revised according to directions, and not all of these possibilities can be included in only five choices. If you should find that you have thought of a sentence that contains none of the words or phrases listed in the choices, you should attempt to rephrase the sentence again so that it includes a word or phrase that is listed. Although the directions may at times require you to change the relationship between parts of the sentence or to make slight changes in meaning in other ways, make only those changes that the directions require; that is, keep the meaning the same, or as nearly the same as the directions permit. If you think that more than one good sentence can be made according to the directions, select the sentence that is most exact, effective, and natural in phrasing and construction.

EXAMPLES

I. Sentence: Coming to the city as a young man, he found a job as a newspaper reporter.
   Directions: Substitute He came for Coming.
   A. and so he found   B. and found
   C. and there he had found   D. and then finding
   E. and had found

Your rephrased sentence will probably read: "He came to the city as a young man and found a job as a newspaper reporter." This sentence contains the correct answer: B. and found. A sentence which used one of the alternate phrases would change the meaning or intention of the original sentence, would be a poorly written sentence, or would be less effective than another possible revision.

II. Sentence: Owing to her wealth, Sarah had many suitors.
Directions: Begin with Many men courted.
A. so   B. while   C. although   D. because   E. and

Your rephrased sentence will probably read: "Many men courted Sarah because she was wealthy." This new sentence contains only choice D, which is the correct answer. None of the other choices will fit into an effective, correct sentence that retains the original meaning.

16. The archaeologists could only mark out the burial site, for then winter came.
Begin with Winter came before.
A. could do nothing more
B. could not do anything
C. could only do
D. could do something
E. could do anything more

17. The white reader often receives some insight into the reasons why black men are angry from descriptions by a black writer of the injustice they encounter in a white society.
Begin with A black writer often gives.
A. when describing
B. by describing
C. he has described
D. in the descriptions
E. because of describing

18. The agreement between the university officials and the dissident students provides for student representation on every university committee and on the board of trustees.
Substitute provides that for provides for.
A. be
B. are
C. would have
D. would be
E. is to be

19. English Romanticism had its roots in German idealist philosophy, first described in England by Samuel Coleridge.
Begin with Samuel Coleridge was the first in.
A. in which English
B. and from it English
C. where English
D. the source of English
E. the birth of English

20. Four months have passed since his dismissal, during which time Alan has looked for work daily.
Begin with Each day.
A. will have passed
B. that have passed
C. that passed
D. were to pass
E. had passed

KEY (CORRECT ANSWERS)

1.	B	11.	D
2.	E	12.	A
3.	D	13.	B
4.	C	14.	E
5.	A	15.	A
6.	B	16.	E
7.	B	17.	B
8.	A	18.	A
9.	C	19.	D
10.	E	20.	B